# SOAP-MAKING MANUAL

# SOAP-MAKING MANUAL

**A practical handbook on the raw materials, their manipulation, analysis and control in the modern soap plant.**

BY

E. G. THOMSSEN PH. D.

KALPAZ

ISBN: 978-93-5128-971-5(HB)

First Published in 1922
Indian Reprint in 2017

*Published by*

Kalpaz Publications
C-30, Satyawati Nagar,
Delhi – 110052
E-mail: kalpaz@hotmail.com
Website: kalpazpublications.com
Ph.: +91-9212142040

**Cataloging in Publication Data—DK**
Courtesy: D.K. Agencies (P) Ltd. <docinfo@dkagencies.com>

**Thomssen, Edgar George,** 1886- **author.**
Soap-making manual : a practical handbook on the raw materials, their manipulation, analysis and control in the modern soap plant / By E.G. Thomssen (Ph. D.).
pages cm
"First published in 1922"—Title page verso.
Includes index.
ISBN 9789351289715 (HB)

1. Soap. I. Title.

TP991.T46 2017 DDC 668.12 23

# PREFATORY NOTE.

The material contained in this work appeared several years ago in serial form in the American Perfumer and Essential Oil Review. Owing to the numerous requests received, it has been decided to now place before those interested, these articles in book form. While it is true that the works pertaining to the soapmaking industry are reasonably plentiful, books are quite rare, however, which, in a brief volume, will clearly outline the processes employed together with the necessary methods of analyses from a purely practical standpoint. In the work presented the author has attempted to briefly, clearly, and fully explain the manufacture of soap in such language that it might be understood by all those interested in this industry. In many cases the smaller plants find it necessary to dispense with the services of a chemist, so that it is necessary for the soapmaker to make his own tests. The tests outlined, therefore, are given as simple as possible to meet this condition. The formulae submitted are authentic, and in many cases are now being used in soapmaking.

In taking up the industry for survey it has been thought desirable to first mention and describe the raw materials used; second, to outline the processes of manufacture; third, to classify the methods and illustrate by formulae the composition of various soaps together with their mode of manufacture; fourth, to enumerate the various methods of glycerine recovery, including the processes of saponification, and, fifth, to give the most important analytical methods which are of value to control the process of manufacture and to determine the purity and fitness of the raw material entering into it.

It is not the intention of the author to go into great detail in this work, nor to outline to any great extent the theoretical side of the subject, but rather to make the work as brief as possible, keeping the practical side of the subject before him and not going into concise descriptions of machinery as is very usual in works on this subject. Illustrations are merely added to show typical kinds of machinery used.

The author wishes to take this opportunity of thanking Messrs. L. S. Levy and E. W. Drew for the reading of proof, and Mr. C. W. Aiken of the Houchin-Aiken Co., for his aid in making the illustrations a success, as well as others who have contributed in the compiling of the formulae for various soaps. He trusts that this work may prove of value to those engaged in soap manufacture.

E. G. T.

January, 1922

# TABLE OF CONTENTS.

## CHAPTER V.

# TABLE OF CONTENTS

## CHAPTER VII

# CHAPTER I

## Raw Materials Used in Soap Making.

Soap is ordinarily thought of as the common cleansing agent well known to everyone. In a general and strictly chemical sense this term is applied to the salts of the non-volatile fatty acids. These salts are not only those formed by the alkali metals, sodium and potassium, but also those formed by the heavy metals and alkaline earths. Thus we have the insoluble soaps of lime and magnesia formed when we attempt to wash in "hard water"; again aluminum soaps are used extensively in polishing materials and to thicken lubricating oils; ammonia or "benzine" soaps are employed among the dry cleaners. Commonly, however, when we speak of soap we limit it to the sodium or potassium salt of a higher fatty acid.

It is very generally known that soap is made by combining a fat or oil with a water solution of sodium hydroxide (caustic soda lye), or potassium hydroxide (caustic potash). Sodium soaps are always harder than potassium soaps, provided the same fat or oil is used in both cases.

The detergent properties of soap are due to the fact that it acts as an alkali regulator, that is, when water comes into contact with soap, it undergoes what is called hydrolytic dissociation. This means that it is broken down by water into other substances. Just what these substances are is subject to controversy, though it is presumed caustic alkali and the acid alkali salt of the fatty acids are formed.

### OILS AND FATS.

There is no sharp distinction between fat and oil. By "oil" the layman has the impression of a liquid which at warm temperature will flow as a slippery, lubricating, viscous fluid; by "fat" he understands a greasy, solid substance unctuous to the touch. It thus becomes necessary to differentiate the oils and fats used in the manufacture of soap.

Inasmuch as a soap is the alkali salt of a fatty acid, the oil or fat from which soap is made must have as a constituent part, these fatty acids. Hydrocarbon oils or paraffines, included in the term "oil," are thus useless in the process of soap-making, as far as entering into chemical combination with the caustic alkalis is concerned. The oils and fats which form soap are those which are a combination of fatty acids and glycerine, the glycerine being obtained as a by-product to the soap-making industry.

### NATURE OF A FAT OR OIL USED IN SOAP MANUFACTURE.

Glycerine, being a tryhydric alcohol, has three atoms of hydrogen which are replaceable by three univalent radicals of the higher members of the fatty acids, *e. g.*,

$$C_3H_5\begin{matrix}OH\\OH\\OH\end{matrix} + 3\ ROH = C_3H_5\begin{matrix}OR\\OR\\OR\end{matrix} + 3\ H_2O$$

Glycerine plus 3 Fatty Alcohols equals Fat or Oil plus 3 Water.

Thus three fatty acid radicals combine with one glycerine to form a true neutral oil or fat which are called triglycerides. The fatty acids which most commonly enter into combination of fats and oils are lauric, myristic, palmitic, stearic and oleic acids and form the neutral oils or triglycerides derived from these, *e. g.*, stearin; palmatin, olein. Mono and diglycerides are also present in fats.

### SAPONIFICATION DEFINED.

When a fat or oil enters into chemical combination with one of the caustic hydrates in the presence of water, the process is called "saponification" and the new compounds formed are soap and glycerine, thus:

$$C_3H_5\begin{matrix}OR\\OR\\OR\end{matrix} + 3\ NaOH = C_3H_5\begin{matrix}OH\\OH\\OH\end{matrix} + 3\ NaOR$$

Fat or Oil plus 3 Sodium Hydrate equals Glycerine plus 3 Soap.

It is by this reaction almost all of the soap used today is made.

There are also other means of saponification, as, the hydrolysis of an oil or fat by the action of hydrochloric or sulfuric acid, by autoclave and by ferments or enzymes. By these latter processes the fatty acids and glycerine are obtained directly, no soap being formed.

### FATS AND OILS USED IN SOAP MANUFACTURE.

The various and most important oils and fats used in the manufacture of soap are, tallow, cocoanut oil, palm oil, olive oil, poppy oil, sesame oil, soya bean oil, cotton-seed oil, corn oil and the various greases. Besides these the fatty acids, stearic, red oil (oleic acid) are more or less extensively used. These oils, fats and fatty acids, while they vary from time to time and to some extent as to their color, odor and consistency, can readily be distinguished by various physical and chemical constants.

Much can be learned by one, who through continued acquaintance with these oils has thoroughly familiarized himself with the indications of a good or bad oil, by taste, smell, feel and appearance. It is, however, not well for the manufacturer in purchasing to depend entirely upon these simpler tests. Since he is interested in the yield of glycerine, the largest possible yield of soap per pound of soap stock and the general body and appearance of the finished product, the chemical tests upon which these depend should be made. Those especially important are the acid value, percentage unsaponifiable matter and titer test.

A short description of the various oils and fats mentioned is sufficient for their use in the soap industry.

*Tallow* is the name given to the fat extracted from the solid fat or "suet" of cattle, sheep or horses. The quality varies greatly, depending upon the seasons of the year, the food and age of the animal and the method of rendering. It comes to the market under the distinction of edible and inedible, a further distinction being made in commerce as beef tallow, mutton tallow or horse tallow. The better quality is white and bleaches whiter upon exposure to air and light, though it usually has a yellowish tint, a well defined grain and a clean odor. It consists chiefly of stearin, palmitin and olein. Tallow is by far the most extensively used and important fat in the making of soap.

In the manufacture of soaps for toilet purposes, it is usually necessary to produce as white a product as possible. In order to do this it often is necessary to bleach the tallow before saponification. The method usually employed is the Fuller's Earth process.

### FULLER'S EARTH PROCESS FOR BLEACHING TALLOW.

From one to two tons of tallow are melted out into the bleaching tank. This tank is jacketed, made of iron and provided with a good agitator designed to stir up sediment or a coil provided with tangential downward opening perforations and a draw-off cock at the bottom. The coil is the far simpler arrangement, more cleanly and less likely to cause trouble. By this arrangement compressed air which is really essential in the utilization of the press (see later) is utilized for agitation. A dry steam coil in an ordinary tank may be employed in place of a jacketed tank, which lessens the cost of installation.

The tallow in the bleaching tank is heated to 180° F. (82° C.) and ten pounds of dry salt per ton of fat used added and thoroughly mixed by agitation. This addition coagulates any albumen and dehydrates the fat. The whole mass is allowed to settle over night where possible, or for at least five hours. Any brine which has separated is drawn off from the bottom and the temperature of the fat is then raised to 160° F. (71° C.).

Five per cent. of the weight of the tallow operated upon, of dry Fuller's earth is now added and the whole mass agitated from twenty to thirty minutes.

The new bleached fat, containing the Fuller's earth is pumped directly to a previously heated filter press and the issuing clear oil run directly to the soap kettle.

One of the difficulties experienced in the process is the heating of the press to a temperature sufficient to prevent solidification of the fat without raising the press to too great a temperature. To overcome this the first plate is heated by wet steam. Air delivered from a blower and heated by passage through a series of coils raised to a high temperature by external application of heat (superheated steam) is then substituted for the steam. The moisture produced by the condensation of the steam is vaporized by the hot air and carried on gradually to each succeeding plate where it again condenses and vaporizes. In this way the small quantity of water is carried through the entire press, raising its temperature to 80°-100° C. This temperature is subsequently maintained by the passage of hot air. By this method of heating the poor conductivity of hot air is overcome through the intermediary action of a liquid vapor and the latent heat of steam is utilized to obtain the initial rise in temperature. To heat a small press economically where conditions are such that a large output is not required the entire press may be encased in a small wooden house which can be heated by steam coils. The cake in the press is heated for some time after the filteration is complete to assist drainage. After such treatment the cake should contain approximately 15 per cent. fat and 25 per cent. water. The cake is now removed from the press and transferred to a small tank where it is treated with sufficient caustic soda to convert the fat content into soap.

Saturated brine is then added to salt out the soap, the Fuller's earth is allowed to settle to the bottom of the tank and the soap which solidifies after a short time is skimmed off to be used in a cheap soap where color is not important. The liquor underneath may also be run off without disturbing the sediment to be used in graining a similar cheap soap. The waste Fuller's earth contains about 0.1 to 0.3 per cent. of fat.

### METHOD FOR FURTHER IMPROVEMENT OF COLOR.

A further improvement of the color of the tallow may be obtained by freeing it from a portion of its free fatty acids, either with or without previous Fuller's earth bleaching.

To carry out this process the melted fat is allowed to settle and as much water as possible taken off. The temperature is then raised to 160° F. with dry steam and enough saturated solution of soda ash added to remove 0.5 per cent. of the free fatty acids, while agitating the mass thoroughly mechanically or by air. The agitation is continued ten minutes, the whole allowed to settle for two hours and the foots drawn off. The soap thus formed entangles a large proportion of the impurities of the fat.

### VEGETABLE OILS.

*Cocoanut Oil,* as the name implies, is obtained from the fruit of the cocoanut palm. This oil is a solid, white fat at ordinary temperature, having a bland taste and a characteristic odor. It is rarely adulterated and is very readily saponified. In recent years the price of this oil has increased materially because cocoanut oil is now being used extensively for edible purposes, especially in the making of oleomargarine. Present indications are that shortly very little high grade oil will be employed for soap manufacture since the demand for oleomargarine is constantly increasing and since new methods of refining the oil for this purpose are constantly being devised.

The oil is found in the market under three different grades: (1) Cochin cocoanut oil, the choicest oil comes from Cochin (Malabar). This product, being more carefully cultivated and refined than the other grades, is whiter, cleaner and contains a smaller percentage of free acid. (2) Ceylon cocoanut oil, coming chiefly from Ceylon, is usually of a yellowish tint and more acrid in odor than Cochin oil. (3) Continental cocoanut oil (Copra, Freudenberg) is obtained from the dried kernels, the copra. which are shipped to Europe in large quantities, where the oil is extracted. These dried kernels yield 60 to 70 per cent oil. This product is generally superior to the Ceylon oil and may be used as a very satisfactory substitute for Cochin oil, in soap manufacture, provided it is low in free acid and of good color. The writer has employed it satisfactorily in the whitest and finest of toilet soaps without being able to distinguish any disadvantage to the Cochin oil. Since continental oil is usually cheaper than Cochin oil, it is advisable to use it, as occasion permits.

Cocoanut oil is used extensively in toilet soap making, usually in connection with tallow. When used alone the soap made from this oil forms a lather, which comes up rapidly but which is fluffy and dries quickly. A pure tallow soap lathers very much slower but produces a more lasting lather. Thus the advantage of using cocoanut oil in soap is seen. It is further used in making a cocoanut oil soap by the cold process also for "fake" or filled soaps. The fatty acid content readily starts the saponification which takes place easily with a strong lye (25°-35° B.). Where large quantities of the oil are saponified care must be exercised as the soap formed suddenly rises or puffs up and may boil over. Cocoanut oil soap takes up large quantities of water, cases having been cited where a 500 per cent. yield has been obtained. This water of course dries out again upon exposure to the air. The soap is harsh to the skin, develops rancidity and darkens readily.

*Palm Kernel Oil,* which is obtained from the kernels of the palm tree of West Africa, is used in soap making to replace cocoanut oil where the lower price warrants its use. It resembles cocoanut oil in respect to saponification and in forming a very similar soap. Kernel oil is white in color, has a pleasant nutty odor when fresh, but rapidly develops free acid, which runs to a high percentage.

*Palm Oil* is produced from the fruit of the several species of the palm tree on the western coast of Africa generally, but also in the Philippines. The fresh oil has a deep orange yellow tint not destroyed by saponification, a sweetish taste and an odor of orris root or violet which is also imparted to soap made from it. The methods by which the natives obtain the oil are crude and depend upon a fermentation, or putrefaction. Large quantities are said to be wasted because of this fact. The oil contains impurities in the form of fermentable fibre and albuminous matter, and consequently develops free fatty acid rapidly. Samples tested for free acid have been found to have hydrolized completely and one seldom obtains an oil with low acid content Because of this high percentage of free fatty acid, the glycerine yield is small, though the neutral oil should produce approximately 12 per cent. glycerine. Some writers claim that glycerine exists in the free state in palm oil. The writer has washed large quantities of the oil and analyzed the wash water for glycerine. The results showed that the amount present did not merit its recovery. Most soap makers do not attempt to recover the glycerine from this oil, when used alone for soap manufacture.

There are several grades of palm oil in commerce, but in toilet soap making it is advisable to utilize only Lagos palm oil, which is the best grade. Where it is desired to maintain the color of the soap this oil produces, a small quantity of the lower or "brass" grade of palm oil may be used, as the soap made from the better grades of oil gradually bleaches and loses its orange yellow color.

Palm oil produces a crumbly soap which cannot readily be milled and is termed "short." When used with tallow and cocoanut oil, or 20 to 25 per cent. cocoanut oil, it produces a very satisfactory toilet soap. In the saponification of palm oil it is not advisable to combine it with tallow in the kettle, as the two do not readily mix.

Since the finished soap has conveyed to it the orange color of the oil, the oil is bleached before saponification. Oxidation readily destroys the coloring matter, while heat and light assist materially. The methods generally employed are by the use of oxygen developed by bichromates and hydrochloric acid and the direct bleaching through the agency of the oxygen of the air.

### CHROME BLEACHING OF PALM OIL.

The chrome process of bleaching palm oil is more rapid and the oxygen thus derived being more active will bleach oils which air alone cannot. It depends upon the reaction:

$$Na_2Cr_2O_7 + 8HCl = Cr_2Cl_6 + 2NaCl + 7O.$$

in which the oxygen is the active principle. In practice it is found necessary to use an excess of acid over that theoretically indicated.

For the best results an oil should be chosen containing under 2 per cent. impurities and a low percentage of free fatty acids. Lagos oil is best adapted to these requirements. The oil is melted by open steam from a jet introduced through the bung, the melted oil and condensed water running to the store tank through two sieves (about 1/8 inch mesh) to remove the fibrous material and gross impurities The oil thus obtained contains fine earthy and fibrous material and vegetable albuminous matter which should be removed, as far as possible, since chemicals are wasted in their oxidation and they retard the bleaching. This is best done by boiling the oil for one hour with wet steam and 10 per cent. solution of common salt (2 per cent. dry salt on weight of oil used) in a lead-lined or wooden tank. After settling over night the brine and impurities are removed by running from a cock at the bottom of the vat and the oil is run out into the bleaching tank through an oil cock, situated about seven inches from the bottom.

The bleaching tank is a lead-lined iron tank of the approximate dimensions of 4 feet deep, 4 feet long and 3½ feet wide, holding about 1½ tons. The charge is one ton. A leaden outlet pipe is fixed at the bottom, to which is attached a rubber tube closed by a screw clip. A plug also is fitted into the lead outlet pipe from above. Seven inches above the lower outlet is affixed another tap through which the oil is drawn off.

The tank is further equipped with a wet steam coil and a coil arranged to allow thorough air agitation, both coils being of lead. A good arrangement is to use one coil to deliver either air or steam. These coils should extend as nearly as possible over the entire bottom of the tank and have a number of small downward perforations, so as to spread the agitation throughout the mass.

The temperature of the oil is reduced by passing in air

to 110° F. and 40 pounds of fine common salt per ton added through a sieve. About one-half of the acid (40 pounds of concentrated commercial hydrochloric acid) is now poured in and this is followed by the sodium bichromate in concentrated solution, previously prepared in a small lead vat or earthen vessel by dissolving 17 pounds of bichromate in 45 pounds commercial hydrochloric acid. This solution should be added slowly and should occupy three hours, the whole mass being thoroughly agitated with air during the addition and for one hour after the last of the bleaching mixture has been introduced. The whole mixture is now allowed to settle for one hour and the exhausted chrome liquors are then run off from the lower pipe to a waste tank. About 40 gallons of water are now run into the bleached oil and the temperature raised by open steam to 150° to 160° F. The mass is then allowed to settle over night.

One such wash is sufficient to remove the spent chrome liquor completely, provided ample time is allowed for settling. A number of washings given successively with short periods of settling do not remove the chrome liquors effectually. The success of the operation depends entirely upon the completeness of settling.

The wash water is drawn off as before and the clear oil run to storage tanks or to the soap kettle through the upper oil cock.

The waste liquors are boiled with wet steam and the oil skimmed from the surface, after which the liquors are run out through an oil trap.

By following the above instructions carefully it is possible to bleach one ton of palm oil with 17 pounds of bichromate of soda and 85 pounds hydrochloric acid.

The spent liquors should be a bright green color. Should they be of a yellow or brownish shade insufficient acid has been allowed and more must be added to render the whole of the oxygen available.

If low grade oils are being treated more chrome will be necessary, the amount being best judged by conducting the operation as usual and after the addition of the bichromate, removing a sample of the oil, washing the sample and noting the color of a rapidly cooled sample.

A little practice will enable the operator to judge the correspondence between the color to be removed and the amount of bleaching mixture to be added.

To obtain success with this process the method of working given must be adhered to even in the *smallest detail.* This applies to the temperature at which each operation is carried out particularly.

### AIR BLEACHING OF PALM OIL.

The method of conducting this process is identical with the chrome process to the point where the hydrochloric acid is to be added to the oil. In this method no acid or chrome is necessary, as the active bleaching agent is the oxygen of the air.

The equipment is similar to that of the former process, except that a wooden tank in which no iron is exposed will suffice to bleach the oil in. The process depends in rapidity upon the amount of air blown through the oil and its even distribution. Iron should not be present or exposed to the oil during bleaching, as it retards the process considerably.

After the impurities have been removed, as outlined under the chrome process, the temperature of the oil is raised by open steam to boiling. The steam is then shut off and air allowed to blow through the oil until it is completely bleached, the temperature being maintained above 150° F. by occasionally passing in steam. Usually a ton of oil is readily and completely bleached after the air has been passed through it for 18 to 20 hours, provided the oil is thoroughly agitated by a sufficient flow of air.

If the the oil has been allowed to settle over night, it is advisable to run off the condensed water and impurities by the lower cock before agitating again the second day.

When the oil has been bleached to the desired color, which can be determined by removing a sample and cooling, the mass is allowed to settle, the water run off to a waste tank from which any oil carried along may be skimmed off and the supernatant clear oil run to the storage or soap kettle.

In bleaching by this process, while the process consumes more time and is not as efficient in bleaching the lower grade oils, the cost of bleaching is less and with a good oil success is more probable, as there is no possibility of any of the chrome liquors being present in the oil. These give the bleached oil a green tint when the chrome method is improperly conducted and they are not removed.

Instead of blowing the air through it, the heater oil may be brought into contact with the air, either by a paddle wheel arrangement, which, in constantly turning, brings the oil into contact with the air, or by pumping the heated oil into an elevated vessel, pierced with numerous fine holes from which the oil continously flows back into the vessel from which the oil is pumped. While in these methods air, light and heat act simultaneously in the bleaching of the oil, the equipment required is too cumbersome to be practical.

Recent investigations[1] in bleaching palm oil by oxygen have shown that not only the coloring matter but the oil itself was affected. In bleaching palm oil for 30 hours with air the free fatty acid content rose and titer decreased considerably.

[1]Seifensieder Zeit, 1913, 40, p. 687, 724, 740.

*Olive Oil*, which comes from the fruit of the olive trees, varies greatly in quality, according to the method by which it is obtained and according to the tree bearing the fruit. Three hundred varieties are known in Italy alone. Since the larger portion of olive oil is used for edible purposes, a lower grade, denatured oil, denatured because of the tariff, is used for soap manufacture in this country. The oil varies in color from pale green to golden yellow. The percentage of free acid in this oil varies greatly, though the oil does not turn rancid easily. It is used mainly in the manufacture of white castile soap.

Olive oil foots, which is the oil extracted by solvents after the better oil is expressed, finds its use in soap making mostly in textile soaps for washing and dyeing silks and in the production of green castile soaps.

Other oils, as poppy seed oil, sesame oil, cottonseed oil, rape oil, peanut (arachis) oil, are used as adulterants for olive oil, also as substitutes in the manufacture of castile soap, since they are cheaper than olive oil.

*Cottonseed Oil* is largely used in the manufacture of floating and laundry soaps. It may be used for toilet soaps where a white color is not desired, as yellow spots appear on a finished soap in which it has been used after having been in stock a short time.

*Corn Oil and Soya Bean Oil* are also used to a slight extent in the manufacture of toilet soaps, although the oils form a soap of very little body. Their soaps also spot yellow on aging.

Corn oil finds its greatest use in the manufacture of soap for washing automobiles. It is further employed for the manufacture of cheap liquid soaps.

*Fatty Acids* are also used extensively in soap manufacture. While the soap manufacturer prefers to use a neutral oil or fat, since from these the by-product glycerine is obtained, circumstances arise where it is an advantage to use the free fatty acids. Red oil (oleic acid, elaine) and stearic acid are the two fatty acids most generally bought for soap making. In plants using the Twitchell process, which consists in splitting the neutral fats and oils into fatty acids and glycerine by dilute sulphuric acid and producing their final separation by the use of so-called aromatic sulphonic acids, these fatty acids consisting of a mixture of oleic, stearic, palmitic acids, etc., are used directly after having been purified by distillation, the glycerine being obtained from evaporating the wash water.

Oleic acid (red oil) and stearic acid are obtained usually by the saponification of oils, fats and greases by acid, lime or water under pressure or Twitchelling. The fatty acids thus are freed from their combination with glycerine and solidify upon cooling, after which they are separated from the water and pressed at a higher or lower temperature. The oleic acid, being liquid at ordinary temperature, together with some stearic and palmitic acid, is thus pressed out. These latter acids are usually separated by distillation, combined with the press cake further purified and sold as stearic acid.

The red oil, sometimes called saponified red oil, is often semi-solid, resembling a soft tallow, due to the presence of stearic acid. The distilled oils are usually clear, varying in color from light to a deep brown. Stearic acid, which reaches the trade in slab form, varies in quality from a soft brown, greasy, crumbly solid of unpleasant odor to a snow white, wax-like, hard, odorless mass. The quality of stearic acid is best judged by the melting point, since the presence of any oleic acid lowers this. The melting point of the varieties used in soap manufacture usually ranges from 128° to 132° F. Red oil is used in the manufacture of textile soaps, replacing olive oil foots soap for this purpose, chlorophyll being used to color the soap green. Stearic acid, being the hard firm fatty acid, may be used in small quantities to give a better grade of soap body and finish. In adding this substance it should always be done in the crutcher, as it will not mix in the kettle. It finds its largest use for soap, however, in the manufacture of shaving soaps and shaving creams, since it produces the non-drying creamy lather so greatly desired for this purpose. Both red oil and stearic acid being fatty acids, readily unite with the alkali carbonates, carbon dioxide being formed in the reaction and this method is extensively used in the formation of soap from them.

### RANCIDITY OF OILS AND FATS.

Rancidity in neutral oils and fats is one of the problems the soap manufacturer has to contend with. The mere saying that an oil is rancid is no indication of its being high in free acid. The two terms rancidity and acidity are usually allied. Formerly, the acidity of a fat was looked upon as the direct measure of its rancidity. This idea is still prevalent in practice and cannot be too often stated as incorrect. Fats and oils may be *acid,* or *rancid,* or *acid and rancid.* In an acid fat there has been a hydrolysis of the fat and it has developed a rather high percentage of free acid. A rancid fat is one in which have been developed compounds of an odoriferous nature.. An acid and rancid fat is one in which both free acid and organic compounds of the well known disagreeable odors have been produced.

It cannot be definitely stated just how this rancidity takes place, any more than just what are the chemical products causing rancidity. The only conclusion that one may draw is that the fats are first hydrolyzed or split up into glycerine and free fatty acids. This is followed by an oxidation of the products thus formed.

Moisture, air, light, enzymes (organized ferments) and bacteria are all given as causes of rancidity.

It seems very probable that the initial splitting of the fats is caused by enzymes, which are present in the seeds and fruits of the vegetable oils and tissue of animal fats, in the presence of moisture. Lewkowitsch strongly emphasizes this point and he is substantiated in his idea by other authorities. Others hold that bacteria or micro-organisms are the cause of this hydrolysis, citing the fact that they have isolated various micro-organisms from various fats and oils. The acceptance of the bacterial action would explain the various methods of preservation of oils and fats by the use of antiseptic preparations. It cannot, however, be accepted as a certainty that bacteria cause the rancidity of fats.

The action of enzymes is a more probable explanation.

The hydrolysis of fats and oils is accelerated when they are allowed to remain for some time in the presence of organic non-fats. Thus, palm oil, lower grades of olive oil, and tallow, which has been in contact with the animal tissue for a long time, all contain other nitrogenous matter and exhibit a larger percentage of free fatty acid than the oils and fats not containing such impurities.

Granting this initial splitting of the fat into free fatty acids and glycerine, this is not a sufficient explanation. The products thus formed must be acted upon by air and light. It is by the action of these agents that there is a further action upon the products, and from this oxidation we ascertain by taste and smell (chemical means are still unable to define rancidity) whether or not a fat is rancid. While some authorities have presumed to isolate some of these products causing rancidity, we can only assume the presence of the various possible compounds produced by the action of air and light which include oxy fatty acids, lactones, alcohols, esters, aldehydes and other products.

The soap manufacturer is interested in rancidity to the extent of the effect upon the finished soap. Rancid fats form darker soaps than fats in the neutral state, and very often carry with them the disagreeable odor of a rancid oil. Further, a rancid fat or oil is usually high in free acid. It is by no means true, however, that rancidity is a measure for acidity, for as has already been pointed out, an oil may be rancid and not high in free acid.

The percentage of free fatty acid is of even greater importance in the soap industry. The amount of glycerine yield is dependent upon the percentage of free fatty acid and is one of the criterions of a good fat or oil for soap stock.

### PREVENTION OF RANCIDITY.

Since moisture, air, light and enzymes, produced by the presence of organic impurities, are necessary for the rancidity of a fat or oil, the methods of preventing rancidity are given. Complete dryness, complete purification of fats and oils and storage without access of air or light are desirable. Simple as these means may seem, they can only be approximated in practice. The most difficult problem is the removal of the last trace of moisture. Impurities may be lessened very often by the use of greater care. In storing it is well to store in closed barrels or closed iron tanks away from light, as it has been observed that oils and fats in closed receptacles become rancid less rapidly than those in open ones, even though this method of storing is only partially attained. Preservatives are also used, but only in edible products, where their effectiveness is an open question.

### CHEMICAL CONSTANTS OF OILS AND FATS.

Besides the various physical properties of oils and fats,

such as color, specific gravity, melting point, solubility, etc., they may be distinguished chemically by a number of chemical constants. These are the iodine number, the acetyl value, saponification number, Reichert-Meissl number for volatile acids, Hehner number for insoluble acids. These constants, while they vary somewhat with any particular oil or fat, are more applicable to the edible products and are criterions where any adulteration of fat or oil is suspected. The methods of carrying out the analyses of oils and fats to obtain these constants are given in the various texts* on oils and fats, and inasmuch as they are not of great importance to the soap industry they are merely mentioned here.

### OIL HARDENING OR HYDROGENATING.

It is very well known that oils and fats vary in consistency and hardness, depending upon the glycerides forming same. Olein, a combination of oleic acid and glycerine, as well as oleic acid itself largely forms the liquid portion of oils and fats. Oleic acid ($C_{18}H_{34}O_2$) is an unsaturated acid and differs from stearic acid $C_{18}H_{36}O_2$), the acid forming the hard firm portion of oils and fats, by containing two atoms of hydrogen less in the molecule. Theoretically it should be a simple matter to introduce two atoms of hydrogen into oleic acid or olein, and by this mere addition convert liquid oleic acid and olein into solid stearic acid and stearine.

For years this was attempted and all attempts to apply the well known methods of reduction (addition of hydrogen) in organic chemistry, such as treatment with tin and acid, sodium amalgam, etc., were unsuccessful. In recent years, however, it has been discovered that in the presence of a catalyzer, nickel in finely divided form

*Official Methods, see Bull. 107, A. O. A. C., U. S. Dept. Agricult.

or the oxides of nickel are usually employed, the process of hydrogenating an oil is readily attained upon a practical basis.

The introduction of hardened oils has opened a new source of raw material for the soap manufacturer in that it is now possible to use oils in soap making which were formerly discarded because of their undesirable odors. Thus fish or train oils which had up to the time of oil hydrogenating resisted all attempts of being permanently deodorized, can now be employed very satisfactorily for soap manufacture. A Japanese chemist, Tsujimoto[1] has shown that fish oils contain an unsaturated acid of the composition $C_{18}H_{28}O_2$, for which he proposed the name clupanodonic acid. By the catalytic hardening of train oils this acid passes to stearic acid and the problem of deodorizing these oils is solved.[2]

At first the introduction of hardened oils for soap manufacture met with numerous objections, due to the continual failures of obtaining a satisfactory product by the use of same. Various attempts have now shown that these oils, particularly hardened train oils, produce extraordinarily useful materials for soap making. These replace expensive tallow and other high melting oils. It is of course impossible to employ hardened oils alone, as a soap so hard would thus be obtained that it would be difficultly soluble in water and possess very little lathering quality. By the addition of 20-25% of tallow oil or some other oil forming a soft soap a very suitable soap for household use may be obtained. Ribot[3] discusses this matter fully. Hardened oils readily saponify, may be

---

[1]Journ. Coll. of Engin. Tokyo Imper. Univ. (1906), p. 1. Abs. Chem. Revue f. d. Fett-u. Harz, Ind. 16, p. 84; 20, p. 8.

[2] Meyerheim—Fort. der Chem., Physik. und Physik. Chem. (1913), 8. 6, p. 293-307.

[3] Seifs. Ztg. (1913), 40, p. 142.

perfumed without any objections and do not impart any fishy odor to an article washed with same. Meyerheim[4] states that through the use of hydrogenated oils the hardness of soap is extraordinarily raised, so that soap made from hardened cottonseed oil is twelve times as hard as the soap made from ordinary cottonseed oil. This soap is also said to no longer spot yellow upon aging, and as a consequence of its hardness, is able to contain a considerably higher content of rosin through which lathering power and odor may be improved. Hardened oils can easily be used for toilet soap bases, provided they are not added in too great a percentage.

The use of hardened oils is not yet general, but there is little doubt that the introduction of this process goes a long way toward solving the problem of cheaper soap material for the coap making industry.

### GREASE.

Grease varies so greatly in composition and consistency that it can hardly be classed as a distinctive oil or fat. It is obtained from refuse, bones, hides, etc., and while it contains the same constituents as tallow, the olein content is considerably greater, which causes it to be more liquid in composition. Grease differs in color from an off-white to a dark brown. The better qualities are employed in the manufacture of laundry and chip soap, while the poorer qualities are only fit for the cheapest of soaps used in scrubbing floors and such purposes. There is usually found in grease a considerable amount of gluey matter, lime and water. The percentage of free fatty acid is generally high.

The darker grades of grease are bleached before being used. This is done by adding a small quantity of sodium nitrate to the melted grease and agitating, then

[4] Loc. cit.

removing the excess saltpeter by decomposing with sulphuric acid. A better method of refining, however, is by distillation. The chrome bleach is also applicable.

### ROSIN (COLOPHONY, YELLOW ROSIN, RESINA).

Rosin is the residue which remains after the distillation of turpentine from the various species of pines. The chief source of supply is in the States of Georgia North and South Carolina. It is a transparent, amber colored hard pulverizable resin. The better grades are light in color and known as water white (w. w.) and window glass (w. g.). These are obtained from a tree which has been tapped for the first year. As the same trees are tapped from year to year, the product becomes deeper and darker in color until it becomes almost black.

The constituents of rosin are chiefly (80-90%) abietic acid or its anhydride together with pinic and sylvic acids. Its specific gravity is 1.07-1.08, melting point about 152.5 C., and it is soluble in alcohol, ether, benzine, carbon disulfide, oils, alkalis and acetic acid. The main use of rosin, outside of the production of varnishes, is in the production of laundry soaps, although a slight percentage acts as a binder and fixative for perfumes in toilet soaps and adds to their detergent properties. Since it is mainly composed of acids, it readily unites with alkaline carbonates, though the saponification is not quite complete and the last portion must be completed through the use of caustic hydrates, unless an excess of 10% carbonate over the theoretical amount is used. A lye of 20° B. is best adapted to the saponification of rosin when caustic hydrates are employed for this purpose, since weak lyes cause frothing. While it is sometimes considered that rosin is an adulterant for soap, this is hardly justifiable, as it adds to the cleansing properties of soap. Soaps containing rosin are of the well known yellowish color common to ordinary laundry soaps. The price of rosin has so risen in the last few years that it presents a problem of cost to the soap manufacturer considering the price at which laundry soaps are sold.

### ROSIN SAPONIFICATION.

As has been stated, rosin may be saponified by the use of alkaline carbonates. On account of the possibility of the soap frothing over, the kettle in which the operation takes place should be set flush with the floor, which ought to be constructed of cement. The kettle itself is an open one with round bottom, equipped with an open steam coil and skimmer pipe, and the open portion is protected by a semi-circular rail. A powerful grid, having a 3-inch mesh, covers one-half of the kettle, the sharp edges protruding upwards.

The staves from the rosin casks are removed at the edge of the kettle, the rosin placed on the grid and beaten through with a hammer to break it up into small pieces.

To saponify a ton of rosin there are required 200 lbs. soda ash, 1,600 lbs. water and 100 lbs. salt. Half the water is run into the kettle, boiled, and then the soda ash and half the salt added. The rosin is now added through the grid and the mixture thoroughly boiled. As carbon dioxide is evolved by the reaction the boiling is continued for one hour to remove any excess of this gas. A portion of the salt is gradually added to grain the soap well and to keep the mass in such condition as to favor the evolution of gas. The remainder of the water is added to close the soap and boiling continued for one or two hours longer. At this point the kettle must be carefully watched or it will boil over through the further escape of carbon dioxide being hindered. The mass, being in a frothy condition, will rapidly settle by controlling the flow of steam. The remaining salt is then scattered in and the soap allowed to settle for two hours or longer. The lyes are then drained off the top. If the rosin soap is required for toilet soaps, it is grained a second time. The soap is now boiled with the water caused by the condensation of the steam, which changes it to a half grained soap suitable for pumping. A. soap thus made contains free soda ash 0.15% or less, free rosin about 15%. The mass is then pumped to the kettle containing the soap to which it is to be added at the proper stage. The time consumed in thus saponifying rosin is about five hours.

### NAPHTHENIC ACIDS.

The naphtha or crude petroleum of the various provinces in Europe, as Russia, Galacia, Alsace and Roumania yield a series of bodies of acid character upon refining which are designated under the general name of naphthenic acids. These acids are retained in solution in the alkaline lyes during the distillation of the naphtha in the form of alkaline naphthenates. Upon adding dilute sulphuric acid to these lyes the naphthenates are decomposed and the naphthenic acids float to the surface in an oily layer of characteristic disagreeable odor and varying from yellow to brown in color[1]. In Russia particularly large quantities of these acids are employed in the manufacture of soap.

The soaps formed from naphthenic acids have recently been investigated[2] and found to resemble the soaps made from cocoanut oil and palm kernel oil, in that they are

[1] Les Matieres Graisses (1914), 7, 69, p. 3367.
[2] Zeit. f. Angew. Chem. (1914), 27, 1, p. 2-4.

difficult to salt out and dissociate very slightly with water, The latter property makes them valuable in textile industries when a mild soap is required as a detergent, e. g., in the silk industry. These soaps also possess a high solvent power for mineral oils and emulsify very readily. The mean molecular weight of naphthenic acids themselves is very near that of the fatty acids contained in cocoanut oil, and like those of cocoanut oil a portion of the separated acids are volatile with steam. The iodine number indicates a small content of unsaturated acids.

That naphthenic acids are a valuable soap material is now recognized, but except in Russia the soap is not manufactured to any extent at the present time.

### ALKALIS.

The common alkali metals which enter into the formation of soap are sodium and potassium. The hydroxides of these metals are usually used, except in the so called carbonate saponification of free fatty acids in which case sodium and potassium carbonate are used. A water solution of the caustic alkalis is known as lye, and it is as lyes of various strengths that they are added to oils and fats to form soap. The density or weight of a lye is considerably greater than that of water, depending upon the amount of alkali dissolved, and its weight is usually determined by a hydrometer. This instrument is graduated by a standardized scale, and while all hydrometers should read alike in a liquid of known specific gravity, this is generally not the case, so that it is advisable to check a new hydrometer for accurate work against one of known accuracy. In this country the Baumé scale has been adopted, while in England a different graduation known as the Twaddle scale is used. The strength of a lye or any solution is determined by the distance the instrument sinks into the solution, and we speak of the strength of a solution as so many degrees Baumé or Twaddle which are read to the point where the meniscus of the lye comes on the graduated scale. Hydrometers are graduated differently for liquids of different weights. In the testing of lyes one which is graduated from 0° to 50° B. is usually employed.

*Caustic soda* is received by the consumer in iron drums weighing approximately 700 lbs. each. The various grades are designated as 60, 70, 74, 76 and 77%. These percentages refer to the percentage of sodium oxide ($Na_2O$) in 100 parts of pure caustic soda formed by the combination of 77½ parts of sodium oxide and 22½ parts of water, 77½% being chemically pure caustic soda. There are generally impurities present in commercial caustic soda. These consist of sodium carbonate, sodium chloride or common salt and sometimes lime. It is manufactured by treating sodium carbonate in an iron vessel with calcium hydroxide or slaked lime, or by electrolysis of common salt. The latter process has yet been unable to compete with the former in price. Formerly all the caustic soda used in soap making was imported, and it was only through the American manufacturer using a similar container to that used by foreign manufacturers that they were able to introduce their product. This prejudice has now been entirely overcome and most of the caustic soda used in this country is manufactured here.

### CAUSTIC POTASH.

The output of the salts containing potassium is controlled almost entirely by Germany. Formerly the chief source of supply of potassium compounds was from the burned ashes of plants, but about fifty years ago the inexhaustible salt mines of Stassfurt, Germany, were discovered. The salt there mined contains, besides the chlorides and sulphates of sodium, magnesium, calcium and other salts, considerable quantities of potassium chloride, and the Stassfurt mines at present are practically the entire source of all potassium compounds, in spite of the fact that other localities have been sought to produce these compounds on a commercial basis, especially by the United States government.

After separating the potassium chloride from the magnesium chloride and other substances found in Stassfurt salts the methods of manufacture of caustic potash are identical to those of caustic soda. In this case, however, domestic electrolytic caustic potash may be purchased cheaper than the imported product and it gives results equal to those obtained by the use of the imported article, opinions to the contrary among soap makers being many. Most of the caustic potash in the United States is manufactured at Niagara Falls by the Niagara Alkali Co., and the Hooker Electrochemical Co., chlorine being obtained as a by-product. The latter concern employs the Townsend Cell, for the manufacture of electrolytic potash, and are said to have a capacity for making 64 tons of alkali daily.

Since the molecular weight of caustic potash (56) is greater than that of caustic soda (40) more potash is required to saponify a pound of fat. The resulting potash soap is correspondingly heavier than a soda soap. When salt is added to a potassium soap double decomposition occurs, the potassium soap being transformed to a sodium soap and the potassium uniting with the chlorine to form potassium chloride. This was one of the earliest methods of making a hard soap, especially in Germany, where potash was derived from leeching ashes of burned wood and plants.

### SODIUM CARBONATE (SODA ASH).

While carbonate of soda is widely distributed in nature the source of supply is entirely dependent upon the manufactured product. Its uses are many, but it is especially important to the soap industry in the so called carbonate saponification of free fatty acids, as a constituent of soap powders, in the neutralization of glycerine lyes and as a filler for laundry soaps.

The old French Le Blanc soda process, which consists in treating common salt with sulphuric acid and reducing the sodium sulphate (salt cake) thus formed with carbon in the form of charcoal or coke to sodium sulphide, which when treated with calcium carbonate yields a mixture of calcium sulphide and sodium carbonate (black ash) from which the carbonate is dissolved by water, has been replaced by the more recent Solvay ammonia soda process. Even though there is a considerable loss of salt and the by-product calcium chloride produced by this process is only partially used up as a drying agent, and for refrigerating purposes, the Le Blanc process cannot compete with the Solvay process, so that the time is not far distant when the former will be considered a chemical curiosity. In the Solvay method of manufacture sodium chloride (common salt) and ammonium bicarbonate are mixed in solution. Double decomposition occurs with the formation of ammonium chloride and sodium bicarbonate. The latter salt is comparatively difficultly soluble in water and crystallizes out, the ammonium chloride remaining in solution. When the sodium bicarbonate is heated it yields sodium carbonate, carbon dioxide and water; the carbon dioxide is passed into ammonia which is set free from the ammonium chloride obtained as above by treatment with lime (calcium oxide) calcium chloride being the by-product.

Sal soda or washing soda is obtained by recrystallizing a solution of soda ash in water. Large crystals of sal soda containing but 37% sodium carbonate are formed.

### POTASSIUM CARBONATE.

Potassium carbonate is not extensively used in the manufacture of soap. It may be used in the forming of soft soaps by uniting it with free fatty acids. The methods of manufacture are the same as for sodium carbonate, although a much larger quantity of potassium carbonate than carbonate of soda is obtained from burned plant ashes. Purified potassium carbonate is known as *pearl ash.*

### ADDITIONAL MATERIAL USED IN SOAP MAKING.

Water is indispensable to the soap manufacturer. In the soap factory *hard* water is often the cause of much trouble. Water, which is the best solvent known, in passing through the crevices of rocks dissolves some of the constituents of these, and the water is known as hard. This hardness is of two kinds, *temporary* and *permanent.* Temporarily hard water is formed by water, which contains carbonic acid, dissolving a portion of calcium carbonate or carbonate of lime. Upon boiling, the carbonic acid is driven from the water and the carbonate, being insoluble in carbon dioxide free water, is deposited. This is the cause of boiler scale, and to check this a small amount of sal ammoniac may be added to the water, which converts the carbonate into soluble calcium chloride and volatile ammonium carbonate. Permanent hardness is caused by calcium sulphate which is soluble in 400 parts of water and cannot be removed by boiling.

The presence of these salts in water form insoluble lime soaps which act as inert bodies as far as their value for the common use of soap is concerned. Where the percentage of lime in water is large this should be removed.

A method generally used is to add about 5% of 20° B. sodium silicate to the hard water. This precipitates the lime and the water is then sufficiently pure to use.

*Salt,* known as sodium chloride, is used to a large extent in soap making for "salting out" the soap during saponification, as well as graining soaps. Soap ordinarily soluble in water is insoluble in a salt solution, use of which is made by adding salt to the soap which goes into solution and throws any soap dissolved in the lyes out of solution. Salt may contain magnesium and calcium chlorides, which of course are undesirable in large amounts. The products on the market, however, are satisfactory, thus no detail is necessary.

*Filling materials* used are sodium silicate, or water glass, talc, silex, pumice, starch, borax, tripoli, etc.

Besides these other materials are used in the refining of the oils and fats, and glycerine recovery, such as Fuller's earth, bichromates of soda or potash, sulphate of alumina, sulphuric and hydrochloric acids and alcohol.

A lengthy description of these substances is not given, as their modes of use are detailed elsewhere.

# CHAPTER II

## Construction and Equipment of a Soap Plant.

No fixed plan for the construction and equipment of a soap plant can be given. The specifications for a soap factory to be erected or remodeled must suit the particular cases. Very often a building which was constructed for a purpose other than soap manufacture must be adapted for the production of soap. In either case it is a question of engineering and architecture, together with the knowledge obtained in practice and the final decision as to the arrangement is best solved by a conference with those skilled in each of these branches.

An ideal soap plant is one in which the process of soap making, from the melting out of the stock to the packing and shipping of the finished product, moves downward from floor to floor, since by this method it is possible to utilize gravitation rather than pumping liquid fats and fluid soaps. Convenience and economy are obtained by such an arrangement.

The various machinery and other equipment for soap manufacture are well known to those connected with this industry. It varies, of course, depending upon the kind of soap to be manufactured, and full descriptions of the necessary machinery are best given in the catalogs issued by the manufacturers of such equipment, who in this country are most reliable.

To know just what equipment is necessary can very easily be described by a brief outline of the process various soaps undergo to produce the finished article. After the saponification has taken place in the *soap kettle* the molten soap is run directly into the soap *frames,* which consist of an oblong compartment, holding anywhere from 400 to 1,200 pounds, with removable steel sides and mounted upon trucks, in which it solidifies. In most cases it is advisable to first run the soap into a *crutcher* or mixer which produces a more homogeneous mass than if this operation is omitted. Color and perfume may also be added at this point, although when a better grade of perfume is added it must be remembered that there is considerable loss due to volatilization of same. When a *drying machine* is employed the molten soap is run directly upon the rollers of this machine, later adding about 1.0% zinc oxide to the soap from which it passes continuously through the drying chamber and is emitted in chip form ready for milling. After the soap has been framed, it is allowed to cool and solidify, which takes several days, and then the sides of the frame are stripped off. The large solid cake is cut with wires by hand or by a *slabber* into slabs of any desired size. These slabs are further divided into smaller divisions by the *cutting table.* In non-milled soaps (laundry soaps, floating soaps, etc.), these are pressed at this stage, usually by automatic presses, after a thin hard film has been formed over the cake by allowing it to dry slightly. In making these soaps they are not touched by hand at any time during the operation, the pressing, wrapping and packing all being done by machinery. For a milled soap the large slabs are cut into narrow oblong shapes by means of the cutting table to readily pass into the feeder of the *chipper,* the chips being spread upon *trays* and dried in a *dry house* until the moisture content is approximately 15%.

The process of milling is accomplished by passing the dried soap chips through a *soap mill,* which is a machine consisting of usually three or four contiguous, smooth, granite rollers operated by a system of gears and set far enough apart to allow the soap to pass from a hopper to the first roller, from which it is constantly conveyed to each succeeding roller as a thin film, and finally scraped from the last roller to fall into the *milling box* in thin ribbon form. These mills are often operated in tandem, which necessitates less handling of soap by the operator. The object of milling is to give the soap a glossy, smooth finish and to blend it into a homogeneous mass. The perfume, color, medication or any other material desired are added to the dried soap chips prior to milling. Some manufacturers use an *amalgamator* to distribute these uniformly through the soap, which eliminates at least one milling. When a white soap is being put through the mill, it is advisable to add from 0.5% to 1% of a good, fine quality of zinc oxide to the soap, if this substance has not been previously added. This serves to remove the yellowish cast and any translucency occasioned by plodding. Too great a quantity of this compound added, later exhibits itself by imparting to the soap a dead white appearance. Inasmuch as the milling process is one upon which the appearance of a finished cake of toilet soap largely depends, it should be carefully done. The number of times a soap should be milled depends upon the character of a soap being worked. It should of course be the object to mill with as high a percentage of moisture as possible. Should the soap become too dry it is advisable to add water directly, rather than wet soap, since water can more easily be distributed through the mass. As a general statement it may be said it is better policy to overmill a soap, rather than not mill it often enough.

After the soap has been thoroughly milled it is ready for plodding. A *plodder* is so constructed as to take the soap ribbons fed into the hopper by means of a worm screw and continuously force it under great pressure through a jacketed cylinder through which cold water circulates in the rear to compensate the heat produced by friction and hot water at the front, to soften and polish the soap which passes out in solid form in bars of any shape and size depending upon the form of the *shaping plate* through which it is emitted. The bars run upon a *roller board,* are cut into the required length by a special *cake cutting table,* allowed to dry slightly and pressed either automatically or by a foot power *press* in any suitable soap *die.* The finished cake is then ready for wrapping and after due time in stock reaches the consumer.

Besides the various apparatus mentioned above there are many other parts for the full equipment of a modern soap plant, such as remelters, pumps, mixers, special tanks, power equipment, etc. As has been stated, however, practical experience will aid in judging the practicability as to installation of these. The various methods of powdering soap are, however, not generally known. Where a coarse powder is to be produced, such as is used for common washing powders, no great difficulty is experienced with the well known Blanchard mill. In grinding soap to an impalpable powder the difficulties increase. The methods adapted in pulverizing soaps are by means of disintegrators, pebble mills and chaser mills. The disintegrator grinds by the principle of attrition, that is, the material is reduced by the particles being caused to beat against each other at great velocity; a pebble mill crushes the substance by rubbing it between hard pebbles in a slowly revolving cylinder; the chaser mill first grinds the material and then floats it as a very fine powder above a curb of fixed height. The last method is particularly adapted for the finest of powder (140 mesh and over).

# CHAPTER III

## Classification of Soap-Making Methods.

In the saponification of fats and oils to form soap through the agency of caustic alkalis, as has been stated, the sodium or potassium salts of the mixed fatty acids are formed. Sodium soaps are usually termed hard soaps, and potassium soaps soft. There are, however, a great many varieties of soaps the appearance and properties of which depend upon their method of manufacture and the oils or fats used therein.

The various methods adopted in soap making may be thus classified:

1. Boiling the fats and oils in open kettles by open steam with indefinite quantities of caustic alkali solutions until the finished soap is obtained; ordinarily named *full boiled soaps.* These may be sub-divided into (a) hard soaps with sodium hydrate as a base, in which the glycerine is recovered from the spent lyes; (b) hard soaps with soda as a base, in which the glycerine remains in the soap, e. g., marine cocoanut oil soaps; (c) soft potash soaps, in which the glycerine is retained by the soap.

2. Combining the required amount of lye for complete saponification of a fat therewith, heating slightly with dry heat and then allowing the saponification to complete itself. This is known as the *cold process.*

3. Utilizing the fatty acid, instead of the neutral fat, and combining it directly with caustic alkali or carbonate, which is incorrectly termed *carbonate saponification,* since it is merely neutralizing the free fatty acid and thus is not a saponification in the true sense of the word. No glycerine is directly obtained by this method, as it is

usually previously removed in the clearage of the fat by either the Twitchell or autoclave saponification method.

In the methods thus outlined the one most generally employed is the full boiled process to form a sodium soap. This method of making soap requires close attention and a knowledge which can only be obtained by constant practice. The stock, strength of lyes, heat, amount of salt or brine added, time of settling, etc., are all influencing factors.

The principles involved in this process are briefly these: The fat is partly saponified with weak lyes (usually those obtained from a previous boiling in the strengthening change are used), and salt is added to grain the soap. The mass is then allowed to settle into two layers. The upper layer is partly saponified fat; the lower layer, or spent lye, is a solution of salt, glycerine, and contains any albuminous matter or any other impurity contained in the fat. This is known as the *killing* or glycerine change. Strong lyes are now added and the fat entirely saponified, which is termed the *strengthening change.* The mass is then allowed to settle and the fluid soap run off above the "nigre." This operation is called the finish or *finishing* change.

The method may be more fully illustrated by a concrete example of the method of manufacture of a tallow base:

Charge—

| | |
|---|---|
| Tallow ........................ | 88 per cent. |
| Cocoanut oil.................... | 10 per cent. |
| Rosin w. w...................... | 2 per cent. |
| Amount charge............ | 10 tons |

About five tons of tallow and one ton of cocoanut oil are pumped or run into the soap kettle and brought to a boil with wet steam until it briskly comes through the hot fat. The caustic soda (strengthening lyes from former boilings may be used here) is gradually added by the distributing pipe, any tendency to thicken being checked by the introduction of small quantities of brine ("salt pickle"). If the lye is added too rapidly the soap assumes a granular appearance, indicating that the addition of same must be discontinued. Water should then be added and the mass boiled through until it again closes. When the addition of the proper amount of caustic soda is nearing its completion the soap gradually thins. The steam is now cut down to about one turn of the valve, and brine is rapidly added or salt shoveled in. In ten to fifteen minutes the steam again breaks through and, from the appearance of the soap, it can be seen whether sufficient brine has been added. A sample taken out by means of a long wooden paddle should show the soap in fine grains with the lyes running from it clear. The steam is then shut off and the soap allowed to settle from one and one-half to two hours. In all settlings the longer time this operation is permitted to continue, the better will the subsequent operations proceed.

The mixture now consists of a partly saponified layer of fat above the spent lyes. The lyes are drawn off until soap makes its appearance at the exit pipe. The valve is then closed and the soap blown back into the kettle by steam. The lyes thus obtained are known as *spent lyes*, from which the glycerine is recovered. They should show an alkalinity of approximately 0.5 per cent. if the operation is carefully carried out.

The remaining tallow is now added and the above operations repeated.

After the spent lyes have been drawn off, the soap is closed with water and the proper percentage of rosin soap previously formed, or rosin itself is added to the mass in the kettle. More lye is then allowed to flow in until the mixture is up to "strength." This is usually tested by the "bite" on the tongue of a small cooled sample. After boil ing until the steam comes through, the mass is grained with salt as before and allowed to settle one and one-half to three hours. These lyes, known as *strengthening lyes* are run to storage to be used subsequently with fresh fat to take up the caustic soda contained therein.

The soap is now ready for finishing and is first boiled through and tried for strength. A drop of phenolphthalein (1 per cent. phenolphthalein in 98 per cent. alcohol) is allowed to drop on the molten soap taken up on a trowel. The red color should be instantly produced and develop to a full deep crimson in a few seconds, or more lye must be added until this condition is realized. Should it flash a deep crimson immediately it is on the strong side. This cannot be conveniently remedied; it can only serve as a guide for the next boil, but in any case it is not of any serious consequence, unless it is too strong.

With the steam on, the soap is now examined with a trowel which must be thoroughly heated by working it about under the surface of the hot soap. The appearance of the soap as it runs from the face of the trowel indicates its condition. It is not possible to absolutely describe the effect, which can only be properly judged by practice, yet the following points may serve as a guide. The indications to be noticed are the shape and size of the flakes of soap as the sample on the trowel breaks up and runs from the hot iron surface, when the latter is turned in a vertical position, as well as the condition of the iron surface from which the soap flakes have fallen. A closed soap will run slowly into a homogeneous sheet, leaving the trowel's surface covered with a thin layer of transparent soap; a grained mass will run rapidly down in tiny grains, about one-half an inch in diameter or less, leaving the hot trowel absolutely dry. The object of the finish is to separate the soaps of the lower fatty acids from those of the higher, and both from excess of liquid. A point midway between "open" and "closed" is required to arrive at this point.

Having arrived at the above condition, the soap is allowed to settle anywhere from one to three days and then run off through the skimmer pipes to the nigre and framed or pumped to the tank feeding the drying machine.

The stock thus obtained should be fairly white, depending upon the grade of tallow used and slightly alkaline to an alcoholic phenolphthalein solution. If removed at exactly the neutral point or with a content of free fat the soap will sooner or later develop rancidity. The soap thus obtained is an ordinary tallow base, and the one by far greatest used in the manufacture of toilet soaps. The percentage of cocoanut oil indicated is not fixed and may readily be varied, while in fine toilet soap the rosin is usually eliminated.

In the manufacture of full boiled soda soaps in which no glycerine is obtained as a by-product, it being retained in the soap itself, the soap formed is known as a "run" soap. The process is used most extensively in the manufacture of marine soaps by which the method may be best illustrated. This soap is known as marine soap because of its property of readily forming a lather with salt water and is mostly consumed aboard vessels.

Marine soaps are manufactured by first placing in the kettle a calculated amount of lye of 25 deg. to 35 deg. B., depending upon the amount of moisture desired in the finished soaps, plus a slight excess required to saponify a known weight of cocoanut oil. With open steam on, the cocoanut oil is then gradually added, care being taken that the soap does not froth over. Saponification takes place readily and when the oil is entirely saponified the finished soap is put through the process known as running. This consists in constantly pumping the mass from the skimmer pipe back into the top of the kettle, the object being to prevent any settling of the nigre or lye from the soap, as well as producing a homogeneous mass. It is customary to begin the saponification in the morning, which should be completed by noon. The soap is then run for about three hours and framed the next morning. After having remained in the frame the time required to solidify and cool, the soap is slabbed and cut into cakes. This process is difficult to carry out properly, and one not greatly employed, although large quantities of marine soap are purchased by the government for use in the navy and must fulfill certain specifications required by the purchasing department.

In making potash soaps it is practically impossible to obtain any glycerine directly because of the pasty consistency of the soap, and no graining is possible because the addition of salt to a soft soap, as already explained, would form a soda soap. Large quantities of soft soaps are required for the textile industries who desire mostly a strong potash soap, and the large number of automobiles in use at the present time has opened a field for the use of a soft soap for washing these. A soap for this purpose must be neutral so as not to affect the varnish or paint of automobiles.

A suitable soap for textile purposes may be made as follows:

| | |
|---|---|
| Red oil | 80 parts |
| House grease | 20 parts |
| Caustic soda lye, 36 degs. B. | 3 parts |
| Carbonate of potash | 5½ parts |
| Caustic potash | 23¼ parts |

Olive oil, corn oil, soya bean oil, olive oil foots or cottonseed oil may replace any of the above oils. A large quantity of cottonseed oil will cause the soap to fig.

To carry out the process, the caustic potash and carbonate of potash are dissolved and placed in the kettle together with the soda lye, and the oils added. This is most satisfactorily accomplished by being finished the day before the boiling is begun. The next day the boiling is begun and water added to bring the soap up to the desired percentage of fatty acid, due allowance being made for the water formed by the condensation of the open steam in boiling. Care must be taken that the soap in the kettle does not swell and run over during the saponification. A good procedure is to use open steam for a period of about two hours, then close the valve and allow the saponification to continue without boiling, and repeat this until it is entirely saponified. After the saponification has been completed the soap is briskly boiled all day and the proper corrections made; that is, if too alkaline, more oil is added, and if free fat is present, more potash. About 2 per cent. carbonate of potash is the proper amount for a soap containing 50 per cent. fatty acid. The soap is sampled by allowing it to drop on a clean, cold glass surface. In so doing, the soap should not slide or slip over the glass surface when pressed thereon, but should adhere to the glass, or it is too alkaline. A sample worked between the fingers showing too much stringiness should have more strong potash and oil added. A sample taken out in a pail and allowed to cool over night will serve as a guide as to the body of the soap in the kettle. When the soap has thus been properly finished it is run into barrels.

For an automobile soap the following is a good working formula:

| | |
|---|---|
| Corn oil..................... | 1,000 parts |
| Potash lye, 31½ degs. B....... | 697 parts |

Proceed as in the directions just given for textile soap in placing charge in the kettle. When the kettle is boiling up well, shut off the steam and the saponification will complete itself. The soap may be run into the barrels the next day.

A heavy soap with a smaller percentage of fat may be made as follows:

| | |
|---|---|
| Corn oil...................... | 1,000 parts |
| Potash lye, 24½ degs. B....... | 900 parts |

Boil until the soap bunches, and shovel the finished soap into barrels. Upon standing it will clear up. By the addition of more water the yield of soap per pound of oil may be run up to 300 per cent.

After soft soaps have been allowed to stand for some time the phenomenon known as "figging" often occurs. This term is applied to a crystalline-like formation, causing spots of a star-like shape throughout the soap. This is undoubtedly due to the stearine content of the soap crystallizing out as it cools, and forming these peculiarly-shaped spots. It more generally occurs in the winter and may be produced artificially by adding a small quantity of soda to the potash lye before saponification.

The oils usually employed in the manufacture of potash soaps are cottonseed oil, corn oil, soya bean oil, olive oil foots, red oil, cocoanut oil, grease and the various train oils. The usual percentage yield is from 225 per cent. to 300 per cent., based upon the weight of oil used. In calculating the weight of a soft soap it is to be remembered that since potassium has a higher molecular weight (56) than sodium (40), the corresponding soap formed is that much greater in weight when compared with a sodium soap. Rosin may be added to soft soaps as a cheapening agent.

## COLD PROCESS.

The cold process for manufacturing soap is the simplest method of soap making, and the equipment required is small when compared to the other methods. All the more expensive equipment that is necessary is a crutcher, a tank to hold the lye, frames, a slabber or cutting table, and a press. Yet, in spite of the simplicity of thus making soap, the disadvantages are numerous for the production of a good piece of soap. The greatest difficulty is to obtain a thorough combination of oil or fat and lye so that there will not be an excess of one or the other in the finished soap. At its best there is either a considerable excess of free fat which later exhibits itself in producing rancidity or uncombined caustic, which produces an unpleasant effect on the skin when the soap is consumed for washing. The latter objection, of course, can only be applied to toilet soaps.

Cocoanut oil is used very largely in the manufacture of cold-made soaps as it is well adapted for this purpose, although it is by no means true that other oils may not be employed. Since by this process of manufacture no impurity contained in the fat or oil is removed in the making of the soap, it is necessary that in order to obtain a fine finished product, any impurity contained in these may be removed if present, or that the fats be as pure as can be obtained. If inedible tallow is used for cold-made soap, it is advisable to bleach it by the Fuller's Earth Process.

The carrying out of this method is best illustrated by an example of a cold-made cocoanut oil soap.

Charge:

| | |
|---|---|
| Cochin cocoanut oil............ | 846 parts |
| Lye (soda), 35 degs. B......... | 470 parts |
| Water ......................... | 24 parts |

The oil is run into the crutcher and the temperature of the oil raised to 100 degs. F. by dry steam. The lye and water are at room temperature. After all the oil is in the crutcher, the lye and water are slowly added to prevent any graining of the soap. Toward the end the lye may be added more rapidly. When all the lye is in, the mass is crutched for about three hours, or until upon stopping the crutcher a finger drawn over the surface of the soap leaves an impression. If this condition is not realized, the soap must be mixed until such is the case. Having arrived at this point, the mixture is dropped into a frame which should remain uncovered. The heat produced by the further spontaneous saponification will cause the soap to rise in the middle of the frame. After having set for some days it is ready to be slabbed and cut into cakes.

A potash soap may be made by the cold process just as readily as a soda soap. Soaps of this type may be made by either of these formulae in a crutcher:

| | |
|---|---|
| Olive oil foots | 600 |
| Potash lye, 18 degs. B. hot, 20 degs. B. cold | 660 |
| or | |
| Corn oil | 800 |
| Rosin | 200 |
| Potash lye, 27 degs. B | 790 |
| Water | 340 |

Heat the oils to 190 degs. F., add the lye and crutch until the soap begins to bunch, when it is ready to be run into barrels where the saponification will be completed.

Semi-boiled soaps differ from those made by the cold process in temperature. In making semi-boiled soaps the fats are usually heated to 140° F. The addition of the lye raises the temperature to 180°—200° F. when saponification takes place.

### CARBONATE SAPONIFICATION.

The method of the formation of soap by the utilization of the fatty acid directly, from which the glycerine has already been removed by some method of saponification other than with caustic soda, and neutralizing this with alkali, is becoming increasingly popular. The glycerine is more easily recovered from a previous cleavage of the fats or oils, but a soap made from the mixed fatty acids thus obtained is seldom white in color and retains an unpleasant odor. Since soda ash or sodium carbonate is cheaper than caustic soda and readily unites with a fatty acid, it is used as the alkali in the carbonate saponification. The process is similar to that already given under Rosin Saponification. About 19 per cent. by weight of the fatty acids employed of 58 per cent. soda ash is dissolved in water until it has a density of 30 degs. B., and the solution is run into the kettle, which is usually equipped with a removable agitator. The fatty acids, previously melted, are then slowly added while the mixture is boiled with open steam and agitated with the stirring device. The fatty acids instantly unite with the carbonate and rise in the kettle, due to the generation of carbon dioxide, and care must be exercised to prevent boiling over. After all the fatty acid has been added, and the mass is boiled through the saponification must be completed with caustic soda, as there is as yet no practical method known which will split a fat entirely into fatty acid and glycerine. Thus about 10 per cent. of the fatty acids are true neutral fats and require caustic soda for their saponification. This is then added and the soap completed, as in full-boiled soaps.

In carrying out this method upon a large scale, large

quantities of carbon dioxide are formed during the boiling of the soap, which replaces a quantity of the air contained therein. The kettle room should therefore be well ventilated, allowing for a large inflow of fresh air from out of doors.

# CHAPTER IV

## Classification of Soaps.

In considering the many different varieties of soaps, their classification is purely an arbitrary one. No definite plan can be outlined for any particular brand to be manufactured nor can any very sharp distinction be drawn between the many soaps of different properties which are designated by various names. It is really a question to what use a soap is to be put, and at what price it may be sold. There is, of course, a difference in the appearance, form and color, and then there are soaps of special kinds, such as floating soaps, transparent soaps, liquid soaps, etc., yet in the ultimate sense they are closely allied, because they are all the same chemical compound, varying only in their being a potash or soda soap, and in the fatty acids which enter into combination with these alkalis. Thus we can take a combination of tallow and cocoanut oil and make a great many presumably different soaps by combining these substances with caustic soda, by different methods of manufacture and by incorporating various other ingredients, as air, to form a floating soap, alcohol to make a transparent soap, dyestuffs to give a different color, etc., but essentially it is the same definite compound.

The manufacturer can best judge the brand of soaps he desires to manufacture, and much of his success depends upon the name, package, shape, color or perfume of a cake of soap. It is the consumer whom he must please and many of the large selling brands upon the market today owe their success to the above mentioned details. The great majority of consumers of soap know very little concerning soap, except the fact that it washes or has a pleasant odor or looks pretty, and the manufacturer of soap must study these phases of the subject even more carefully than the making of the soap itself.

For a matter of convenience we will classify soap under three general divisions:

I. Laundry soaps, including chip soaps, soap powders and scouring soaps.

II. Toilet soaps, including floating soap, castile soap, liquid soap, shaving soap, etc.

III. Textile soaps.

## LAUNDRY SOAP.

The most popular household soap is laundry soap. A tremendous amount of this soap is consumed each day in this country, and it is by far manufactured in larger quantities than any other soap. It is also a soap which must be sold cheaper than any other soap that enters the home.

The consumers of laundry soap have been educated to use a full boiled settled rosin soap and to make a good article at a price this method should be carried out, as it is the one most advisable to use. The composition of the fats entering into the soap depends upon the market price of these, and it is not advisable to keep to one formula in the manufacture of laundry soap, but rather to adjust the various fatty ingredients to obtain the desired results with the cheapest material that can be purchased. It is impossible to use a good grade of fats and make a profit upon laundry soap at the price at which it must be retailed. The manufacturer of this grade of soap must look to the by-product, glycerine, for his profit and he is fortunate indeed if he realizes the entire benefit of this and still produces a superior piece of laundry soap.

## SEMI-BOILED LAUNDRY SOAPS.

It is advantageous at times to make a laundry soap by a method other than the full boiled settled soap procedure as previously outlined. This is especially the condition in making a naphtha soap, in which is incorporated naphtha, which is very volatile and some of the well known manufacturers of this class of soap have adopted this process entirely. A laundry soap containing rosin cannot be advantageously made by the cold process, as the soap thus made grains during saponification and drops a portion of the lye and filling materials. By making a semiboiled soap this objection is overcome. The half boiled process differs from the cold process by uniting the fats and alkalis at a higher temperature.

To carry out this process the following formulae have been found by experience to give satisfactory results.

| I. | lbs. |
|---|---|
| Tallow | 100 |
| Rosin | 60 |
| Soda Lye, 36° B. | 80 |

| II. | |
|---|---|
| Tallow | 100 |
| Rosin | 60 |
| Silicate of Soda | 25 |
| Soda Lye, 36° B. | 85 |

| III. | |
|---|---|
| Tallow | 100 |
| Rosin | 100 |
| Lye, 36° B. | 105 |
| Silicate of Soda | 25 |
| Sal Soda Solution | 20 |

In any of these formulas the sodium silicate (40° B.) may be increased to the same proportion as the fats used. By so doing, however, twenty pounds of 36° B. lye must be added for every hundred pounds of silicate additional to that indicated or in other words, for every pound of silicate added 20 per cent. by weight of 36° B. lye must be put into the mixture. The rosin may also be replaced by a previously made rosin soap.

To make a semi-boiled soap, using any of the above formulae, first melt the rosin with all or part of the fat, as rosin when melted alone readily decomposes. When the mixture is at 150° F. run it into the crutcher and add the lye. Turn on sufficient dry steam to keep the temperature of the soap at about 150° F. in the winter or 130° F. in summer. After the mass has been mixed for half an hour, by continuously crutching the soap it will at first thicken, then grain and it may again become thick before it becomes smooth. When the mass is perfectly smooth and homogeneous drop into a frame and crutch in the frame by hand to prevent streaking. After standing the required length of time the soap is finished into cakes as usual.

### SETTLED ROSIN SOAP.

Settled rosin soaps are made from tallow, grease, cottonseed oil, bleached palm oils of the lower grades, corn oil, soya bean oil, arachis oil, distilled garbage grease, cotton seed foots or fatty acids together with an addition of rosin, varying from 24 per cent. to 60 per cent. of the fatty acids which should titer from 28 to 35. A titer lower than 28 will prevent the finished kettle of soap from being capable of later taking up the filling materials. As has already been stated under hardened oils, these being very much higher in titer allow a greater percentage of rosin to be added. Thus hardened fish oils and cottonseed oil are gradually being more extensively employed in soaps of this character.

The procedure of handling the kettle is similar to that given under full boiled soap. The stock is steamed out into a settling tank and allowed to settle over night, after which it is pumped into the soap kettle. Having stocked the kettle, open steam is turned on and 10°-12° B. lye is run in, while using a steam pressure of ninety to one hundred pounds in order to prevent too great a quantity of condensation of the steam, the water thus being formed weakening the lye. If a steam pressure of fifty to sixty pounds is available, a stronger lye (20° B.) should be added. Care must be taken not to allow the lye to flow in too rapidly or the soap will not grain. The saponification is only attained by prolonged boiling with sufficient lye of proper strength. When saponification has taken place, the mass begins to clear and a sample taken out with a paddle and cooled should show a slight pink with a 1 per cent. alcoholic phenolphthalein solution.

It may be stated here that in using this indicator or any other to test the alkalinity of soap, the soap should always be cooled and firm, as whenever water is present, the dissociation of the soap thereby will always react alkaline. When this state is reached the mass is ready for graining, which is accomplished by distributing salt brine or pickle or spreading dry salt over the surface of the soap. The kettle is then thoroughly boiled until the mass shows a soft curd and the lye drops clearly from a sample taken out with a trowel or paddle. The steam is then shut off and the soap allowed to settle over night. The lyes are then run off to the spent lye tank for glycerine recovery. In saponifying a freshly stocked kettle it is apt to bunch. To prevent this salt is added at various times to approximately one per cent. of the fat used.

If, by any possibility the soap has bunched, this condition may be remedied by the addition of more strong lye and boiling until it is taken up. To work a kettle to its full capacity it is advisable to make two "killing" changes. First add about 75 per cent. of the fat and grain as directed. Run off the spent lyes and then add the remainder of the stock and repeat the process. When the spent lye has been run to storage, the open steam is again turned on and 18° B lye gradually allowed to run in. The rosin is now broken up and put into the kettle, or a previously made rosin soap is pumped in.

Lye is then added until the soap has a sharp taste after about three hours of continous boiling, or when the soap is in the closed state. More lye should then be run into the kettle to grain the soap well, the grain not being too small. Then allow the soap to settle over night and draw off the strengthening lye. The next day again boil up the kettle and add water until the soap thins out and rises or swells high in the kettle. A sample taken out at this stage upon a hot trowel should run off in large flakes. The surface of the soap should be bright and shiny.

If the sample clings to the trowel, a slight addition of lye will remedy this defect. The kettle is then allowed to rest, to drop the nigre and to cool for some time, depending upon the size of the kettle. The proper temperature is such that after having been pumped to the crutcher and the filling materials having been added, a thermometer placed into the mass should indicate 128°-135° F. after the crutcher has run from ten to fifteen minutes. The filling material may consist of from 7-9 per cent. of sal soda solution, 36°-37° B. warm or just enough to close up the soap and make it rise high in the center of a screw crutcher and make it cling close to a warm trowel. Other fillers such as outlined below are added at this point.

An addition of from 2-3 per cent. of a special mineral oil for this purpose will impart a finish to the soap and 3-5 per cent. starch added prevents the soap from cracking in the frames. Other filling material as silicate of soda, borax, talc or silex are used. After the filling material has been thoroughly crutched through the soap it is framed, and. after being several days in the frame to solidify and cool the soap is ready for slabbing, pressing and wrapping.

In order to more definitely illustrate the composition of the mixture of fats and oils entering into the formation of a laundry soap a typical formula may be given for such a soap containing 40 per cent. rosin added to the amount of fats used:

| | lbs. |
|---|---|
| Grease | 7,000 |
| Tallow | 4,000 |
| Corn Oil | 7,000 |
| Cottonseed Oil | 3,000 |
| Rosin | 8,400 |

The following have been found to be satisfactory filling materials and are calculated upon the basis of a 1,400-pound frame of soap.

| I. | lbs. |
|---|---|
| Sodium Silicate, 38°-40° B. | 100 |
| Mineral Oil | 25 |
| Sal Soda Solution, 36° B. | 80 |
| Borax | 1 |

| II. | |
|---|---|
| Sal Soda Solution, 36° B. | 80 |
| Mineral Oil | 25 |
| Sodium Silicate | 60 |

III.

| | |
|---|---|
| Soda Ash | 10 |
| Sal Soda | 55 |
| Sodium Silicate | 115 |
| Mineral Oil | 40 |
| Brine (Saturated Solution) | 10 |

IV.

| | |
|---|---|
| Sodium Silicate | 100 |
| Silex or Talc | 200 |
| Soda Ash | 50 |

V.

| | |
|---|---|
| Sal Soda Solution, 36° B. | 90 |
| Sodium Silicate | 50-60 |
| Mineral Oil | 25 |
| Borax Solution, 25° B. (hot) | 15 |

### CHIP SOAP.

Chip soap is used extensively in laundries but is also used largely in other branches. It may be made either as a settled soap or by the cold made process.

To make a full boiled settled chip soap, proceed as directed under settled laundry soap. The kettle is stocked with light grease or a mixture of grease with corn oil or other cheap oils. For this kind of soap the rosin is eliminated.

Chip soap may be filled as well as laundry soap. This is done in the crutcher and the following adulterations are suitable.

| | lbs. |
|---|---|
| Settled Soap | 700 |
| Soda Ash | 35 |
| Sodium Silicate | 215 |

or

| | |
|---|---|
| Settled Soap | 700 |

| | |
|---|---|
| Silicate of Soda | 560 |
| Soda Ash | 18 |
| Carbonate of Potash, 26° B. | 50 |

The cheapest method of drying is by running this soap through a drying machine and this is the procedure usually carried out for making dried chip soap.

### COLD MADE CHIP SOAPS.

To make chip soaps by the cold process a sweet tallow of low percentage of free fatty acid should be employed. The tallow is heated to 120° to 135° F. and the lye run in slowly at first and then the silicate of soda is added. The mass is then mixed until a finger drawn through the soap leaves a slight impression, then dropped into frames or barrels. Soaps containing a small percentage of fat should be well covered in the frame for twenty-four hours to retain their heat and insure proper saponification. The following formulae are suitable:

| I. | lbs. |
|---|---|
| Tallow | 1,200 |
| Soda Lye, 35° B. | 850 |
| Sodium Silicate | 750 |

| II. | |
|---|---|
| Tallow | 475 |
| Ceylon Cocoanut Oil | 100 |
| Soda Lye, 37° B. | 325 |
| Potash Lye, 37° B. | 56 |

| III. | |
|---|---|
| Tallow | 500 |
| Soda Lye, 37½° B. | 297 |
| Sodium Silicate | 416 |
| Potash Lye, 37½° B. | 37½ |

IV.

| | |
|---|---|
| Tallow | 450 |
| Soda Lye, 37½° B. | 255 |
| Sodium Silicate | 450 |
| Potash Lye, 37½° B. | 50 |

V.

| | |
|---|---|
| Tallow | 450 |
| Soda Lye, 35° B. | 470 |
| Sodium Silicate | 650 |

VI.

| | |
|---|---|
| Tallow | 420 |
| Sodium Silicate | 600 |
| Soda Lye, 37½° B. | 270 |

#### UNFILLED CHIP SOAP.

A very good grade of chip soap is made by employing no filling material whatsoever, but unfortunately the price of this soap has been cut to such an extent that these can not compete with a filled chip. A number of the best soaps of this kind are made from a settled soap using a light grease with corn oil. A soap of this nature is made as follows.

| | lbs. |
|---|---|
| Settled Soap | 800 |
| Sal Soda Solution, 36°-37° B. | 252 |
| Soda Ash | 182 |

If this soap is run into frames it may be stripped and chipped in two days.

#### SOAP POWDERS.

Soap powders have become so great a convenience as a general cleansing agent that to eliminate them from the household necessities would mean much unnecessary energy and work to the great number of consumers of this product. They may be manufactured so heaply and still be efficient, that their use has almost become universal for cleansing and scouring purposes. The uses to which soap and scouring powders are adapted are too well known to enter into a description of their employment. Since they offer a greater profit to the manufacturer than ordinary household soap, many brands are extensively advertised.

Numerous combinations for soap powders might be cited and it is a simple matter to vary the ingredients as to fat content and manufacture a powder of this sort as low as a cent a pound. Many substances are incorporated with soap, such as salt, soda ash, tripoli, crushed volcanic deposits, ground feldspar, infusorial earth of various kinds, silex, etc. In addition to these various fillers, compounds with true cleansing and bleaching properties, in addition to soap, are added, such as the salts of ammonium (sal ammoniac, carbonate of ammonia), sodium perborate and the peroxides of various metals. The public, however, have been accustomed to receive a large package of soap or scouring powder for a small amount of money and it is a difficult matter for the manufacturer to add more expensive substances of this nature to his product, to increase its efficiency, without raising the price or decreasing the size of the package.

In manufacturing soap powders, the dried soap chips might be mixed with the filler and alkali and then pulverized. This method is not extensively employed nevertheless. The process which is the most economical is one whereby the ingredients are mixed in a specially adapted mixer for heavy material until dry and then run directly to the crusher and pulverizer, after which it is automatically packed, sealed and boxed.

Another method of procedure is to run out the mixture from the crutcher to the frames, which are stripped before the soap cools, and is cut up at once, for if it hardens it could not be cut with wires. It is better, however, to run the mixture into sheets upon a specially constructed floor and break up the mass when cool.

Formulae for soap powders which have been found to be suitable for running dry in the mixer follow:

I

| | |
|---|---|
| Soda ash, 58 per cent | 42 lbs. |
| Silica | 220 " |
| Settled soap (usually cottonseed) | 25 " |
| Salt | 10 " |

II

| | |
|---|---|
| Soap (settled cottonseed) | 40 lbs. |
| Soda ash, 58 per cent | 60 " |

III

| | |
|---|---|
| Settled soap | 100 lbs. |
| Soda ash, 58 per cent | 400 " |

Fillers in varying proportions may replace the soda ash in the above formulae. It is of course understood that the soap has been previously made and run as molten soap into the crutcher.

The following soap powders will not dry up in the crutcher upon running, but are of the class which may be framed or run on the floor to solidify:

I

| | |
|---|---|
| Soap | 850 lbs. |
| Filler | 400 " |
| Sal soda solution, 20 degs. B. | 170 " |

II

| | |
|---|---|
| Soap | 650 lbs. |
| Filler | 550 " |
| Sal soda solution, 20 degs. B | 340 " |

III

| | |
|---|---|
| Soap | 80 lbs. |
| Filler | 550 " |
| Sal soda solution | 170 " |

IV

| | |
|---|---|
| Soap (settled tallow) | 800 lbs. |
| Filler | 400 " |
| Sal soda solution | 170 " |
| Water | 100 " |

V

First saponify 100 parts house grease and 100 parts ordinary grease and make a run soap. Then use in crutcher either:

| | |
|---|---|
| Soap | 400 lbs. |
| Filler | 575 " |
| Hot water | 60 " |

or

| | |
|---|---|
| Soap | 200 lbs. |
| Hot water | 200 " |
| Filler | 625 " |

It would be a simple matter to write numerous additional formulae, but the above are typical. The manufacturer must judge for himself just what filling material to use. The filler indicated in the above formulae is therefore left open. A few formulae for more expensive powders than those given recently appeared among others in the "Seifensieder Zeitung"*:

*Seifensieder Ztg., 40, 47, 1266 (1913).

I

| | |
|---|---|
| Powdered soap | 90 lbs. |
| Sodium perborate | 10 " |

The perborate should be added when the powder is perfectly dry or it loses its bleaching properties.

II

Soap powder, 20 per cent. fat.

| | |
|---|---|
| Cocoanut oil fatty acids | 25 lbs. |
| Olein | 25 " |
| Bone fat | 70 " |
| Soda lye, 30 degs. B | 90 " |
| Water | 150 " |
| Ammonium carbonate | 125 " |

III

Soap powder, 10 per cent. fat.

| | |
|---|---|
| Cocoanut oil fatty acids | 20 lbs. |
| Olein | 10 " |
| Bone fat | 20 " |
| Soda lye, 30 degs. B | 30 " |
| Water | 175 " |
| Ammonium carbonate | 175 " |

#### LIGHT OR FLUFFY POWDERS.

Light or fluffy powders containing 35-45% moisture can be made in two ways. The first method requiring a minimum equipment is to mix the powder and sal soda in a mixer, allow it to stand in frames for a week to crystallize or spread it on the floor for a few hours to dry and then grinding it.

The continuous method finishes the powder in a few minutes and with a minimum amount of labor. By this process the various ingredients, soap, soda ash solution, etc., are measured, run by gravity into the mixer, mixed and the molten mass run over the crystallizer or chilling rolls thru which either cold water or brine is pumped. From the roll the powder is scraped off clean ab y knife, passes to a screen which sends the tailings to a grinder, falls into a storage bin from whence it is weighed and packed by an automatic weighing machine into cartons made up in most cases by another machine. Due to the large percentage of moisture contained in these soap powders the carton is generally wrapped in wax paper to aid in the prevention of the escape of moisture.

### SCOURING POWDERS.

Scouring powders are very similar to soap powders and differ only in the filler used. We have already considered these fillers under scouring soap, from which they do not differ materially. They are usually insoluble in water to aid in scouring. The mixer used for substances of this kind in incorporating the soap and alkali must be of strong construction.

### SCOURING SOAP.

Scouring soaps resemble soap powders very closely in their composition, in that they are a combination of soap and filling material. Since more lather is required from a scouring soap than in soap powders, a cocoanut oil soap is generally used. The usual filling material used is silex. The greatest difficulty in the manufacture of scouring soap is the cracking of the finished cake. This is usually due to the incorporation of too great an amount of filler, or too high a percentage of moisture.

In manufacturing these soaps the cocoanut oil is saponified in the crutcher with 38 degs. B. lye, or previously saponified as a run soap, as already described under "Marine Soaps." To twenty-five parts of soap are added a percentage of 38 degs. B. sal soda or soda ash solution, together with a small quantity of salt brine. To this mixture in the crutcher seventy-five parts of silex are then added, and a sufficient amount of hot water to make the mass flow readily. Care must be exercised to not add too great a quantity of water or the mass will crack when it cools. The mass is then framed and cut before it sets, or poured into molds and allowed to set. While silex is the most extensively used filler for scouring soaps, it is feasible to incorporate other substances of like character, although it is to be remembered that the consumer is accustomed to a white cake, such as silex produces. Any other material used to replace silex should also be as fine as this product.

### FLOATING SOAP.

Floating soap occupies a position midway between laundry and toilet soap. Since it is not highly perfumed and a large piece of soap may be purchased for small cost, as is the case with laundry soap, it is readily adaptable to general household use. Floating soap differs from ordinary soap in having air crutched into it which causes the soap to float in water. This is often advantageous, especially as a bath soap, and undoubtedly the largest selling brand of soap on the American market today is a floating soap.

In the manufacture of floating soap a high proportion of cocoanut oil is necessary. A most suitable composition is one part cocoanut oil to one part of tallow. This is an expensive stock for the highest grade of soap and is usually cheapened by the use of cottonseed or various other liquid oils. Thus it is possible to obtain a floating soap from a kettle stocked with 30 per cent. cocoanut oil, 15 per cent. cottonseed oil and 55 per cent. tallow. With this quality of soap, however, there is a possibility of sweating and rancidity, and of the soap being too soft and being poor in color.

The process of manufacture is to boil the soap in an ordinary soap kettle, after which air is worked into the hot soap by a specially constructed crutcher, after which the soap is framed, slabbed, cut into cakes and pressed.

Concerning the boiling of the soap, the saponification must be carefully carried out, as the high proportion of cocoanut oil may cause a violent reaction in the kettle causing it to boil over.

The method of procedure is the same as for a settled soap up to the finishing. When the mass is finally settled after the finish, the soap should be more on the "open" side, and the object should be to get as long a piece of goods as possible.

Due to its high melting point, a much harder crust forms on the surface of a floating soap and in a greater proportion than on a settled soap during the settling. In a large kettle, in fact, it has been found impossible to break through this crust by the ordinary procedure to admit the skimmer pipe. Much of the success of the subsequent operations depends upon the completeness of the settling, and in order to overcome the difficulties occasioned by the formation of the crust everything possible should be done in the way of covering the kettle completely to enable this period of settling to continue as long as possible.

When the soap is finished it is run into a specially constructed U-shape crutcher, a Strunz crutcher is best adapted to this purpose, although a rapidly revolving upright screw crutcher has been found to give satisfaction upon a smaller scale, and a sufficient quantity of air beaten into the soap to make it light enough to float. Care must be taken not to run the crutcher too rapidly or the soap will be entirely too fobby. During this operation the mass of soap increases in bulk, and after it has been established how much air must be put into the soap to satisfy the requirements, this increase in bulk is a criterion to estimate when this process is completed.

It is of course understood that the longer the crutching continues the greater quantity of air is incorporated and the increase of volume must be established for a particular composition by sampling, cooling the sample rapidly and seeing if it floats in water. If the beating is continued too long an interval of time, the finished soap is too spongy and useless.

The temperature of the mass during crutching is most important. This must never exceed 158 degrees F. At 159 degrees F. the operation is not very successful, yet the thermometer may indicate 140 degrees F. without interfering with this operation. If, however, the temperature drops too low, trouble is liable to be met with, by the soap solidifying too quickly in the frames.

When the crutching is completed, the soap is allowed to drop into frames through the valve at the bottom of the crutcher and rapidly crutched by the hand in the frames to prevent large air spaces and then allowed to cool. It is an improvement to jolt the frames as they are drawn away as this tends to make the larger air bubbles float to the surface and thus reduce the quantity of waste. When the soap has cooled, the frame is stripped and the soap slabbed as usual. At this point a layer of considerable depth of spongy soap will be found to have formed. This of course must be cut away and returned to the kettle. The last few slabs are also often rejected, inasmuch as the weight of the soap above them has forced out so much of the air that the soap no longer floats. As a fair average it may be estimated that not more than 50 to 60 per cent. of the soap in the kettle will come out as finished cakes.

the remaining 40 to 50 per cent. being constituted by the heavy crust in the kettle, the spongy tops, the botton slabs and scrapings. This soap is of course reboiled and consequently not lost, but the actual cakes obtained are produced at a cost of practically double labor.

It is advisable to add a small quantity of soap blue color to the mass while crutching to neutralize the yellowish tint a floating soap is liable to have.

Some manufacturers add a percentage of carbonate of soda, about 3 per cent., to prevent the soap from shrinking. Floating soap may also be loaded with sodium silicate to the extent of about 5 per cent.

### TOILET SOAP.

It is not a simple matter to differentiate between toilet soaps and various other soaps, because numerous soaps are adaptable to toilet purposes. While some soaps of this variety are manufactured by the cold made or semi-boiled process, and not milled, the consumer has become accustomed to a milled soap for general toilet use.

The toilet base most extensively employed is a tallow and cocoanut base made as a full boiled settled soap. The manufacture of this base has already been outlined and really needs no further comment except that it is to be remembered that a suitable toilet soap should contain no great excess of free alkali which is injurious to the skin. Cochin cocoanut oil is preferable to the Ceylon cocoanut oil or palm kernel oil, to use in conjunction with the tallow, which should be a good grade and color if a white piece of goods is desired. The percentage of cocoanut oil may be anywhere from 10 to 25 per cent., depending upon the kind of lather required, it being remembered that cocoanut oil increases the lathering power of the soap.

In addition to a tallow base, numerous other oils are

used in the manufacture of toilet soaps, especially palm oil, palm kernel oil, olive oil and olive oil foots, and to a much less extent arachis or peanut oil, sesame oil and poppy seed oil, oils of the class of cottonseed, corn and soya bean oils are not adapted to manufacturing a milled soap, as they form yellow spots in a finished cake of soap which has been kept a short time.

Palm oil, especially the Lagos oil, is much used in making a palm base. As has already been stated, the oil is bleached before saponification. A palm base has a yellowish color, a sweetish odor, and a small quantity added to a tallow base naturally aids the perfume. It is especially good for a violet soap. The peculiarity of a palm oil base is that this oil makes a short soap. By the addition of some tallow or twenty to twenty-five per cent. of cocoanut oil, or both, this objection is overcome. It is a good plan in using a straight palm base to add a proportion of yellow color to hold the yellowish tint of this soap, as a soap made from this oil continues bleaching upon exposure to air and light.

Olive oil and olive oil foots are used most extensively in the manufacture of castile soaps. The peculiarity of an olive oil soap is that it makes a very slimy lather, and like palm oil gives the soap a characteristic odor. An olive oil soap is usually considered to be a very neutral soap and may readily be superfatted. Much olive oil soap is used in bars or slabs as an unmilled soap and it is often made by the cold process. Peanut oil or sesame and poppy seed oil often replaces olive oil, as they form a similar soap to olive oil.

In the manufacture of a toilet soap it is hardly practical to lay down a definite plan for the various bases to be made. From the combination of tallow, palm oil, cocoanut oil, palm kernel oil, olive oil and olive oil foots, a great many bases of different proportions might be given. The simplest method is to make a tallow base, a palm base and an olive oil base. Then from these it is an easy matter to weigh out any proportion of these soap bases and obtain the proper mixture in the mill. If, however, as is often the case, a large quantity of soap base of certain proportions of these, four or even more of these fats and oils is required, it is not only more economical to stock the kettle with the correct proportion of these oils, but a more thorough mixture is thus obtained by saponifying these in the kettle. In view of the fact that it is really a question for the manufacturer to decide for himself what combination of oils he desires for a particular soap we will simply outline a few typical toilet soap bases in their simplest combination. It is understood that these soaps are suitable for milled soaps and are to be made as fully boiled settled soaps. Palm kernel oil may be substituted for cocoanut oil in all cases.

TALLOW BASE.

Tallow .......................... 75-90 parts
Cocoanut oil .................... 25-10 parts

PALM BASE.

Bleached Lagos palm oil......... 75-80 parts
Cocoanut oil .................... 25-20 parts

or

Tallow .......................... 30 parts
Palm oil ........................ 60 parts
Cocoanut oil .................... 10 parts

OLIVE OIL BASE (WHITE).

Olive oil ....................... 75-90 parts
Cocoanut oil .................... 25-10 parts

or

| | |
|---|---|
| Olive oil | 40 parts |
| Tallow | 40 parts |
| Cocoanut | 20 parts |

Where a green olive oil base is desired, olive oil foots are substituted for the olive oil. Peanut oil may replace the olive oil or part of it, the same being true of sesame oil and poppy seed oil.

### PALM AND OLIVE BASE.

| | |
|---|---|
| Palm oil | 50 parts |
| Olive oil | 30 parts |
| Cocoanut oil | 20 parts |

or

| | |
|---|---|
| Palm oil | 20 parts |
| Olive oil | 10 parts |
| Tallow | 50 parts |
| Cocoanut oil | 20 parts |

### CHEAPER TOILET SOAPS.

It is often necessary to manufacture a cheaper grade of soap for toilet purposes to meet the demand of a certain class of trade as well as for export. To accomplish this it is of course necessary to produce a very inferior product and run down the percentage of fatty acids contained in the soaps by the addition of fillers or to use cheaper oils in manufacturing. The most simple method of filling a soap is to load it at the mill with some substance much less expensive than the soap itself. Many of the cheaper toilet soaps, however, are not milled and it is, therefore, necessary to follow out some other procedure.

Milled soaps, as has just been stated, are loaded at the mill. The consumers of cheaper toilet soaps in this country are accustomed to a milled soap and this grade of soap for home consumption is very often filled with numerous substances, but most generally by adding starch and talc. The addition of such materials of course later exhibit themselves by imparting to the cake of soap a dead appearance. Talc is more readily detected in the soap than starch by washing with it, as talc is insoluble and imparts a roughness to the soap, like sand or pumice, as the soap wears down. It may readily be added to 20 per cent. by weight. Starch is to be preferred to talc, in loading a soap, as it is not so readily noticeable in washing. It leaves the cake itself absolutely smooth although the lather formed is more shiny. This substance may be employed to as high a percentage as one-third the weight of the soap. It is, of course, possible to cheapen the best soap base by this method and the price may be further lowered by using the less expensive oils and fats to make the soap base.

### RUN AND GLUED UP SOAPS.

A very cheap grade of soap may be made by making a run soap and adding the filler e. g. sodium silicate in the kettle during saponification. The percentage of fatty acids may be brought down to 10 per cent., although of course a soap of this type shrinks a whole lot upon exposure.

In making a "glued up" soap the procedure is the same for making the soap itself as with a settled soap, except that the soap is finished "curd" and later filled in the crutcher. The percentage of fatty acids in a soap of this type is seldom below 50 per cent.

The method of "gluing up" a soap is best illustrated by a typical soap of this character in which the kettle is charged with the following stock.

| | | |
|---|---|---|
| Bleached palm oil | 5 | parts |
| Distilled grease | 2 | " |
| Cotton oil foots stock, 63% fatty acid. | 1 | " |
| Rosin | 4 | " |

The palm oil is first run into the kettle, saponified and washed to extract any glycerine, then the rest of the fats and finally the rosin. The soap is then finished and settled as with a boiled settled soap. To assure success it is absolutely necessary that the soap settle as long a period as possible, or until the temperature is about 150 degs. F. The ideal temperature for carrying out the "gluing up" process is 140 degs. F., as at a lower temperature than this the soap is liable to cool too quickly and not be thoroughly glued up. A higher temperature than 150 degs. F. causes delay in that the soap does not properly take the filler at a higher temperature and the soap must be kept in the crutcher until the temperature drops to the right point.

The soap is run into the crutcher and the percentage of fatty acids run down to 50-55 per cent. with one of the following mixtures:

Sodium silicate, 59½° B.............. 1 part
Potassium carbonate, 51° B.......... 1 "

or

Sodium silicate, 59½° B.............. 1 part
Potassium carbonate, 51° B........... 1 "
Sodium sulfate, 28° B................ 1 "

From 230 to 300 pounds of either of these mixtures are required for a crutcher holding 2,600 pounds of soap.

The crutching is continued until the mass is well "spiked," that is to say, a freshly broken surface of the soap, as the crutcher blade is jerked away, stands up like shattered sheets in triangular form (Δ Δ Δ), which retain their shape perfectly. When this condition is realized the soap is run into frames which are carefully crutched by hand to remove any air spaces. The surface of the soap is then smoothed down and heaped up in the center. After standing a day to contract, the surface is again leveled and a snugly-fitting board placed on the top of the soap upon which a weight is placed or upon which the workman treads and stamps until the surface is flat, thus assuring the further removal of air spaces. The soap remains in the frame from six to eight days and is then slabbed, barred and pressed by the usual method employed for soaps thus handled without milling.

In a soap of this nature no hard and fast rule can be laid down as to the quantity of solution to be used for "gluing up" or the strength of the solution. In a soap of the type described the most satisfactory appearing cake will be obtained from a soap containing 58 per cent. fatty acids. That is to say, about 8 per cent. to 10 per cent. filling solution is added per hundred pounds of soap. The filling solutions given are very satisfactory. Carbonate of soda should be avoided in connection with sodium silicate as the property of efflorescing on the surface of the finished cake after a short time will prove detrimental. To assure successful gluing up it is advisable to experiment upon a small scale to determine the exact extent to which the filling solution should be diluted. Various proportions of water are added to a certain quantity of the filled soap. After the soap has been filled in a small receptacle a sample is taken and rubbed between the fingers. If the freshly exposed surface is smooth and glossy, the filling solution is weak enough, if rough it is too strong. It is of course understood that the temperature must be correct, 140 degs. to 150 degs. F., or the soap will be rough. By this means the operator can readily judge the correct strength of his filling solution. When properly carried out a perfectly satisfactory soap is obtained.

### CURD SOAP.

The object of a soap which is finished "curd" or grained, is to obtain a harder piece of goods from low titer fat or to increase the percentage of fatty acids in the finished soap. This is still another method of producing a cheap grade of soap as by its adoption the cheaper oils and fats may be used to obtain a firm piece of soap.

A typical charge for curd soap is:

| | |
|---|---|
| Red oil | 63 parts |
| Tallow | 10 " |
| Rosin | 27 " |

Cotton seed foots may be employed in place of red oil and a tallow of too high titer is not suitable for this kind of soap.

The red oil and tallow are first saponified with 15 degs. B. lye, boiler pressure 80-90 pounds, 18 degs. B. lye for lower steam pressure, and two washings given to extract the glycerine. The rosin is added at the strengthening change and at the finish the soap is "pitched," that is to say, the soap is settled over night only. The next day the lyes are drawn off and a portion of the nigre pumped to another kettle which prevents later streaking of the soap. The soap is then boiled with 18 degs. B. lye as with another strengthening change under closed steam. Salt brine or "pickle," 15 degs. B. is then added and the mass boiled with closed steam until the brine reaches a density of 18 degs. B. and the kettle pumped the next day. A soap of this type requires either hand or power crutching to assure homogeneity and prevention of streaks. To obviate any air spaces it is advisable to place over the top of the frame a tightly-fitted board which is heavily weighted down. This soap is also pressed without any milling.

### COLD MADE TOILET SOAPS.

Comparatively little toilet soap is made by the cold or semi-boiled processes. While these are the simplest methods of manufacturing soaps the drawbacks of using them are numerous and only in a few cases are they very extensively employed. To make a toilet soap by the cold process a combination of good grade tallow and cocoanut oil is required. It requires 50 per cent. by weight of 36 degs. B. lye to saponify a given weight of tallow and 50 per cent. of 38 degs. B. lye for cocoanut oil. The lyes are used full strength or may be reduced slightly with water and the method of procedure is the same as already given in the general directions for cold made soaps.

Cold made soaps are readily filled with sodium silicate which is added at the same time the stock is put into the crutcher. In adding the silicate it is necessary to add additional lye to that required for saponifying the fats, about 20 per cent. of 36 degs. B. lye is the proper amount. There is of course a certain amount of shrinking due to the addition of this filler and the finished cake is exceedingly hard, yet the author has seen a good looking cake of cheap soap made from as high a proportion as 420 parts of tallow to 600 parts of silicate.

Cold made soaps are usually pressed without milling, although it is readily feasible to mill a cold made soap provided it is not a filled soap such as has just been described.

### PERFUMING AND COLORING TOILET SOAPS.

Equally important as the soap itself or even to a greater extent is the perfume of a toilet soap. A prominent manufacturer recently made the statement, which is often the truth, that it makes no difference to the public what kind of soap you give them, as long as you put plenty of odor into it. The perfuming of soaps is an art in itself and a subject to be treated by one versed in this particular branch. We can only take into account the importance of the perfume as related to toilet soap not only, but the necessity of adding a certain proportion of the cheaper products of odoriferous nature to laundry soap to cover and disguise the odor of even this type of soap.

The price of a cake of toilet soap to a great extent depends upon the perfume, and the manufacturer should aim to give the best possible perfume for a certain price. He should not allow his personal likes or dislikes to enter into the judgment of whether an odor is good or not, but submit it to a number of persons to obtain the concensus of opinion. In giving or selling a piece of soap to the consumer, it is second nature for him to smell it, and in the great majority of cases his opinion is formed not from any quality the soap itself may have during use, but from the odor. This only emphasizes the fact that the perfume must be pleasing, not to one person, but to the majority, and many brands owe their popularity to nothing more than the enticing perfume.

Perfuming of soap is closely allied to the soap making industry, but as stated a branch in itself. It is, therefore, not our purpose to give numerous formulae of how to perfume a soap, but rather to advise to go for information to some one who thoroughly understands the characteristics of the numerous essential oils and synthetics and give positive information for the particular odor desired. Under no circumstances is it advisable to purchase a perfume already compounded, but since all perfumes are a blend of several or many essential oils and synthetics, it is a more positive assurance of obtaining what is desired, by purchasing the straight oils and blending or mixing them as one desires.

The perfume is added to a milled soap just before the milling process in the proper proportion per hundred pounds of soap. In cold made or unmilled soaps it is added in the crutcher while the soap is still hot. By this method, of course, a proportion of the perfume is lost due to its being more or less volatile.

### COLORING SOAP.

While much toilet soap is white or natural in color, many soaps are also artificially colored. The soap colors used for this purpose are mostly aniline dyestuffs. The price of these dyestuffs is no criterion as to their quality, as the price is usually regulated by the addition of some inert, water soluble substance like common salt or sugar.

The main properties that a dyestuff suitable for producing a colored soap should have are fastness to light and to alkali. They should further be of such a type that the color does not come off and stain a wash cloth or the hands when the soap is used and should be soluble in water. Under no circumstances is it advisable to add these in such a quantity that the lather produced in the soap is colored. It is customary to first dissolve the dye in hot water as a standardized solution. This can then be measured out in a graduate and added to the soap the same time as the perfume is put in. About one part of color to fifty parts of water is the propor proportion to obtain a perfect solution, though this is by no means fixed. In making up a solution thus it is an improvement to add to the same about one-half of one per cent. of an alkali either as the hydroxide or carbonate. Then, if there is any possibility of change of color due to alkalinity of the soap, it will exhibit itself before the color is added.

A particularly difficult shade to obtain is a purple, as there is up to the present time no purplish aniline color known which is fast to light. Very good results in soap may be obtained by mixing a fast blue, as ultramarine or cobalt blue, with a red as rhodamine or eosine.

Inasmuch as the colors for soap have been carefully tested by most of the dyestuff manufacturers, and their information, usually reliable, is open to any one desiring to know about a color for soap, it is better to depend upon their experience with colors after having satisfied one's self that a color is what it is represented for a particular shade, than to experiment with the numerous colors one's self.

### MEDICINAL SOAPS.

Soap is often used for the conveyance of various medicants, antiseptics or other material presumably beneficial for treatment of skin diseases. While soap is an ideal medium for the carrying of such materials, it is an unfortunate condition that when incorporated with the soap, all but a very few of the numerous substances thus employed lose their medicinal properties and effectiveness for curing skin disorders, as well as any antiseptic value the substance may have. Soap is of such a nature chemically that many of the substances used for skin troubles are either entirely decomposed or altered to such an extent so as to impair their therapeutic value. Thus many of the claims made for various medicated soaps fall flat, and really have no more antiseptic or therapeutic merit than ordinary soap which in itself has certain germicidal and cleaning value.

In medicating a soap the material used for this purpose is usually added at the mill. A tallow and cocoanut oil base is best adapted for a soap of this type. The public have been educated more or less to the use of colored soap to accentuate its medicinal value, and green is undoubtedly the most popular shade. This inference, however, is by no means true for all soaps of this character. Possibly the best method of arranging these soaps is briefly to outline some medicinal soaps.

### SULPHUR SOAPS.

The best known sulphur soaps contain anywhere from one to 20 per cent. of flowers of sulphur. Other soaps contain either organic or inorganic sulphur compounds.

### TAR SOAP.

The tar used in the manufacturing of tar soap is obtained by the destructive distillation of wood, the pine tar being the most extensively employed. While the different wood tars contain numerous aromatic compounds, such as phenols, phenyl oxides, terpenes and organic acids, these are present in such a slight proportion so as to render their effectiveness practically useless. It has, therefore, been tried to use these various compounds contained in the tar themselves to make tar soap really effective, yet tar is so cheap a substance that it is usually the substance used for medicating a tar soap. About 10 per cent. of tar is usually added to the soap with 2 ounces of lamp black per hundred pounds of soap.

### SOAPS CONTAINING PHENOLS.

Phenol (Carbolic Acid) is most extensively used in soaps of this kind, which are called carbolic soaps. Carbolic soaps are generally colored green and contain from 1 to 5 per cent. phenol crystals.

The cresols are also extensively used for making soaps named carbolic. These substances impart more odor to the soap and really have more disinfecting powers than phenol when incorporated with soap.

Other soaps, containing the phenol group, which are well known are resorcinol soap, salol soap, thymol soap, naphthol soap, etc. From one to five per cent of the compound after which the soap is named is usually incorporated with the soap.

### PEROXIDE SOAP.

Hydrogen peroxide in itself is an excellent disinfectant. It loses all its medicinal value, however, when added to the soap. To overcome this objection various metallic peroxides are added to the soap, as sodium peroxide, zinc peroxide and barium peroxide. These generate hydrogen peroxide by the addition of water. Sodium perborate is also used in peroxide soaps, as this substance is decomposed by water into hydrogen peroxide and sodium metaborate.

### MERCURY SOAPS.

Mercuric chloride (corrosive sublimate) is most extensively used for the production of mercury soaps. Because of its extremely poisonous properties care should be taken in using it. Since it really eventually loses any antiseptic value in the soap through forming an insoluble mercury soap it might better be omitted entirely.

### LESS IMPORTANT MEDICINAL SOAPS.

While the above mentioned soaps are probably the best known medicated soaps, there are numerous other soaps which may be classed under these kinds of soaps. Thus we have cold cream soap, which can be made by adding Russian Mineral Oil, 1 to 5 per cent., to the soap; witch hazel soap, made by the addition of extract of witch hazel; iodine soap, made by adding iodine or iodoform; formaldehyde soap, made by adding formaldehyde; tannin soaps, made by adding tannin. In fact, there have been incorporated in soap so great a number of substances that the list might be greatly enlarged.

Medicated soaps are not only used in solid form, but in powder, paste and liquid soap as well. The only difference in a soap like those just referred to is that the medicant is incorporated with these forms of soaps as convenience directs.

## CASTILE SOAP.

A pure castile soap should be made from olive oil. This, however, is not always the case, as a number of oils as well as tallow are used to adulterate this oil to cheapen it, and there are even some soaps called castile which contain no olive oil at all. Most of the pure castile soap used in this country is imported, as it is a difficult matter for the American manufacturer to compete with the pure imported castile soap, since both labor and oil itself are so much cheaper in the vicinities of Europe where this oil is produced, that this advantage is more than compensated by the carrying and custom charges by importing the castile soap.

Castile soap may be made either by the full boiled or cold process. There are numerous grades of olive oil, and those used for soap making are denatured to lower the duty charges. Olive oil makes a hard white soap, usually sold in bars, and olive oil foots a green soap, due to the coloring matter contained in this oil.

To make a boiled castile soap, a composition of 10 per cent. Cochin cocoanut oil and 90 per cent. olive oil may be used. To cheapen this, peanut oil (Arachis oil) may entirely replace the olive oil, or about 20 per cent. of corn or soya bean oil may be added. The oils are saponified as usual in making a settled soap and to prevent rancidity the soap is boiled near the finish for some time in the closed state with sufficient excess of alkali to give it a sharp taste, then grained with lye, the lye drawn off, closed with water and then grained with salt. This process is repeated until the desired strength is reached. The last graining should not be too great, and on the last change the soap should not be thinned out, as it will contain too great a quantity of water when slabbed.

In making a cold castile soap the usual method is pursued as already directed under cold made soap. When the soap is taken from the crutcher it is advisable, however, to keep the soap in the frame well covered to assure complete saponification. Some manufacturers use very small frames which are placed into compartments, well insulated to retain heat. Several formulae for cold made castile soaps, follow. It may be noted that some of these contain practically no olive oil.

I

| | |
|---|---|
| Olive oil | 2030 |
| Palm kernel | 674 |
| Soda lye, 35 per cent. B | 1506 |

II

| | |
|---|---|
| Olive oil | 2030 |
| Cochin cocoanut oil | 674 |
| Soda lye, 36 per cent. B | 1523 |
| Sodium Silicate | 82 |

III

| | |
|---|---|
| Palm kernel oil | 1578 |
| Tallow | 940 |
| Olive oil | 7 |
| Sodium silicate, 20 per cent. B | 190 |
| Soda lye, 36 per cent. B | 1507 |

IV

| | |
|---|---|
| Olive oil (yellow) | 1000 |
| Soda lye, 37 per cent. B | 500 |

V

| | |
|---|---|
| Olive oil | 90 |
| or | |
| Palm kernel<br>Cochin or cocoanut oil | 10 |
| Lye, 37 per cent. B | 51 |

If any of the soaps containing a high proportion of cocoanut oil are boiled the soap will float. It is therefore necessary to keep the temperature as low as possible.

ESCHWEGER SOAP (BLUE MOTTLED).

Eschweger soap is a colored mottled or marbled soap made to a very slight extent in this country. Inasmuch as it has been introduced to the export trade, it is made for this purpose by some manufacturers. A high percentage of cocoanut oil is usually used together with tallow and grease. About one-third of each is a typical formula. In a soap of this character the fact that cocoanut oil soap takes up a large quantity of water and salts of various kinds and is difficult to salt out is made use of. The tallow and grease are first saponified as usual, then the cocoanut oil is pumped and saponified. When the saponification is nearly completed either silicate or carbonate of soda or common salt are added to make the soap "short" so as to form the mottle. The finishing of a soap of this type can only be gained by practice and it is rather difficult to explain the exact appearance of the kettle at this stage. The surface of the soap should be bright and lustrous with the steam escaping in numerous places in rose-like formation. A sample on the trowel should have a slight sharpness to the tongue and be plastic. When the soap slides from the trowel it should break short. When the soap has reached this stage the desired coloring matter, usually ultramarine, is added to the soap either in the kettle or crutcher and the soap framed. The yield is 200-215 pounds per hundred pounds of stock.

Several modifications of this general method for Eschweger soap are used by adopting the half boiled or cold process.

### Transparent Soap.

Transparent soap is really not a most desirable soap for toilet purposes, as it contains an excess of free alkali. It has, nevertheless, met with public approval because of the fact it is novel in being transparent. Except for this fact very little merit can be claimed for a soap of this kind.

The transparency of soap is generally due to the presence of alcohol, sugar or glycerine in the soap when it is made It is very essential in a soap of this character, where lightness and clearness of color are desired, that the material for making the soap be carefully selected as to color and purity. The perfumes also play an important part in the color of the soap and many of the tinctures, balsams and infusions used in perfuming soap may eventually cause trouble by spotting. If the soap is artificially colored, which is almost always the case, the dyestuffs used for this purpose should have careful attention and only those should be used which are known to resist the action of alkalis. Where rosin is used this product must be of the better grade. Distilled water is always preferable for use in transparent soap. The government permits the use of a specially denatured alcohol. This alcohol is not taxed and consists of grain (ethyl) alcohol denatured with 5 per cent. wood (methyl) alcohol. Some soapmakers prefer to use a more expensive refined methyl alcohol, but outside of adding to the cost of the soap, there is no particular advantage. The glycerine should be chemically pure. As to the oils and fats these should be low in acid and of good color. Under no circumstances should the crutcher or kettle in which the soap is made be rusty or unclean in any way. For a light soap enameled utensils are to be preferred.

To obtain transparency in soap the following general methods may be given.

1. Where the transparency is due to sugar.
2. Where alcohol and glycerine produce transparency.
3. Where (1) or (2) is supplemented by the use of castor oil.
4. Where transparency depends upon the percentage of fatty acid in a soap and the number of times the soap is milled.

Under the first method at least 25 per cent. of the charge should be cocoanut oil, the other constituent being tallow or any fat or oil capable of giving a sufficiently hard soap. The soap is boiled and finished as usual, then run to the crutcher to be mixed with a strong cane sugar solution, containing 10-20 per cent. sugar of the weight of the soap. The sugar is dissolved in its own weight of water and the solution heated to 175 degs. F. before being very slowly added to the soap. As the water evaporates, soaps of this type show spots due to the sugar thus being thrown out of solution.

Transparent soap made under the second method may be saponified as usual and consist of any good toilet base. The soap is run to the crutcher and mixed with 95 per cent. alcohol in the proportion of one part alcohol to two parts of fatty acid contained in the soap together with glycerine in the same proportion.

By the third method castor oil alone may be used to make the soap or added to any of the above bases up to 33⅓ per cent. of the charge. If castor oil only is used, but 2 per cent. or 3 per cent. of sugar is required.

In the last method a combination of 80 per cent. tallow, very low in free acid, 20 per cent. cocoanut oil and 5 per cent. W. W. rosin is a suitable charge. The saponification and finishing is carried out as with a full boiled soap. The soap is then placed into a jacketed vessel, provided with dry-steam coils, by which the excess water is evaporated from the soap until it contains 73 per cent. fatty acids. When the thick mass reaches this stage it is framed and when cool is suitable for obtaining a semi transparency which now depends upon the number of times the soap is milled, it being, of course, inferred that no solid matter of any sort be added to the soap.

## Cold Made Transparent Soap.

While transparent soaps may be made by the above general methods they are usually made by the semi-boiled or cold process. By this process a more satisfactory soap is obtained and it is more simple to carry out. A detailed description of this method is best and most easily given by using a typical formula.

Charge:

| | | |
|---|---|---|
| Tallow | 193½ | lbs. |
| Cochin Cocoanut Oil | 169½ | " |
| Castor Oil | 89½ | " |
| Soda Ash | 7¾ | " |
| Soda Lye, 36 degs. B. | 256 | " |
| Sugar (Cane) | 198 | " |
| Alcohol | 126 | " |
| Water (Distilled) | 80 | " |

To proceed, first place into a crutcher or jacketed kettle the oils and fat and heat to 140 degs. F. Then add the soda ash dissolved in about 30 pounds of the water, after which the lye is added and the mass stirred until a finger or stick run over the surface leaves an imprint. Where the soap has reached this stage, it is well covered and allowed to stand about two hours or until it bulges in the center, after which the rest of the water which should contain no lime or other mineral substance and which is preferably distilled water, is added. The sugar is then slowly shoveled in while the mass is stirring and finally the alcohol is poured in. The heat is then increased to 160 degs. F. by dry steam and the soap crutched until dissolved. Under no circumstances should any soap be allowed to remain above the surface of the mass on the sides of the mixer. This crutching operation consumes about one hour, and when finished the soap should stand in the vessel about half an hour when a small sample is taken out to cool. This sample should be clear and show an excess of alkali. If it is not clear more alcohol is added, if not of sufficient strength more lye put in until the desired condition is reached. The perfume and color are now added.

The soap is then framed and allowed to set after which it is cut, allowed to dry slightly and then pressed. To obtain a polished cake transparent soaps are often planed before pressing and after pressing polished with a soft cloth, dampened with alcohol. Instead of framing this soap, it is sometimes "tubed," that is to say, the soap from the crutcher is run into specially constructed tubes of a shape near that of the desired cake and allowed to cool, after which it is cut and pressed. All scraps are returned to the crutcher, but in so doing the soap is slightly darkened in color. It is advisable to expôse a finished cake of transparent soap to the air for some time as by so doing it becomes clearer.

Other formulae for cold made transparent soaps made as just outlined follow:

I.

| | | |
|---|---|---|
| Bleached Tallow | 134 | lbs. |
| Cochin Cocoanut Oil | 88 | " |
| Castor Oil | 20 | " |
| W. W. Rosin | 7 | " |
| Cane Sugar | 64 | " |
| Water | 32 | " |
| Glycerine | 34 | " |
| Soda Lye, 38 degs. B. | 135 | " |
| Alcohol | 16 | gal. |

II.

| | | |
|---|---|---|
| Tallow | 211 | lbs. |
| Cochin Cocoanut Oil | 185 | " |
| Castor Oil | 97½ | " |
| Soda Ash | 8½ | " |
| Water | 106 | " |
| Soda Lye, 38 degs. B. | 279 | " |
| Sugar | 216 | " |
| Alcohol | 137 | " |

III.

| | | |
|---|---|---|
| Castor Oil. | 60 | lbs. |
| Cochin Cocoanut Oil | 195 | " |
| Tallow | 120 | " |
| Alcohol | 115 | " |
| Sugar | 90 | " |
| Water | 53 | " |
| Glycerine | 53 | " |
| Soda Lye, 38 degs. B. | 205½ | " |

IV.

| | | |
|---|---|---|
| Tallow | 100 | lbs. |
| Cochin Cocoanut Oil | 100 | " |
| Castor Oil | 60 | " |
| Glycerine | 20 | " |
| Rosin, W. W. | 20 | " |
| Sugar | 40 | " |
| Water | 50 | " |
| Soda Lye, 36 degs. B. | 164 | " |
| Alcohol | 8 | gal. |

V.

| | | |
|---|---|---|
| Tallow | 174 | lbs. |
| Cocoanut Oil | 114 | " |
| Soda Lye, 38 degs. B. | 170 | " |
| Sugar | 80 | " |
| Water | 72 | " |
| Alcohol | 16 | gal. |

Rosin may be added in this formula up to 20 per cent. of fats used and the tallow cut down correspondingly.

### SHAVING SOAPS.

The requirements of a shaving soap are somewhat different than those of other soaps. To be a good shaving soap the lather produced therefrom must be heavy, creamy, but not gummy, and remain moist when formed on the face. The soap itself should be of a soft consistency so as to readily adhere to the face when used in stick form. It should furthermore be neutral or nearly so to prevent the alkali from smarting during shaving.

Shaving soap is made in the form of a stick, and a tablet for use in the shaving mug. Some shavers prefer to have the soap as a powder or cream, which are claimed to be more convenient methods of shaving. While a liquid shaving soap is not as well known because it has not yet become popular, some soap for shaving is made in this form.

Formerly shaving soap was extensively made from a charge of about 80 parts tallow and 20 parts cocoanut oil as a boiled settled soap, but either making the strengthening change with potash lye or using potash lye in saponifying the stock and graining with salt. Soaps for shaving made in this manner are very unsatisfactory, as they do not produce a sufficiently thick or lasting lather and discolor very materially upon ageing. Potassium stearate forms an ideal lather for shaving, but readily hardens and hence needs some of the softer oils, or glycerine incorporated with it to form a satisfactory soap for shaving.

The selection of materials for making a shaving soap is important. The tallow used should be white and of high titer. Cochin cocoanut oil is to be preferred to the other kinds, and the alkalis should be the best for technical use that can be purchased—76 per cent. caustic soda and 88-92 per cent. caustic potash are suitable. By the use of stearic acid it is a simple matter to reach the neutral point which can be carefully approximated.

The following are shaving soap formulae which have been found to give good satisfaction:

| I. | lbs. |
|---|---|
| Tallow | 360 |
| Stearic acid | 40 |
| Soda lye, 41° B. | 147 |
| Potash lye, 34° B. | 87 |
| Water | 32 |
| Gum tragacanth | 1 |

| II. | lbs. |
|---|---|
| Tallow | 282 |
| Cocoanut oil | 60 |

| | |
|---|---|
| Stearic acid | 50 |
| Bayberry wax | 18 |
| Soda lye, 41° B. | 147 |
| Potash lye, 34° B. | 90 |
| Water | 32 |

| III. | lbs. |
|---|---|
| Tallow | 400 |
| Cocoanut oil | 176 |
| Stearic acid | 415 |
| Caustic soda, 40° B. | 182 |
| Caustic potash, 38° B. | 108 |

To proceed, first run into the crutcher the tallow, cocoanut oil and bayberry wax when used, and bring the temperature of the mass up to 140°-160° F. by dry steam. Then add the caustic soda lye and keep on heat with occasional mixing until it is all taken up. When this stage is reached gradually add all but about 5 per cent. of the potash lye, and complete the saponification. This point having been reached, the heat is turned off; the crutcher is run and the stearic acid, previously melted by dry steam in a lead-lined or enameled vessel, is run in in a continuous stream and the crutching continued for fifteen minutes to half an hour. Samples are taken at this time, cooled and tested by alcoholic phenolphthalein solution. If too alkaline more stearic acid is added, if too acid more potash lye from that previously reserved. After each addition of lye or stearic acid the mass is crutched from 10 to 15 minutes longer, another sample is taken, cooled and again tested. When the phenolphthalein shows a very light pink after several minutes, the soap is practically neutral, although at this point one can better judge by dissolving a sample in hot neutralized alcohol made by putting into the alcohol a few drops of phenolphthalein, and then adding weak alkali drop by drop from a burette until a slight pink, not yellow, tint is obtained, and noting the color of the solution. The solution should show a very light pink when the soap is properly neutralized. When this stage is arrived at the gum tragacanth, previously softened in water, is crutched in if it is to be added. The soap is then framed, stripped in three or four days, dried and milled.

The formulae as given are for shaving sticks, and do not readily press unless thoroughly dried. A more satisfactory result is obtained by adding at the mill 25 per cent. of white tallow base to obtain a satisfactory mug soap.

### SHAVING POWDER.

Shaving powder differs from the soaps just described in being pulverized, usually adding up to 5 per cent. starch to prevent caking. Any of the above soaps, dried bone dry, with or without the addition of tallow base make a satisfactory powder for shaving.

### SHAVING CREAM.

Shaving cream is now a very popular shaving medium due to the rapidity and convenience with which one can shave by the use of this product. Formerly shaving cream was made from the liquid oils like olive oil and a soft fat like lard, together with cocoanut oil. Now, however, most of the popular shaving creams are made from stearic acid and cocoanut oil, as a far superior product is obtained by the use of these substances. By using these a more satisfactory cream is obtained, and it is far more convenient to make. The lather also produced therefrom is more suitable for shaving, being thick, creamy and remaining moist.

A few typical formulae for shaving creams of this type are as follows:

| I. | lbs. |
|---|---|
| Cochin cocoanut oil | 26 |
| Stearic acid | 165 |
| Caustic potash lye, 50° B | 69 |
| Glycerine C. P | 76 |
| Water | 38 |

| II. | lbs. |
|---|---|
| Cochin cocoanut oil | 18 |
| Stearic acid | 73 |
| Caustic potash lye, 39° B | 54 |
| Glycerine | 33 |
| Water | 27 |

| III. | lbs. |
|---|---|
| Cochin cocoanut oil | 18 |
| Stearic acid | 73 |
| Caustic potash lye, 39° B | 54 |
| Glycerine | 20 |
| Water | 40 |

| and | lbs. |
|---|---|
| Stearic acid | 60 |
| Glycerine C. P | 85 |
| Water | 165 |
| Sodium carbonate | 50 |
| Borax | 1 |

To make a shaving cream by Formula I or II, the cocoanut oil and glycerine are first put into a suitable mixing apparatus or crutcher, and heated to 120° F. A part or all the potash lye is then added and the cocoanut oil saponified. The rest of the potash lye and the water are then added, and with the mixer running the stearic acid, previously melted in a lead-lined or enameled vessel, is then poured in in a stream and the mass stirred until smooth, care being exercised not to aerate it too much. The cream is then tested for alkalinity, the best method being by that described under shaving soap, in which the sample is dissolved in alcohol. Because of the large quantity of water present, phenolphthalein is unsatisfactory, as dissociation of the soap may show a pink indication in spite of the fact the mass is on the acid side. For a quick method of testing the bite on the tongue is a satisfactory criterion. If a cooled sample bites the tongue more stearic acid is added until there is a 3% excess of this. When the proper neutralization has taken place the cream is perfumed and framed in a special frame, or it may be allowed to cool in the mixer and perfumed the next day. When cool the cream is strained, or put through an ointment mill, after which it is ready to fill into tubes.

The procedure for the first part of Formula III is the same as that just given. The second part of the formula is made the same as a vanishing cream for toilet purposes. To make this, first melt the stearic acid as already directed. Dissolve the sodium carbonate and borax in water and when dissolved add the glycerine and stir. Then heat this solution to about 100°-120° F. and while stirring in a suitable mixing machine into which this solution has been poured after being heated, or better still in which it has been heated by dry steam, add the stearic acid. Continue mixing until smooth and then allow to cool, or run into frames to cool.

When the shaving cream and vanishing cream are both cool, they are mixed in the proportion of one of the former to two of the latter. It is claimed that in thus making a shaving cream a smoother product is obtained, although it may be said that the vanishing cream is merely a soft soap and the ultimate result is the same as though the various ingredients were added in one operation, rather than making two separate products and then mixing them, thereby considerably increasing the cost of manufacture.

### PUMICE OR SAND SOAPS.

Pumice and sand are at times added to soap to aid in the removal of dirt in cleansing the hands. In some cases these soaps are made in the form of a cake, in others they are sold in cans in the form of a paste.

A hand paste is usually made by merely dissolving ordinary tallow base in two or three times its weight of hot water and mixing in the desired quantity of pumice or sand and in some instances adding a little glycerine to keep it soft or a solvent of some kind for grease. It may also be made by directly incorporating any of these in a potash soap.

A cold made or semi-boiled cocoanut or palm kernel oil soap is the base used to add the pumice or sand to in making a cake soap of this sort. The following formulae serve as a guide for these soaps.

I.

| | |
|---|---|
| Palm Kernel or Ceylon Cocoanut Oil.... | 705 lbs. |
| Pumice (Powdered) .................. | 281 " |
| Soda Lye, 38° B...................... | 378 " |

II.

| | |
|---|---|
| Cocoanut Oil ......................... | 100 " |
| Soda Lye, 38° B...................... | 55 " |
| Water ................................ | 6 " |
| Silver Sand (fine).................... | 60 " |

To proceed place the oil in a crutcher and heat to 140° F. Sift in the pumice and mix thoroughly. The lye is then added which causes a curdling of the grain. The stirring is continued until the grain closes and the soap is smooth, after which the desired perfume is added and the soap dropped into a frame and crutched by hand. When the soap is set, it is slabbed, cut into cakes, dried slightly and pressed.

### LIQUID SOAPS.

Liquid soaps are merely solutions of a potash soap, usually cocoanut oil soap, although corn oil is used to make a cheap soap. One of the difficulties encountered in liquid soap is to keep it clear. At a low temperature a sediment is often formed, but this can be overcome by the use of sugar and filtering the soap through a filter press at a low temperature. In order to prevent the soap from freezing, it is necessary to lower the freezing point by the addition of glycerine or alcohol.

To make liquid soap by any of the formulae given below, the oil is first run into a jacketed kettle with a stirring device, and heated to about 120° F. The potash lye is then added and the oil saponified. When the saponification takes place, especially when cocoanut oil is used, the mass swells rapidly and may foam over the sides of the kettle unless water is used to check this, or a kettle of about four to five times the capacity of the total charge of soap is used. When the saponification has occurred, the sugar, borax and glycerine are added, the water run in and the mixture stirred until the soap is thoroughly dissolved. Heat aids materially in dissolving the soap. The soap is then allowed to cool and if color or perfume is to be added this is stirred in, after which the soap is cooled and filtered or else run directly into barrels.

Tallow is not suitable for making a clear liquid soap since it is too high in stearine which when formed into the stearate makes an opaque solution. The formulae herewith given have been found to give good practical results.

| I. | lbs. |
|---|---|
| Cocoanut oil | 130 |
| Caustic potash lye, 28° B. | 135 |
| Sugar | 72 |
| Borax | 2 |
| Water | 267 |

| II. | lbs. |
|---|---|
| Corn oil | 130 |
| Caustic potash lye, 26° B. | 135 |
| Sugar | 72 |
| Borax | 2 |
| Water | 267 |

| III. | lbs. |
|---|---|
| Cocoanut oil | 100 |
| Caustic potash lye, 28° B. | 102 |
| Glycerine | 100 |
| Sugar | 70 |
| Water | 833 |

Formulae I and II contain about 20 per cent. fatty acids. It is possible, of course, to either increase or decrease the percentage of fatty acid by varying the amount of water. The water used in making liquid soaps, of course, should be soft, for hard water forms insoluble soaps which precipitate and cause a sediment.

### USE OF HARDENED OILS IN TOILET SOAPS.

While the introduction of the hydrogenation of oils is a decided advance in the production of suitable cheaper oils for soap making, comparatively little hardened oil is employed for soap making in America up to the present time. In Europe, however, considerable advance has been made by the use of such oils for manufacturing soap therefrom and a number of plants turn out large quantities of hydrogenated oils for soap making as well as for edible purposes. Recently a company has been formed in this country for hardening oils and it is very probable that the future will see this material extensively used in our own country, as these appear to be the one present hope of the soap manufacturer as a check on the ever increasing cost of fats and oils now used in making soap.

It is an unfortunate condition that hydrogenated oils produced abroad are sold under names which give absolutely no indication as to the oil which has been hardened. The softer and cheaper oils like fish oil, linseed oil, cottonseed oil, etc., are generally hardened for soap manufacture to different degrees of hardness. While it is impossible to definitely state just what products as Candelite, Talgol, Krutolin or several other coined names of hardened oils are, various investigators have experimented with them as to their adaptability for producing toilet soaps and found that suitable toilet soaps may be made from them. While many objections were at first met with concerning soaps made from these products, as to their unsatisfactory saponification, the poor lathering quality of the soaps and their odor and consequent difficulty in perfuming, the results of most investigators along these lines indicate that these in many cases were due to prejudice against or unfamiliarity with handling oils of this type for soap making.

In manufacturing soap from hardened oils it is usually

necessary to incorporate with the charge lard, tallow, tallow oil or some other soft oil of this nature. Satisfactory bases for toilet soaps, made as boiled settled soap by the use of Talgol (undoubtedly hardened fish oil), are said to be made by the formulae* below.

I.

| | |
|---|---|
| Tallow | 45 parts |
| Talgol | 40 " |
| Cocoanut Oil | 15 " |

II.

| | |
|---|---|
| Cocoanut Oil (Ceylon) | 6 " |
| Tallow | 12 " |
| Talgol, Extra | 12 " |

The method of boiling a soap of this type does not differ materially from that of making settled tallow soap base. The soap itself has a different odor than a straight tallow base, but is said to make a very satisfactory soap for milling and to be of good appearance.

Satisfactory transparent soaps are made from the hardened oil Candelite, which replaces the tallow in transparent soap formulae such as have already been given in the section under "Transparent Soaps." The method of manufacturing a soap by the use of this product varies in no way from the usual method employed for making these soaps.

Since hydrogenated oils are high in stearine, their use in shaving soaps is a decided advantage. It has previously been pointed out that potassium stearate forms an ideal lather for shaving, and in the hydrogenating process the olein is converted to stearine. Thus a hardened

*Seifensieder Ztg. (1913), p. 334 and 338.
" " (1912), p. 1229 and 1257.

oil is advantageous in a shaving soap. As an example of a cold made soap for shaving the following may be taken.†

| | |
|---|---|
| Talgol Extra | 50 lbs. |
| Cocoanut Oil | 10 " |
| Lard | 10 " |
| Soda Lye, 38° B. | 20 " |
| Potash Lye, 37° B. | 21 " |

This soap may be made in a crutcher by the method generally used in making soap by the cold process.

### TEXTILE SOAPS.

Soap is a very important product to every branch of the textile industry. For woolen fabrics it is used for scouring, fulling and throwing the wool; in the silk industry it is necessary for degumming the raw silk, as well as for dyeing; in the cotton mills it is used to finish cotton cloth and to some extent in bleaching; it is, furthermore, employed in a number of ways in the manufacture of linen. Large quantities of soap are thus consumed in an industry of so great an extent and the requirements necessitate different soaps for the different operations. We will, therefore, consider these in detail.

### SCOURING AND FULLING SOAPS FOR WOOL.

The soaps used to scour wool and for fulling the woven cloth are usually made as cheaply as possible. They are, however, generally pure soaps, as filling material such as sodium silicate does not readily rinse out of the wool and if used at all must be added very sparingly. Both cold made and boiled settled soaps are made for this purpose. The soap is generally sold in barrels, hence is run directly to these from the crutcher or soap kettle. As cold made soaps the following serve for wool scouring or fulling.

†Seifensieder Ztg. (1912), p. 954.

CLASSIFICATION OF SOAPS

I.

| | |
|---|---|
| Palm Oil | 200 lbs. |
| Bone Grease | 460 " |
| Soda Lye, 36° B | 357 " |
| Water | 113 " |
| Soda Ash | 50 " |
| Citronella | 2 " |

II.

| | |
|---|---|
| Palm Oil (Calabar, unbleached) | 155 " |
| House Grease | 360 " |
| Soda Lye, 36° B | 324 " |
| Water | 268 " |
| Sodium Silicate | 83 " |

III.

| | |
|---|---|
| House Grease | 185 " |
| Palm Oil (unbleached) | 309 " |
| Soda Lye, 36° B | 309 " |
| Water | 391 " |
| Soda Ash | 70 " |
| Sodium Silicate | 60 " |
| Corn Starch | 10 " |

These soaps are made in a crutcher by the usual process for cold-made soaps, crutched until smooth, dropped into a barrel and crutched by hand the next day or just before cooling.

As a settled soap for these operations the following charge is typical:

| | |
|---|---|
| Palm Oil | 34 parts |
| Cottonseed foots or its equivalent in fatty acids | 33 " |
| Rosin | 10 " |
| House Grease | 23 " |

The method of boiling such a soap is the same as for any settled soap up to the strengthening change. When this stage is reached, sufficient lye is added to strengthen the kettle strongly. It is then boiled down with closed steam on salt brine or "pickle" until a sample of the lye taken from the bottom stands at 16°-22° B. The soap is then run into barrels and after standing therein for a day is hand crutched until cool to prevent streaking of the soap.

Besides a soap of this type a settled tallow chip soap is used.

### WOOL THROWER'S SOAP.

Soaps for wool throwing are sometimes made from olive oil foots but these are often objected to because of the sulphur-like odor conveyed to the cloth due to the method by which this oil is extracted with carbon disulphide. A potash soap hardened somewhat with soda is also used. As a formula for a suitable soap of this type this may be given.

| | |
|---|---|
| Olive Oil Foots | 12 parts |
| Corn Oil | 46 " |
| House Grease | 20 " |
| Soda Lye, 36° B. | 3 " |
| Potassium Carbonate (dry) | 5¾ " |
| Potassium Hydrate (solid) | 23 " |

This soap is made as a "run" soap by the general directions already given for a soap thus made. The kettle is boiled with open and closed steam, adding water very slowly and aiming to obtain a 220-225 per cent. yield or fatty acid content of the finished soap of 46 per cent. When the soap is finished a sample cooled on a plate of glass should be neither slippery or short, but should string slightly. The finished soap is run directly into barrels.

A soap for wool throwing by the semi-boiled process may be made from olive oil foots in a crutcher thus:

| | |
|---|---|
| Olive Oil Foots | 600 lbs. |
| Potash Lye, 20° B. | 660 " |

The oil is heated to 180° F., the lye added and the mass stirred until it bunches, when it is dropped into barrels.

### WORSTED FINISHING SOAPS.

For the finishing of worsted cloth soaps high in cocoanut oil or palm kernel oil are preferred. These soaps are finished very neutral, being made as settled soaps, but given an extra wash change after strengthening strongly. They are then finished as usual and run into barrels. If framed too hot, the high percentage of cocoanut oil causes mottling, which is prevented by crutching by hand until the temperature of the soap is 140°-145° F. Some typical charges, all of which are saponified with soda lye, follow:

I.

| | |
|---|---|
| Palm Kernel Oil | 60 parts |
| Corn Oil | 40 " |

II.

| | |
|---|---|
| Palm Kernel Oil | 30 " |
| Red Oil (single pressed) | 70 " |

III.

| | |
|---|---|
| Red Oil | 33⅓ " |
| Corn Oil | 33⅓ " |
| Cocoanut Oil or Palm Kernel Oil | 33⅓ " |

### SOAPS USED IN THE SILK INDUSTRY.

Soap is used to a very large extent in silk mills, both for

degumming the raw silk and in silk dyeing. Raw silk consists of the true silk fibre known as fibroin and a gummy coating, sericin, which dulls the lustre of the silk unless removed. For this purpose a slightly alkaline olive oil foots soap is best adapted, although palm oil and peanut oil soaps are sometimes used, as well as soaps made from a combination of house grease to the extent of 30 per cent., together with red oil or straight olein soaps, both of which are artificially colored green. In using house grease, if 30 per cent. is exceeded in combination with red oil, the titer is raised to such an extent that the soap does not readily rinse from the silk nor dissolve readily. They are also not advisable because they impart a disagreeable odor to the silk.

To make a soap for this purpose from olive oil foots it is made as a settled soap, care being taken to thoroughly boil the mass on the saponification change in the closed state to assure proper saponification. The kettle is usually grained with lye and given a good wash change to remove the excess strength. The change previous to the finish should not be too heavy or too large a nigre results. The lighter the grain is, the better the finished kettle is. A yield of 150 per cent. is usually obtained. This soap is generally run to a frame, slabbed upon cooling and packed directly into wooden cases.

For silk dyeing the above soap is suitable, although any well-made soap of good odor and not rancid is useable. While soap alone is often used in the bath for silk dyeing, certain dyestuffs require the addition of acetic or sulphuric acid, which sets free the fatty acids. If these be of bad odor it is taken up by the silk and is difficult to remove. The most generally used soaps are the just mentioned olive foots soap or a soap made from a good grade red oil.

Both kinds are extensively used.

### SOAPS USED FOR COTTON GOODS.

In the manufacture of cotton goods, as compared to the wool and silk industries, very much less soap is used and it is only applied to the finished fabric either to clean the cloth preparatory to dyeing or to aid in dyeing with certain colors. It is also used in calico printing. For cleansing the cloth ordinary chip soap is suitable although a more alkaline soap finished as a curd soap is an advantage in that the free alkali contained therein aids in removing the dirt and has no harmful effect on the cotton. For dyeing cotton goods or to brighten certain colors after dyeing an olive oil foots soap is most generally employed. In calico printing soap is used to wash and clear the cloth after printing. A soap for this purpose should be easily soluble in water and contain no free alkali, rosin or filler. The best soaps for use in calico printing are either an olive oil foots soap or an olein soap.

### SULPHONATED OILS.

While sulphonated oils are not used to any great extent in the manufacture of soap, they are used very largely in the dyeing and printing of turkey and alizarine reds on cotton as well as other colors. Just what action these oils have is not known. Turkey red oil or sulphonated castor oil is the best known sulphonated oil.

The process of making these oils is simple. The equipment necessary is a wooden tank or barrel of suitable capacity, approximately two and a half times the amount of oil to be treated. There are furthermore required other tanks or vessels to hold the solutions used such as caustic soda, ammonia and acid. The tank to be used for the preparation of sulphonated oil should be provided with a valve at the bottom of the tank and a gauge to measure the quantity of liquid therein.

The process is carried out as follows:

Three hundred pounds of castor oil are placed in the tank and 80 pounds at 66 deg. B. sulphuric acid are weighed out in another vessel. The acid is run into the tank containing the oil in a very thin stream while the oil is well stirred. At no time should the temperature exceed 40 deg. C. This operation should consume at least an hour and stirring should be continued half an hour longer to insure the thorough mixing of the oil with the acid. The mass is then allowed to settle for 24 hours, after which 40 gallons of water are added and the mixture stirred until it has a uniform creamy color indicating no dark streaks. This mixing process should be carefully carried out and when completed allowed to settle 36 hours. At this point the mass will have separated into two layers, the lower layer consisting of a water solution of acid and the upper layer of oil. The former is run out through the valve located at the bottom of the tank. Another wash may now be given or dispensed with as desired. In this wash the addition of salt or sodium sulphate at the rate of 1½ pounds per gallon of water is advisable. A 24 deg. B. caustic soda solution is prepared and added slowly to the acidified oil with constant stirring. The mass first turns creamy, then becomes streaked, increasing in streaks as the caustic solution is poured in, and finally becomes clear and transparent. Water is now added to bring the volume to 75 gallons. The oil is now milky in appearance, but the addition of a little more soda solution restores the transparency.

In some cases ammonia is used in addition to caustic soda in neutralizing the oil. Three-fourths of the amount of caustic soda required to complete the neutralization is first added and then the neutralization is completed with a one to one liquid ammonia and water solution.

# CHAPTER V

## Glycerine Recovery.

The recovery of glycerine is very closely allied with the soap-making industry, because glycerine is the very valuable by-product obtained in the saponification of oils and fats. No soap plant is, therefore, fully equipped unless it has some method whereby the glycerine is recovered and the importance of recovering this product cannot be too strongly emphasized.

It has already been pointed out that neutral fats or the glycerides are a combination of fatty acid with glycerine. These are split apart in the process of saponification. While by the term *saponification* as used in soap making it is inferred that this is the combination of caustic alkalis with the fatty acids to form soap, this term is by no means limited to this method of saponification, as there are various other methods of saponifying a fat. The chemical definition of saponification is the conversion of an ester, of which glycerides are merely a certain type, into an alcohol and an acid or a salt of this acid. Thus, if we use caustic alkali as our saponifying agent for a fat or oil, we obtain the sodium or potassium salt of the higher fatty acids or soap and the alcohol, glycerine. On the other hand, if we use a mineral acid as the saponifying agent, we obtain the fatty acids themselves in addition to glycerine. While the former is by far the most generally employed for making soap, other processes consist in saponifying the fats by some method other than caustic alkalis and then converting the fatty acids into soap by either neutralizing them with sodium or potassium carbonate or hydrate.

It is important to again point out here that fats and oils

develop free fatty acid of themselves and that the development of this acid represents a loss in glycerine. The selection of an oil or fat for soap making should therefore to a large extent be judged as to its adaptability by the free fatty acid content, as the higher this content is, the greater is the loss in the glycerine eventually obtained. Glycerine often represents the only profit to a soap manufacturer. It is indeed necessary to determine the percentage of free fatty acid before purchasing a lot of stock to be made into soap.

In taking up the question of glycerine recovery we will consider the various methods thus:

1. Where the glycerine is obtained from spent lye by saponifying the fats or oils with caustic alkali.

2. Where the glycerine is obtained by saponifying the fats or oils by some other method than the above, of which there are the following:

(a) Twitchell process.
(b) Saponification by lime in autoclave.
(c) Saponification by acid.
(d) Saponification by water in autoclave.
(e) Fermentative (Enzyms)
(f) Krebitz process.

### RECOVERY OF GLYCERINE FROM SPENT LYE.

The spent lye obtained from the glycerine changes in making soap varies greatly, the quality depending upon the stock saponified and the soap maker's care in handling the operation. No two lyes run exactly alike as to proportion of the various ingredients, although they are all similar in containing the same substances either in solution or suspension. Spent lye is a water solution of mainly glycerine, free alkali either as caustic alkali or carbonate and salt, including sodium sulfate, but furthermore contains some soap and albuminous matter either in solution or suspension. Upon standing in the storage tank the greater part of the soap usually separates when the lye cools. In order to assure the greatest economical yield of glycerine by saponifying a fat with caustic soda it is necessary to obtain a proportion of three parts of water to every part of fat made into soap. Test runs have shown that this is the proper proportion and that it is not economical to greatly exceed this amount, and if a much less proportion is used the full yield of glycerine is not obtained.

The spent lyes contain varying amounts of glycerine, the first change being richest in glycerine content, and this being reduced in the subsequent changes. If the lyes always run high in glycerine it is an indication that it is not all being obtained. The usual percentage is from 0.5% to 5% or even more, although the average is somewhere around 2% to 3%. The lye as it comes from the kettle should not contain any more than 0.5% to 0.6% of free alkali calculated as sodium carbonate, $Na_2CO_3$. If the proportion is higher than this, it shows that the saponification has been conducted with too high a proportion of alkali, a condition which should be corrected in the kettle room. An excess of free alkali does not interfere to any great extent with the successful recovery of the glycerine, but is a waste of both alkali and the acid used in neutralizing this. It is, therefore, more economical to run a strong lye over fresh stock and neutralize the alkali thus, rather than treating the lye for glycerine recovery.

Before the spent lye can be run into the evaporator it is necessary to remove the albuminous impurities and soap and to neutralize the excess alkali to between exactly neutral and 0.02% alkalinity. The lye should never be fed into the evaporator in the acid condition.

In order to treat the spent lyes for evaporation, they are first allowed to cool in the storage tank, after which any soap which may have separated is skimmed off and returned to the soap kettle. This lye is then pumped to the treatment tank, an ordinary tank equipped with some method of agitating the liquor, either by a mechanical stirrer, steam blower or compressed air, until it is about two feet from the top.

After the lye has been skimmed off it is thoroughly agitated and a sample taken. The amount of lye in the tank is then calculated. Spent lye is about 1.09 times heavier than water, or weighs about 9 pounds to the gallon. While the sample is being tested for alkalinity it is advisable to add sulfate of alumina, which may be dissolving while the sample is being titrated. This substance should be added in the proportion of anywhere from 6 to 14 pounds per thousand pounds of lye, depending upon the amount of impurities contained therein. For a clean lye six pounds per thousand is sufficient, but for an impure lye a greater quantity is necessary. The sulfate of alumina used should be free from arsenic and sulfides and should contain a minimum amount of grit (silica), as grit reduces the life of the pump valves. This may be estimated with sufficient accuracy by rubbing the filtered-off portions, insoluble in water between the fingers and a plate of glass. The object of adding the sulfate of alumina is to transform the soap contained in the lye into the insoluble aluminum soaps, and at the same time to coagulate the albuminous impurities. It must be remembered that the sulfate of alumina is added only for the fresh lye put into the tank. Thus if there were 10,000 pounds of lye in the treating tank when the fresh lye was run in, and 50,000 pounds when the tank is filled, adding nine pounds of sulfate of alumina per thousand of lye, only 360 pounds would be added or enough for 40,000 pounds. Sulfate of alumina neutralizes one-third of its weight of caustic.

To determine the alkali in the sample, 10 cubic centimeters are pipetted into a beaker, a little distilled water added, then 3 or 4 drops of phenolphthalein indicator. From a burette, quarter normal (N/4) sulfuric acid is added until the pink color is just discharged. When this point is reached 4 to 5 c. c. more of acid are added and the solution is boiled to expel the carbon dioxide. Should the solution turn pink, it is necessary to add more acid. After having boiled for 3 to 4 minutes, N/4 caustic soda is added until the pink color just returns and the amount of caustic soda used is read on the burette. The difference between the number of cubic centimeters of N/4 sulfuric acid and N/4 caustic soda gives the amount of alkali in the sample. By using a 10 c. c. sample and N/4 sulfuric acid and N/4 caustic soda each c. c. obtained by the difference of these two solutions is equal to one-tenth of one per cent. (0.1%) of the total alkali in the lye. As an example, say we first used 7.7 c. c. of N/4 sulfuric acid to just discharge the pink, then added 4 c. c. more, or 11.7 c. c. in total. After boiling it required 5.3 c. c. to bring back a slight pink, the total alkalinity would be 11.7 c. c. — 5.3 c. c. = 6.4 c. c., or 0.64% total alkali in the lye in terms of caustic soda. If there were 40,000 pounds of lye to be treated then we should have to neutralize:

40,000 × .0064 = 256 lbs. alkali. Since sulfate of alumina neutralizes one-third of its weight in caustic, and there are say 9 lbs. of this added per thousand pounds of lye we would add

40,000 × 9 = 360 lbs. of sulfate of alumina. This would neutralize

360 × ⅓ = 120 lbs of alkali. There are then 256 — 120 = 136 lbs. of alkali still to be neutralized. If 60° B. sulfuric acid is used it requires about 1.54 lbs. of acid to one pound of caustic. Therefore to neutralize the caustic soda remaining it requires:

$136 \times 1.54 = 209.44$ lbs. 60° B. sulfuric acid to neutralize the total alkali in the 40,000 pounds of spent lye.

The acid is added and the lye well stirred, after which another sample is taken and again titrated as before. From this titration the amount of acid to be added is again calculated and more acid is added if necessary. Should too much acid have been added, caustic soda solution is added until the lye is between exactly neutral and 0.02% alkaline. The filtered lyes at this stage have a slight yellowish cast.

To be sure that the lyes are treated correctly the precipitation test is advisable. To carry this out filter about 50 c. c. of the treated lye and divide into two portions in a test tube. To one portion add ammonia drop by drop. If a cloudiness develops upon shaking, more alkali is added to the lye in the tank. To the other portion add a few drops of 1 to 5 sulfuric acid and shake the test tube. If a precipitate develops or the solution clouds, more acid is needed. When the lyes are treated right no cloudiness should develop either upon adding ammonia or the dilute acid.

The properly treated lye is then run through the filter press while slightly warm and the filtered lye is fed to the evaporator from the filtered lye tank. The lye coming from the filter press should be clear and have a slight yellowish cast. As the pressure increases it is necessary to clean the press or some of the press cake will pass through the cloths. Where sodium silicate is used as a filler, the silicate scrap should never be returned to the soap kettle until the glycerine lyes have been withdrawn. This practice of some soapmakers is to be strongly censured, as it causes decided difficulty in filtering the lye, since during the treatment of the lye, free silicic acid in colloidal form is produced by the decomposition of the sodium silicate by acid. This often prevents filtering the treated lye even at excess pressure and at its best retards the filtering.

As to the filter press cake, this may be best thrown away in a small factory. Where, however, the output of glycerine is very large it pays to recover both the fatty acids and alumina in the press cakes.

In some cases, especially when the lyes are very dirty and the total residue in the crude glycerine runs high, for which there is a penalty usually attached, a double filtration of the lye is advisable. This is carried out by first making the lye slightly acid in reaction by the addition of alum and acid, then filtering. This filtered lye is then neutralized to the proper point with caustic, as already described, and passed through the filter press again.

While in the method of treating the lyes as given sulfuric acid is used for neutralizing, some operators prefer to use hydrochloric acid, as this forms sodium chloride or common salt, whereas sulfuric acid forms sodium sulfate, having 3/5 the graining power of salt, which eventually renders the salt useless for graining the soap, as the percentage of sodium sulfate increases in the salt. When the salt contains 25 per cent. sodium sulfate it is advisable to throw it away. Sulfuric acid, however, is considerably cheaper than hydrochloric and this more than compensates the necessity of having to eventually reject the recovered salt. It may here also be mentioned that recovered salt contains 5-7 per cent. glycerine which should be washed out in the evaporator before it is thrown away. The following tables give the approximate theoretical amounts of acids of various strengths required to neutralize one pound of caustic soda:

For 1 pound of caustic soda—

3.25 lbs. 18° B. hydrochloric (muriatic) acid are required.<br>
2.92 " 20° B. " " " " "<br>
2.58 " 22° B. " " " " "

For 1 pound of caustic soda—

| | | | |
|---|---|---|---|
| 1.93 lbs. | 50° B. | sulphuric acid | are required. |
| 1.54 " | 60° B. | " " | " |
| 1.28 " | 66° B. | " " | " |

It is, of course, feasible to neutralize the spent lye without first determining the causticity by titrating a sample and this is often the case. The operator under such conditions first adds the sulfate of alumina, then the acid, using litmus paper as his indicator. Comparatively, this method of treatment is much slower and not as positive, as the amount of acid or alkali to be added is at all times uncertain, for in the foaming of the lyes their action on litmus is misleading.

After the lye has been filtered to the filtered lye tank it is fed to the evaporator, the method of operation of which varies somewhat with different styles or makes. When it first enters the evaporator the lye is about 11°-12° B. After boiling the density will gradually rise to 27° B. and remain at this gravity for some time and during which time most of the salt is dropped out in the salt filter. As the lye concentrates the gravity gradually rises to 28°-30° B., which is half crude glycerine and contains about 60 per cent. glycerine. Some operators carry the evaporation to this point and accumulate a quantity of half crude before going on to crude. After half crude is obtained the temperature on the evaporator increases, the vacuum increases and the pressure on the condensation drain goes up (using the same amount of live steam). As the liquor grows heavier the amount of evaporation is less, and less steam is required necessitating the regulation of the steam pressure on the drum. When a temperature of 210° F. on the evaporator, with 26 or more inches vacuum on the pump is arrived at, the crude stage has been reached and the liquor now contains about 80 per cent. glycerine in which shape it is usually sold by soap manufacturers. A greater concentration requires more intricate apparatus. After settling a day in the crude tank it is drummed.

Crude glycerine (about 80 per cent. glycerol) free from salt is 33° B., or has a specific gravity of 1.3. A sample boiled in an open dish boils at a temperature of 155° C. or over.

### TWITCHELL PROCESS.

The Twitchell process of saponification consists of causing an almost complete cleavage of fats and oils by the use of the Twitchell reagent or saponifier, a sulfo-aromatic compound. This is made by the action of concentrated sulfuric acid upon a solution of oleic acid or stearic acid in an aromatic hydrocarbon. From 0.5 per cent. to 3 per cent. of the reagent is added and saponification takes place from 12-48 hours by heating in a current of live steam The reaction is usually accelerated by the presence of a few per cent. of free fatty acids as a starter. Recently the Twitchell double reagent has been introduced through which it is claimed that better colored fatty acids are obtained and the glycerine is free from ash.

The advantages claimed for the Twitchell process as outlined by Joslin[1] are as follows:

1. All the glycerine is separated from the stock before entering the kettle, preventing loss of glycerine in the soap and removing glycerine from spent lye.

2. The liquors contain 15-20 per cent. glycerine whereas spent lyes contain but 3-5 per cent, necessitating less evaporation and consequently being more economical in steam, labor and time.

3. No salt is obtained in the liquors which makes the evaporation cheaper and removes the cause of corrosion of

---

[1]Journ. Ind. Eng. Chem. (1909), I, p. 654.

the evaporator; also saves the glycerine retained by the salt.

4. The glycerine liquors are purer and thus the treatment of the lyes is cheaper and simpler and the evaporation less difficult.

5. The glycerine can readily be evaporated to 90 per cent. crude rather than 80 per cent. crude, thus saving drums, labor in handling and freight. The glycerine furthermore receives a higher rating and price, being known as saponification crude which develops no glycols in refining it.

6. The fatty acids obtained by the Twitchell saponifier may be converted into soap by carbonates, thus saving cost in alkali.

7. There is a decrease in the odor of many strong smelling stocks.

8. The glycerine may be obtained from half boiled and cold made soaps as well as soft (potash) soaps.

While the advantages thus outlined are of decided value in the employment of the Twitchell process, the one great disadvantage is that the fatty acids obtained are rather dark in color and are not satisfactorily employed for the making of a soap where whiteness of color is desired.

To carry out the process the previously heated oil or fat to be saponified is run into a lead lined tank. As greases and tallow often contain impurities a preliminary treatment with sulfuric acid is necessary. For a grease 1.25 per cent. of half water and half 66° B. sulfuric acid is the approximate amount. The undiluted 66° B. acid should never be added directly, as the grease would be charred by this. The grease should be agitated by steam after the required percentage of acid, calculated on the weight of the grease, has been added. The wash lye coming off should be 7°-10° B. on a good clean grease or 15°-22° B. on cotton oil or a poor grease. As has been stated the grease is heated before the acid is added or the condensation of the steam necessitates the addition of more acid. After having boiled for 1-2 hours the grease is allowed to settle for 12 hours and run off through a swivel pipe.

After the grease has been washed, as just explained, and settled, it is pumped into a covered wooden tank containing an open brass coil. Some of the second lye from a previous run is usually left in this tank and the grease pumped into this. The amount of this lye should be about one-third to one-half the weight of the grease so that there is about 60 per cent. by weight of grease in the tank after 24 hours boiling. Where occasions arise when there is no second lye about 50 per cent. by weight of distilled water to the amount of grease is run into the tank to replace the lye. The saponifier is then added through a glass or granite ware funnel after the contents of the tank have been brought to a boil. If the boiling is to be continued 48 hours, 1 per cent. of saponifier is added. For 24 hours boiling add 1.5 per cent. The boiling is continued for 24-48 hours allowing 18 inches for boiling room or the grease will boil over.

After boiling has continued the required length of time the mass is settled and the glycerine water is drawn off to the treatment tank. Should a permanent emulsion have formed, due to adding too great an amount of saponifier, a little sulfuric acid (0.1 per cent.-0.3 per cent.) will readily break this. During the time this is being done the space between the grease and the cover on the tank is kept filled with steam as contact with the air darkens the fatty acids.

To the grease remaining in the tank distilled water (condensed water from steam coils) to one-half its volume is added and the boiling continued 12-24 hours. The grease is then settled and the clear grease run off through a swivel pipe. A layer of emulsion usually forms between the clear grease and lye so that it may easily be determined when the grease has all been run off. To prevent discoloration of the fatty acids it is necessary to neutralize the lye with barium carbonate. The amount of this to be added depends upon the percentage of saponifier used. About 1/10 the weight of saponifier is the right amount. The barium carbonate is added through the funnel at the top of the tank mixed with a little water and the lye tested until it is neutral to methyl orange indicator. When the fatty acids are thus treated they will not darken upon exposure to the air when run off.

Fresh grease is now pumped into the lye or water remaining in the tank and the process repeated.

The glycerine water or first lye is run to the treatment tank, the fat skimmed off and neutralized with lime until it shows pink with phenolphthalein, after having been thoroughly boiled with steam. About 0.25 per cent. lime is the proper amount to add. The mixture is then allowed to settle and the supernatant mixture drawn off and run to the glycerine evaporator feed tank. The lime which holds considerable glycerine is filtered and the liquor added to the other. The evaporation is carried out in two stages. The glycerine water is first evaporated to about 60 per cent. glycerol, then dropped into a settling tank to settle out the calcium sulfate. The clear liquor is then evaporated to crude (about 90 per cent. glycerine) and the sediment filtered and also evaporated to crude.

As to the amount of saponifier to use on various stocks, this is best determined by experiment as to how high a percentage gives dark colored fatty acids. For good stock such as clean tallow, prime cottonseed oil, corn oil, cocoanut oil and stock of this kind 0.75 per cent. saponifier is sufficient. For poorer grades of tallow, house grease, poor cottonseed oil, etc., 1 per cent. saponifier is required and for poorer grade greases higher percentages. The percentage of fatty acids developed varies in various stocks, and also varies with the care that the operation is carried out, but is usually between 85 per cent.-95 per cent. Due to the water taken up in the saponification process there is a yield of about 103 pounds of fatty acids and glycerine for 100 pounds of fat.

The Twitchell reagent has undoubtedly caused a decided advance in the saponification of fats and oils and has been of great value to the soap manufacturer, because with a small expenditure it is possible to compete with the much more expensive equipment necessary for autoclave saponification. The drawback, however, has been that the reagent imparted a dark color to the fatty acids obtained, due to decomposition products forming when the reagent is made, and hence is not suitable for use in soaps where whiteness of color is desired.

There have recently been two new reagents introduced which act as catalyzers in splitting fats, just as the Twitchell reagent acts, but the fatty acids produced by the cleavage are of good color. The saponification, furthermore, takes place more rapidly. These are the Pfeilring reagent and Kontact reagent.

The Pfeilring reagent is very similar to the Twitchell reagent, being made from hydrogenated castor oil and naphthalene by sulfonation with concentrated sulfuric acid. It is manufactured in Germany and is being extensively used in that country with good success.

The Kontact or Petroff reagent, discovered by Petroff in Russia, is made from sulfonated mineral oils. Until very recently it has only been manufactured in Europe, but now that it has been found possible to obtain the proper mineral constituent from American petroleum, it is being manufactured in this country, and it is very probable that it will replace the Twitchell reagent because of the advantages derived by using it, as compared to the old Twitchell reagent.

The method and equipment necessary for employing either the Pfeilring or Kontact reagents is exactly the same as in using the Twitchell process.

### AUTOCLAVE SAPONIFICATION.

While the introduction of the Twitchell process to a great extent replaced the autoclave method of saponification for obtaining fatty acids for soap making, the autoclave method is also used. This process consists in heating the previously purified fat or oil in the presence of lime and water, or water only, for several hours, which causes a splitting of the glycerides into fatty acids and glycerine. The advantage of autoclave saponification over the Twitchell process is that a greater cleavage of the fats and oils results in less time and at a slightly less expense. The glycerine thus obtained is also purer and of better color than that obtained by Twitchelling the fats.

An autoclave or digestor consists of a strongly constructed, closed cylindrical tank, usually made of copper, and is so built as to resist internal pressure. The digestor is usually 3 to 5 feet in diameter and from 18 to 25 feet high. It may be set up horizontally or vertically and is covered with an asbestos jacket to retain the heat. Various inlets and outlets for the fats, steam, etc., as well as a pressure gauge and safety valve are also a necessary part of the equipment.

### LIME SAPONIFICATION.

The saponification in an autoclave is usually carried out by introducing the fats into the autoclave with a percentage of lime, magnesia or zinc oxide, together with water. If the fats contain any great amount of impurities, it is first necessary to purify them either by a treatment with weak sulfuric acid, as described under the Twitchell process, or by boiling them up with brine and settling out the impurities from the hot fat.

To charge the autoclave a partial vacuum is created therein by condensation of steam just before running the purified oil in from an elevated tank. The required quantity of unslaked lime, 2 to 4 per cent. of the weight of the fat, is run in with the molten fat, together with 30 per cent. to 50 per cent. of water. While 8.7 per cent. lime is theoretically required, practice has shown that 2 per cent. to 4 per cent. is sufficient. The digestor, having been charged and adjusted, steam is turned on and a pressure of 8 to 10 atmospheres maintained thereon for a period of six to ten hours. Samples of the fat are taken at various intervals and the percentage of free fatty acids determined. When the saponification is completed the contents of the autoclave are removed, usually by blowing out the digestor into a wooden settling tank, or by first running off the glycerine water and then blowing out the lime, soap and fatty acids. The mass discharged from the digestor separates into two layers, the upper consisting of a mixture of lime soap or "rock" and fatty acids, and the lower layer contains the glycerine or "sweet" water. The glycerine water is first run off through a clearing tank or oil separator, if this has not been done directly from the autoclave, and the mass remaining washed once or twice more with water to remove any glycerine still retained by the lime soap. The calculated amount of sulfuric acid to decompose the lime "rock" is then added, and the mass agitated until the fatty acids contained therein are entirely set free. Another small wash is then given and the wash water added to the glycerine water already run off. The glycerine water is neutralized with lime, filtered and concentrated as in the Twitchell process.

Due to the difficulties of working the autoclave saponification with lime, decomposing the large amount of lime soap obtained and dealing with much gypsum formed thereby which collects as a sediment and necessitates cleaning the tanks, other substances are used to replace lime. Magnesia, about 2 per cent. of the weight of the fat, is used and gives better results than lime. One-half to 1 per cent. of zinc oxide of the weight of the fat is even better adapted and is now being extensively employed for this purpose. In using zinc oxide it is possible to recover the zinc salts and use them over again in the digestor, which makes the process as cheap to work as with lime, with far more satisfactory results.

### ACID SAPONIFICATION.

While it is possible to saponify fats and oils in an autoclave with the addition of acid to the fat, unless a specially-constructed digestor is built, the action of the acid on the metal from which the autoclave is constructed prohibits its use. The acid saponification is therefore carried out by another method.

The method of procedure for acid saponification, therefore, is to first purify the fats with dilute acid as already described. The purified, hot or warm, dry fat is then run to a specially-built acidifier or a lead-lined tank and from 4 per cent. to 6 per cent. of concentrated sulfuric acid added to the fat, depending upon its character, the degree of saponification required, temperature and time of saponification. A temperature of 110 degrees C. is maintained and the mass mixed from four to six hours. The tank is then allowed to settle out the tar formed during the saponification, and the fatty acids run off to another tank and boiled up about three times with one-third the amount of water. The water thus obtained contains the glycerine, and after neutralization is concentrated.

### AQUEOUS SAPONIFICATION.

While lime or a similar substance is ordinarily used to aid in splitting fats in an autoclave, the old water process is still used. This is a convenient, though slower and more dangerous method, of producing the hydrolysis of the glyceride, as well as the simplest in that fatty acids and glycerine in a water solution are obtained. The method consists in merely charging the autoclave with fats and adding about 30 per cent. to 40 per cent. of their weight of water, depending on the amount of free fatty acid and subjecting the charge to a pressure of 150 to 300 pounds, until the splitting has taken place. This is a much higher pressure than when lime is used and therefore a very strong autoclave is required. Since fatty acids and pure glycerine water are obtained no subsequent treatment of the finished charge is necessary except separating the glycerine water and giving the fatty acids a wash with water to remove all the glycerine from them.

### SPLITTING FATS WITH FERMENTS.

In discussing the causes of rancidity of oils and fats it was pointed out that the initial splitting of these is due to enzymes, organized ferments. In the seeds of the castor oil plant, especially in the protoplasm of the seed, the enzyme which has the property of causing hydrolysis of the glycerides is found. The ferment from the seeds of the castor oil plant is now extracted and used upon a commercial basis for splitting fats.

The equipment necessary to carry out this method of

saponification is a round, iron, lead-lined tank with a conical bottom, preferably about twice as long as it is wide. Open and closed steam coils are also necessary in the tank.

The oils are first heated and run into this tank. The right temperature to heat these to is about 1 degree to 2 degrees above their solidification point. For liquid oils 23 degrees C. is the proper heat as under 20 degrees C. the cleavage takes place slowly. Fats titering 44 degrees C. or above must be brought down in titer by mixing with them oils of a lower titer as the ferment or enzyme is killed at about 45 degrees C. and thus loses its power of splitting. It is also necessary to have the fat in the liquid state or the ferment does not act. The proper temperature must be maintained with dry steam.

It is, of course, necessary to add water, which may be any kind desired, condensed, water from steam coils, well, city, etc. From 30 per cent. to 40 per cent., on the average 35 per cent. of water is added, as the amount necessary is regulated so as to not dilute the glycerine water unnecessarily. To increase the hydrolysis a catalyzer, some neutral salt, usually manganese sulfate is added in the proportion of 0.15 per cent. appears to vary directly as the saponification number of the fat or oil. The approximate percentages of fermentive substance to be added to various oils and fats follow:

| | |
|---|---|
| Cocoanut oil | 8 % |
| Palm Kernel oil | 8 % |
| Cottonseed oil | 6-7 % |
| Linseed oil | 4-5 % |
| Tallow oil | 8-10% |

The oil, water, manganese sulfate and ferment having been placed in the tank in the order named, the mixture is agitated with air for about a quarter of an hour to form an even emulsion, in which state the mass is kept by stirring occasionally with air while the saponification is taking place. A temperature is maintained a degree or two above the titer point of the fat with closed steam which may be aided by covering the tank for a period of 24 to 48 hours. The splitting takes place rapidly at first, then proceeds more slowly. In 24 hours 80 per cent. of the fats are split and in 48 hours 85 per cent. to 90 per cent.

When the cleavage has reached the desired point the mass is heated to 80 degrees-85 degrees C. with live or indirect steam while stirring with air. Then 0.1 per cent.-0.15 per cent of concentrated sulfuric acid diluted with water is added to break the emulsion. When the emulsion is broken the glycerine water is allowed to settle out and drawn off. The glycerine water contains 12 per cent. to 25 per cent. glycerine and contains manganese sulfate, sulfuric acid and albuminous matter. Through neutralization with lime at boiling temperature and filtration the impurities can almost all be removed after which the glycerine water may be fed to the evaporator. Should it be desired to overcome the trouble due to the gypsum formed in the glycerine, the lime treatment may be combined with a previous treatment of the glycerine water with barium hydrate to remove the sulfuric acid, then later oxalic acid to precipitate the lime.

The fatty acids obtained by splitting with ferments are of very good color and adaptable for soap making.

### KREBITZ PROCESS.

The Krebitz process which has been used to some extent in Europe is based upon the conversion of the fat or oil into lime soap which is transformed into the soda soap by the addition of sodium carbonate. To carry out the process a convenient batch of, say, 10,000 pounds of fat or oil, is run into a shallow kettle containing 1,200 to 1,400 pounds of lime previously slaked with 3,700 to 4,500 pounds of water. The mass is slowly heated with live steam to almost boiling until an emulsion is obtained. The tank is then covered and allowed to stand about 12 hours. The lime soap thus formed is dropped from the tank into the hopper of a mill, finely ground and conveyed to a leeching tank. The glycerine is washed out and the glycerine water run to a tank for evaporation. The soap is then further washed and these washings are run to other tanks to be used over again to wash a fresh batch of soap. About 150,000 pounds of water will wash the soap made from 10,000 pounds of fat which makes between 15,000 and 16,000 pounds of soap. The first wash contains approximately 10 per cent. glycerine and under ordinary circumstances this only need be evaporated for glycerine recovery.

After extracting the glycerine the soap is slowly introduced into a boiling solution of sodium carbonate or soda ash and boiled until the soda has replaced the lime. This is indicated by the disappearance of the small lumps of lime soap. Caustic soda is then added to saponify the fat not converted by the lime saponification. The soap is then salted out and allowed to settle out the calcium carbonate. This drops to the bottom of the kettle as a heavy sludge entangling about 10 per cent. of the soap. A portion of this soap may be recovered by agitating the sludge with heat and water, pumping the soap off the top and filtering the remaining sludge.

While the soap thus obtained is very good, the percentage of glycerine recovered is greatly increased and the cost of alkali as carbonate is less. The disadvantages are many. Large quantities of lime are required; it is difficult to recover the soap from the lime sludge; the operations are numerous prior to the soap making proper and rather complicated apparatus is required.

## DISTILLATION OF FATTY ACIDS.

The fatty acids obtained by various methods of saponification may be further improved by distillation.

In order to carry out this distillation, two methods may be pursued, first, the continuous method, whereby the fatty acids are continually distilled for five to six days, and, second, the two phase method, whereby the distillation continues for 16 to 20 hours, after which the residue is drawn off, treated with acid, and its distillate added to a fresh charge of fatty acids. The latter method is by far the best, since the advantages derived by thus proceeding more than compensate the necessity of cleaning the still. Better colored fatty acids are obtained; less unsaponifiable matter is contained therein; there is no accumulation of impurities; the amount of neutral fat is lessened because the treatment of the tar with acid causes a cleavage of the neutral fat and the candle tar or pitch obtained is harder and better and thus more valuable.

The stills are usually built of copper, which are heated by both direct fire and superheated steam. Distillation under vacuum is advisable. To begin the distilling operation, the still is first filled with dry hot fatty acids to the proper level. Superheated steam is then admitted and the condenser is first heated to prevent the freezing of the fatty acids, passing over into same. When the temperature reaches 230 deg. C. the distillation begins. At the beginning, the fatty acids flow from the condensor, an intense green color, due to the formation of copper soaps produced by the action of the fatty acids on the copper still. This color may easily be removed by treating with dilute acid to decompose the copper soaps.

In vacuum distillation, the operation is begun without

the use of vacuum. Vacuum is introduced only when the distillation has proceeded for a time and the introduction of this must be carefully regulated, else the rapid influence of vacuum will cause the contents of the still to overflow. When distillation has begun a constant level of fatty acids is retained therein by opening the feeding valve to same, and the heat is so regulated as to produce the desired rate of distillation. As soon as the distillate flows darker and slower, the feeding valve to the still is shut off and the distillation continued until most of the contents of the still are distilled off, which is indicated by a rise in the temperature. Distillation is then discontinued, the still shut down, and in about an hour the contents are sufficiently cool to be emptied. The residue is run off into a proper receiving vessel, treated with dilute acid and used in the distillation of tar.

In the distillation of tar the same method as the above is followed, only distillation proceeds at a higher temperature. The first portion and last portion of the distillate from tar are so dark that it is necessary to add them to a fresh charge of fatty acids. By a well conducted distillation of tar about 50 per cent. of the fatty acids from the tar can be used to mix with the distilled fatty acids. The residue of this operation called stearine pitch or candle tar consists of a hard, brittle, dark substance. Elastic pitch only results where distillation has been kept constant for several days without interrupting the process, and redistilling the tar. In a good distillation the distillation loss is 0.5 to 1.5% and loss in pitch 1.5%. Fatty acids which are not acidified deliver about 3% of pitch. Very impure fats yield even a higher percentage in spite of acidifying. For a long time it was found impossible to find any use for stearine pitch, but in recent years a use has been found for same in the electrical installation of cables.

# CHAPTER VI

## Analytical Methods.

While it is possible to attain a certain amount of efficiency in determining the worth of the raw material entering into the manufacture of soap through organoleptic methods, these are by no means accurate. It is, therefore, necessary to revert to chemical methods to correctly determine the selection of fats, oil or other substances used in soap making, as well as standardizing a particular soap manufactured and to properly regulate the glycerine recovered.

It is not our purpose to cover in detail the numerous analytical processes which may be employed in the examination of fats and oils, alkalis, soap and glycerine, as these are fully and accurately covered in various texts, but rather to give briefly the necessary tests which ought to be carried out in factories where large amounts of soap are made. Occasion often arises where it is impossible to employ a chemist, yet it is possible to have this work done by a competent person or to have someone instruct himself as just how to carry out the more simple analyses, which is not a very difficult matter. The various standard solutions necessary to carrying out the simpler titrations can readily be purchased from dealers in chemical apparatus and it does not take extraordinary intelligence for anyone to operate a burette, yet in many soap plants in this country absolutely no attention is paid to the examining of raw material, though many thousand pounds are handled annually, which, if they were more carefully examined would result in the saving of much more money than it costs to examine them or have them at least occasionally analyzed.

## ANALYSIS OF FATS AND OILS.

In order to arrive at proper results in the analysis of a fat or oil, it is necessary to have a proper sample. To obtain this a sample of several of the packages of oil or fat is taken and these mixed or molten together into a composite sample which is used in making the tests. If the oil or fat is solid, a tester is used in taking the sample from the package and if they are liquid, it is a simple matter to draw off a uniform sample from each package and from these to form a composite sample.

In purchasing an oil or fat for soap making, the manufacturer is usually interested in the amount of free fatty acid contained therein, of moisture, the titer, the percentage of unsaponifiable matter and to previously determine the color of soap which will be obtained where color is an object.

## DETERMINATION OF FREE FATTY ACIDS.

Since the free fatty acid content of a fat or oil represents a loss of glycerine, the greater the percentage of free fatty acid, the less glycerine is contained in the fat or oil, it is advisable to purchase a fat or oil with the lower free acid, other properties and the price being the same.

While the mean molecular weight of the mixed free fatty acids varies with the same and different oils or fats and should be determined for any particular analysis for accuracy, the free fatty acid is usually expressed as oleic acid, which has a molecular weight of 282.

To carry out the analysis 5 to 20 grams of the fat are

weighed out into an Erlenmeyer flask and 50 cubic centimeters of carefully neutralized alcohol are added. In order to neutralize the alcohol add a few drops of phenolphthalein solution to same and add a weak caustic soda solution drop by drop until a very faint pink color is obtained upon shaking or stirring the alcohol thoroughly. The mixture of fat and neutralized alcohol is then heated to boiling and titrated with tenth normal alkali solution, using phenolphthalein as an indicator. As only the free fatty acids are readily soluble in the alcohol and the fat itself only slightly mixes with it, the flask should be well agitated toward the end of the titration. When a faint pink color remains after thoroughly agitating the flask the end point is reached. In order to calculate the percentage of free fatty acid as oleic acid, multiply the number of cubic centimeters of tenth normal alkali used as read on the burette by 0.0282 and divide by the number of grams of fat taken for the determination and multiply by 100.

When dark colored oils or fats are being titrated it is often difficult to obtain a good end point with phenolphthalein. In such cases about 2 cubic centimeters of a 2 per cent. alcoholic solution of Alkali Blue 6 B is recommended.

Another method of directly determining the free fatty acid content of tallow or grease upon which this determination is most often made is to weigh out into an Erlenmeyer flask exactly 5.645 grams of a sample of tallow or grease. Add about 75 cubic centimeters of neutralized alcohol. Heat until it boils, then titrate with tenth normal alkali and divide the reading by 2, which gives the percentage of free fatty acid as oleic. If a fifth normal caustic solution is used, the reading on the burette gives the percentage of free fatty acid directly.

This method, while it eliminates the necessity of calculation, is troublesome in that it is difficult to obtain the exact weight of fat.

### MOISTURE.

To calculate the amount of moisture contained in a fat or oil 5 to 10 grams are weighed into a flat bottom dish, together with a known amount of clean, dry sand, if it is so desired. The dish is then heated over a water bath, or at a temperature of 100-110 degs. C., until it no longer loses weight upon drying and reweighing the dish. One hour should elapse between the time the dish is put on the water bath and the time it is taken off to reweigh. The difference between the weight of the dish is put on the water bath and the time it is taken off when it reaches a constant weight is moisture. This difference divided by the original weight of the fat or oil $\times$ 100 gives the percentage of moisture.

When highly unsaturated fats or oils are being analyzed for moisture, an error may be introduced either by the absorption of oxygen, which is accelerated at higher temperature, or by the formation of volatile fatty acids. The former causes an increase in weight, the latter causes a decrease. To obviate this, the above operation of drying should be carried out in the presence of some inert gas like hydrogen, carbon dioxide, or nitrogen.

### TITER.

The titer of a fat or oil is really an indication of the amount of stearic acid contained therein. The titer, expressed in degrees Centigrade, is the solidification point of the fatty acids of an oil or fat. In order to carry out the operation a Centigrade thermometer graduated in one or two-tenths of a degree is necessary. A thermometer graduated between 10 degs. centigrade to 60 degs. centigrade is best adapted and the graduations should be clear cut and distinct.

To make the determination about 30 grams of fat are roughly weighed in a metal dish and 30-40 cubic centimeters of a 30 per cent. (36 degs. Baumé) solution of sodium hydroxide, together with 30-40 cubic centimeters of alcohol, denatured alcohol will do, are added and the mass heated until saponified. Heat over a low flame or over an asbestos plate until the soap thus formed is dry, constantly stirring the contents of the dish to prevent burning. The dried soap is then dissolved in about 1000 cubic centimeters of water, being certain that all the alcohol has been expelled by boiling the soap solution for about half an hour. When the soap is in solution add sufficient sulphuric acid to decompose the soap, approximately 100 cubic centimeters of 25 degs. Baumé sulphuric acid, and boil until the fatty acids form a clear layer on top of the liquid. A few pieces of pumice stone put into the mixture will prevent the bumping caused by boiling. Siphon off the water from the bottom of the dish and wash the fatty acids with boiling water until free from sulphuric acid. Collect the fatty acids in a small casserole or beaker and dry them over a steam bath or drying oven at 110 degs. Centigrade. When the fatty acids are dry, cool them to about 10 degs. above the titer expected and transfer them to a titer tube or short test tube which is firmly supported by a cork in the opening of a salt mouth bottle. Hang the thermometer by a cord from above the supported tube so it reaches close to the bottom when in the titer tube containing the fatty acids and so that it may be used as a stirrer. Stir the mass rather slowly, closely noting the temperature. The temperature will gradually fall during the stirring operation and finally remain stationary for half a minute or so then rise from 0.1 to 0.5 degs. The highest point to which the mercury rises after having been stationary is taken as the reading of the titer.

### DETERMINATION OF UNSAPONIFIABLE MATTER.

In order to determine the unsaponifiable matter in fats and oils they are first saponified, then the unsaponifiable, which consists mainly of hydrocarbons and the higher alcohols cholesterol or phytosterol, is extracted with ether or petroleum ether, the ether evaporated and the residue weighed as unsaponifiable.

To carry out the process first saponify about 5 grams of fat or oil with an excess of alcoholic potassium hydrate, 20-30 cubic centimeters of a 1 to 10 solution of potassium hydroxide in alcohol until the alcohol is evaporated over a steam bath. Wash the soap thus formed into a separatory funnel of 200 cubic centimeters capacity with 80-100 cubic centimeters water. Then add about 60 cubic centimeters of ether, petroleum ether or 86 degs. gasoline and thoroughly shake the funnel to extract the unsaponifiable. Should the two layers not separate readily, add a few cubic centimeters of alcohol, which will readily cause them to separate. Draw off the watery solution from beneath and wash the ether with water containing a few drops of sodium hydrate and run to another dish. Pour the watery solution into the funnel again and repeat the extraction once or twice more or until the ether shows no discoloration. Combine the ether extractions into the funnel and wash with water until no alkaline reaction is obtained from the wash water. Run the ether extract to a weighed dish, evaporate and dry rapidly in a drying oven. As some of the hydrocarbons are readily volatile at 100 degs. Centigrade, the drying should not be carried on any longer than necessary. The residue is then weighed and the original weight of fat taken divided into the weight of the residue × 100 gives the percentage unsaponifiable.

### TEST FOR COLOR OF SOAP.

It is often desirable to determine the color of the finished soap by a rapid determination before it is made into soap. It often happens, especially with the tallows, that a dark colored sample produces a light colored soap, whereas a bleached light colored tallow produces a soap off shade.

To rapidly determine whether the color easily washes out of the tallow with lye, 100 cubic centimeters of tallow are saponified in an enameled or iron dish with 100 cubic centimeters of 21 degs. Baumé soda lye and 100 cubic centimeters of denatured alcohol. Continue heating over a wire gauze until all the alcohol is expelled and then add 50 cubic centimeters of the 21 degs. Baumé lye to grain the soap. Allow the lyes to settle and with an inverted pipette draw off the lyes into a test tube or bottle. Close the soap with 100 cubic centimeters of hot water and when closed again grain with 50 cubic centimeters of the lye by just bringing to a boil over an open flame. Again allow the lyes to settle and put aside a sample of the lye for comparison. Repeat the process of closing, graining and settling and take a sample of lye. If the lye is still discolored repeat the above operations again or until the lye is colorless. Ordinarily all the color will come out with the third lye. The soap thus obtained contains considerable water which makes it appear white. The soap is, therefore, dried to about 15 per cent. moisture and examined for color. The color thus obtained is a very good criterion as to what may be expected in the soap kettle.

By making the above analyses of fats or oils the main properties as to their adaptability for being made into soap are determined. In some cases, especially where adulteration or mixtures of oils are suspected, it is necessary to further analyze same. The methods of carrying out these analyses are fully covered by various texts on fats and oils and we will not go into details regarding the method of procedure in carrying these out.

### TESTING OF ALKALIS USED IN SOAP MAKING.

The alkalis entering into the manufacture of soap such as caustic soda or sodium hydroxide, caustic potash or potassium hydrate, carbonate of soda or sodium carbonate, carbonate of potash or potassium carbonate usually contain impurities which do not enter into combination with the fats or fatty acids to form soap. It is out of the question to use chemically pure alkalis in soap making, hence it is often necessary to determine the alkalinity of an alkali. It may again be pointed out that in saponifying a neutral fat or oil only caustic soda or potash are efficient and the carbonate contained in these only combines to a more or less extent with any free fatty acids contained in the oils or fats. Caustic soda or potash or lyes made from these alkalis upon exposure to the air are gradually converted into sodium or potassium carbonate by the action of the carbon dioxide contained in the air. While the amount of carbonate thus formed is not very great and is greatest upon the surface, all lyes as well as caustic alkalis contain some carbonate. This carbonate introduces an error in the analysis of caustic alkalis when accuracy is required and thus in the analysis of caustic soda or potash it is necessary to remove the carbonate when the true alkalinity as sodium hydroxide or potassium hydroxide is desired. This may be done by titration in alcohol which has been neutralized.

In order to determine the alkalinity of any of the above mentioned alkalis, it is first necessary to obtain a representative sample of the substance to be analyzed. To do this take small samples from various portions of the package and combine them into a composite sample. Caustic potash and soda are hygroscopic and samples should be weighed at once or kept in a well stoppered bottle. Sodium or potassium carbonate can be weighed more easily as they do not rapidly absorb moisture from the air.

To weigh the caustic soda or potash place about five grams on a watch glass on a balance and weigh as rapidly as possible. Wash into a 500 cubic centimeter volumetric flask and bring to the mark with distilled water. Pipette off 50 cubic centimeters into a 200 cubic centimeter beaker, dilute slightly with distilled water, add a few drops of methyl orange indicator and titrate with normal acid. For the carbonates about 1 gram may be weighed, washed into a 400 cubic centimeter beaker, diluted with distilled water, methyl orange indicator added and titrated with normal acid. It is advisable to use methyl orange indicator in these titrations as phenolphthalein is affected by the carbon dioxide generated when an acid reacts with a carbonate and does not give the proper end point, unless the solution is boiled to expel the carbon dioxide. Litmus may also be used as the indicator, but here again it is necessary to boil as carbon dioxide also affects this substance. As an aid to the action of these common indicators the following table may be helpful:

| *Indicator.* | *Color in Acid Solution.* | *Color in Alkaline Solution.* | *Action of $CO_2$.* |
|---|---|---|---|
| Methyl orange | Red | Yellow | Very slightly acid |
| Phenolphthalein | Colorless | Red | Acid |
| Litmus | Red | Blue | Acid |

It may be further stated that methyl orange at the neutral point is orange in color.

To calculate the percentage of effective alkali from the above titrations, it must be first pointed out that in the case of caustic potash or soda aliquoit portions are taken. This is done to reduce the error necessarily involved by weighing, as the absorption of water is decided. Thus we had, say, exactly 5 grams which weighed 5.05 grams by the time it was balanced. This was dissolved in 500 cubic centimeters of water and 50 cubic centimeters or one tenth of the amount of the solution was taken, or in each 50 cubic centimeters there were 0.505 grams of the sample. We thus reduced the error of weighing by one tenth provided other conditions introduce no errcr. In the case of the carbonates the weight is taken directly.

One cubic centimeter of a normal acid solution is the equivalent of:

| | Grams. |
|---|---|
| Sodium Carbonate, $Na_2CO_3$ | 0.05305 |
| Sodium Hydroxide, NaOH | 0.04006 |
| Sodium Oxide, $Na_2O$ | 0.02905 |
| Carbonate $K_2CO_3$ | 0.06908 |
| Potassium Hydoxide, KOH | 0.05616 |
| Potassium Oxide, $K_2O$ | 0.04715 |

Hence to arrive at the alkalinity we multiply the number of cubic centimeters, read on the burette, by the factor opposite the terms in which we desire to express the alkalinity, divide the weight in grams thus obtained by the original weight taken, and multiply the result by 100, which gives the percentage of alkali in the proper terms. For example, say, we took the 0.505 grams of caustic potash as explained above and required 8.7 cubic centimeter normal acid to neutralize the solution, then

$$8.7 \times .05616 = .4886 \text{ grams KOH in sample}$$

$$\frac{.4886}{.505} \times 100 = 96.73\% \text{ KOH in sample.}$$

Caustic potash often contains some caustic soda, and while it is possible to express the results in terms of KOH, regardless of any trouble that may be caused by this mixture in soap making, an error is introduced in the results, not all the alkali being caustic potash. In such cases it is advisable to consult a book on analysis as the analysis is far more complicated than those given we will not consider it. The presence of carbonates, as already stated, also causes an error. To overcome this the alkali is titrated in absolute alcohol, filtering off the insoluble carbonate. The soluble portion is caustic hydrate and may be titrated as such. The carbonate remaining on the filter paper is dissolved in water and titrated as carbonate.

### SOAP ANALYSIS.

To obtain a sample of a cake of soap for analysis is a rather difficult matter as the moisture content of the outer and inner layer varies considerably. To overcome this difficulty a borer or sampler may be run right through the cake of soap, or slices may be cut from various parts of the cake, or the cake may be cut and run through a meat chopper several times and mixed. A sufficient amount of a homogeneous sample obtained by any of these methods is preserved for the entire analysis by keeping the soap in a securely stoppered bottle.

The more important determinations of soap are moisture, free alkali, or fatty acid, combined alkali and total fatty matter. Besides these it is often necessary to determine insoluble matter, glycerine, unsaponifiable matter, rosin and sugar.

### MOISTURE.

The analysis of soap for moisture, at its best, is most unsatisfactory, for by heating it is impossible to drive off all the water, and on the other hand volatile oils driven off by heat are a part of the loss represented as moisture.

The usual method of determining moisture is to weigh 2 to 3 grams of finely shaved soap on a watch glass and heat in an oven at 105 degrees C. for 2 to 3 hours. The loss in weight is represented as water, although it is really impossible to drive off all the water in this way.

To overcome the difficulties just mentioned either the Smith or Fahrion method may be used. Allen recommends Smith's method which is said to be truthful to within 0.25 per cent. Fahrion's method, according to the author, gives reliable results to within 0.5 per cent. Both are more rapid than the above manipulation. To carry out the method of Smith, 5 to 10 grams of finely ground soap are heated over a sand bath with a small Bunsen flame beneath it, in a large porcelain crucible. The heating takes 20 to 30 minutes, or until no further evidence is present of water being driven off. This may be tested by the fogging of a cold piece of glass held over the crucible immediately upon removing the burner. When no fog appears the soap is considered dry. Any lumps of soap may be broken up by a small glass rod, weighed with the crucible, and with a roughened end to more easily separate the lumps. Should the soap burn, this can readily be detected by the odor, which, of course, renders the analysis useless. The loss in weight is moisture.

By Fahrion's method*, 2 to 4 grams of soap are weighed in a platinum crucible and about three times its weight of oleic acid, which has been heated at 120 degrees C. until all the water is driven off and preserved from moisture, is added and reweighed. The dish is then cautiously heated with a small flame until all the water is driven off and all the soap is dissolved. Care must be exercised not to heat too highly or the oleic acid will decompose. The moment the water is all driven off a clear solution is formed, provided no fillers are present in the soap. The dish is then cooled in a dessicator and reweighed. The loss in weight of acid plus soap is moisture and is calculated on the weight of soap taken. This determination takes about fifteen minutes.

### FREE ALKALI OR ACID.

(a) *Alcoholic Method.*

Test a freshly cut surface of the soap with a few drops of an alcoholic phenolphthalein solution. If it does not turn red it may be assumed free fat is present; should a red color appear, free alkali is present. In any case dissolve 2 to 5 grams of soap in 100 cubic centimeters of neutralized alcohol and heat to boiling until in solution. Filter off the undissolved portion containing carbonate, etc., and wash with alcohol. Add phenolphthalein to the filtrate and titrate with N/10 acid and calculate the per cent. of free alkali as sodium or potassium hydroxide. Should the filtrate be acid instead of alkaline, titrate with N/10 alkali and calculate the percentage of free fatty acid as oleic acid.

The insoluble portion remaining on the filter paper is washed with water until all the carbonate is dissolved. The washings are then titrated with N/10 sulfuric acid

*Zeit. Angew. Chem. 19, 385 (1906).

and expressed as sodium or potassium carbonate. Should borates or silicates be present it is possible to express in terms of these. If borax is present the carbon dioxide is boiled off after neutralizing exactly to methyl orange; cool, add mannite and phenolphthalein and titrate the boric acid with standard alkali.

(b) *Bosshard and Huggenberg Method.*†

In using the alcoholic method for the determination of the free alkali or fat in soap there is a possibility of both free fat and free alkali being present. Upon boiling in an alcoholic solution the fat will be saponified, thus introducing an error in the analysis. The method of Bosshard and Huggenberg overcomes this objection. Their method is briefly as follows:

*Reagents.*

1. N/10 hydrochloric acid to standardize N/10 alcoholic sodium hydroxide.

2. Approximately N/10 alcoholic sodium hydroxide to fix and control the N/40 stearic acid.

3. N/40 stearic acid. Preparation: About 7.1 grams of stearic acid are dissolved in one liter of absolute alcohol, the solution filtered, the strength determined by titration against N/10 NaOH and then protected in a well stoppered bottle, or better still connected directly to the burette.

4. A 10 per cent. solution of barium chloride. Preparation: 100 grams of barium chloride are dissolved in one liter of distilled water and filtered. The neutrality of the solution should be proven as it must be neutral.

5. *a* naphtholphthalein indicator according to Sorenson. Preparation: 0.1 gram of *a* naphtholphthalein is dissolved in 150 cubic centimeters of alcohol and 100 cubic

†Zeit. Angew. Chem. 27, 11-20 (1914).

centimeters of water. For every 10 cubic centimeters of liquid use at least 12 drops of indicator.

6. Phenolphthalein solution 1 gram to 100 cubic centimeter 96 per cent. alcohol.

7. Solvent, 50 per cent. alcohol neutralized.

MANIPULATION.

First—Determine the strength of the N/10 alcoholic sodium hydroxide in terms of N/10 hydrochloric acid and calculate the factor, e. g.:

$$\left.\begin{array}{l}10 \text{ c.c. N/10 alcoholic NaOH} = 9.95 \text{ N/10 HCl} \\ 10 \text{ c.c. N/10 alcoholic NaOH} = 9.96 \text{ N/10 HCl}\end{array}\right\} 9.96$$

The alcoholic N/10 NaOH has a factor of 0.996.

Second—Control the N/40 stearic acid with the above alkali to obtain its factor, e. g.:

$$\left.\begin{array}{l}40 \text{ c.c. N/40 alcoholic stearic acid} = \\ \qquad 10.18 \text{ c.c. N/10 NaOH} \\ 40 \text{ c.c. N/40 alcoholic stearic acid} = \\ \qquad 10.22 \text{ c.c. N/10 NaOH}\end{array}\right\} 10.2$$

$10.2 \times$ F N/10 NaOH (0.996) = Factor N/40 stearic acid

$\therefore$ Factor N/40 stearic acid = 1.016.

Third—About 5 grams of soap are weighed and dissolved in 100 cubic centimeters of 50 per cent. neutralized alcohol in a 250 cubic centimeter Erlenmeyer flask over a water bath and connected with a reflux condensor. When completely dissolved, which takes but a few moments, it is cooled by allowing a stream of running water to run over the outside of the flask.

Fourth—The soap is precipitated with 15 to 20 cubic centimeters of the 10 per cent. barium chloride solution.

Fifth—After the addition of 2 to 5 cubic centimeters of $\alpha$ naphtholphthalein solution the solution is titrated with N/40 alcoholic stearic acid. $\alpha$ naphtholphthalein is red with an excess of stearic acid. To mark the color changes it is advisable to first run a few blanks until the eye has become accustomed to the change in the indicator in the same way. The change from green to red can then be carefully observed.

Let us presume 5 grams of soap were taken for the analysis and 20 cubic centimeters of N/40 stearic acid were required for the titration then to calculate the amount of NaOH since the stearic factor is 1.016.

$20 \times 1.016 = 20.32$ N/40 stearic acid really required.

1 cubic centimeter N/40 stearic acid = 0.02 per cent. NaOH for 5 grams soap.

$\Delta$ 20.32 cubic centimeters N/40 stearic acid = $0.02 \times 20.32$ per cent. NaOH for 5 grams soap.

Hence the soap contains 0.4064 per cent. NaOH.

It is necessary, however, to make a correction by this method. When the free alkali amounts to over 0.1 per cent. the correction is + 0.01, and when the free alkali exceeds 0.4 per cent. the correction is + 0.04, hence in the above case we multiply 0.004064 by 0.04, add this amount to 0.004064 and multiply by 100 to obtain the true percentage. Should the alkalinity have been near 0.1 per cent. we would have multiplied by 0.01 and added this.

If carbonate is also present in the soap, another 5 grams of soap is dissolved in 100 cubic centimeters of 50 per cent. alcohol and the solution titrated directly after cooling with N/40 stearic acid, using $\alpha$ naphtholphthalein or phenolphthalein as an indicator, without the addition of barium chloride. From the difference of the two titrations the alkali present as carbonate is determined.

If the decomposed soap solution is colorless with phenolphthalein, free fatty acids are present, which may be quickly determined with alcoholic N/10 sodium hydroxide.

### INSOLUBLE MATTER.

The insoluble matter in soap may consist of organic or inorganic substances. Among the organic substances which are usually present in soap are oat meal, bran, sawdust, etc., while among the common inorganic or mineral compounds are pumice, silex, clay, talc, zinc oxide, infusorial earth, sand or other material used as fillers.

To determine insoluble matter, 5 grams of soap are dissolved in 75 cubic centimeters of hot water. The solution is filtered through a weighed gooch crucible or filter paper. The residue remaining on the filter is washed with hot water until all the soap is removed, is then dried to constant weight at 105 degrees C. and weighed. From the difference in weight of the gooch or filter paper and the dried residue remaining thereon after filtering and drying, the total percentage of insoluble matter may easily be calculated. By igniting the residue and reweighing the amount of insoluble mineral matter can be readily determined.

### STARCH AND GELATINE.

Should starch or gelatine be present in soap it is necessary to extract 5 grams of the soap with 100 cubic centimeters of 95 per cent. neutralized alcohol in a Soxhlet extractor until the residue on the extraction thimble is in a powder form. If necessary the apparatus should be disconnected and any lumps crushed, as these may contain soap. The residue remaining on the thimble consists of all substances present in soap, insoluble in alcohol. This is dried and weighed so that any percentage of impurities not actually determined can be found by difference. Starch and gelatine are separated from carbonate, sulfate and borate by dissolving the latter out through a filter with cold water. The starch and gelatine thus remaining can be determined by known methods, starch by the method of direct hydrolysis[1] and gelatine by Kjeldahling and calculating the corresponding amount of gelatine from the percentage of nitrogen (17.9%) therein.[2]

### TOTAL FATTY AND RESIN ACIDS.

To the filtrate from the insoluble matter add 40 cubic centimeters of half normal sulfuric acid, all the acid being added at once. Boil, stir thoroughly for some minutes and keep warm on a water bath until the fatty acids have collected as a clear layer on the surface. Cool by placing the beaker in ice and syphon off the acid water through a filter. Should the fatty acids not readily congeal a weighed amount of dried bleached bees-wax or stearic acid may be added to the hot mixture. This fuses with the hot mass and forms a firm cake of fatty acids upon cooling. Without removing the fatty acids from the beaker, add about 300 cubic centimeters of hot water, cool, syphon off the water through the same filter used before and wash again. Repeat washing, cooling and syphoning processes until the wash water is no longer acid. When this stage is reached, dissolve any fatty acid which may have remained on the filter with hot 95 per cent. alcohol into the beaker containing the fatty acids. Evaporate the alcohol and dry the beaker to constant weight over a water bath. The fatty acids thus obtained represent the combined fatty acids, uncombined fat and hydrocarbons.

### DETERMINATION OF ROSIN.

If resin acids are present, this may be determined by the Liebermann-Storch reaction. To carry out this test shake 2 cubic centimeters of the fatty acids with 5 cubic

[1] Bull. 107, Bur. Chem. U. S. Dept. Agriculture.

[2] Richards and Gies Am. J. Physiol. (1902) 7, 129.

centimeters of acetic anhydride; warm slightly; cool; draw off the anhydride and add 1:1 sulfuric acid. A violet color, which is not permanent, indicates the presence of rosin in the soap. The cholesterol in linseed or fish oil, which of course may be present in the soap, also give this reaction.

Should resin acids be present, these may be separated by the Twitchell method, which depends upon the difference in the behavior of the fatty and resin acids when converted into their ethyl esters through the action of hydrochloric acid. This may be carried out as follows:

Three grams of the dried mixed acids are dissolved in 25 cubic centimeters of absolute alcohol in a 100 cubic centimeter stoppered flask; the flask placed in cold water and shaken. To this cooled solution 25 cubic centimeters of absolute alcohol saturated with dry hydrochloric acid is added. The flask is shaken occasionally and the action allowed to continue for twenty minutes, then 10 grams of dry granular zinc chloride are added, the flask shaken and again allowed to stand for twenty minutes. The contents of the flask are then poured into 200 cubic centimeters of water in a 500 cubic centimeter beaker and the flask rinsed out with alcohol. A small strip of zinc is placed in the beaker and the alcohol evaporated. The beaker is then cooled and transferred to a separatory funnel, washing out the beaker with 50 cubic centimeters of gasoline (boiling below 80 degrees C.) and extracting by shaking the funnel well. Draw off the acid solution after allowing to separate and wash the gasoline with water until free from hydrochloric acid. Draw off the gasoline solution and evaporate the gasoline. Dissolve the residue in neutral alcohol and titrate with standard alkali using phenolphthalein as an indicator. One cubic centimeter of normal alkali equals 0.346 grams of rosin. The rosin may be gravimetrically determined by washing the gasoline extract with water, it not being necessary to wash absolutely free from acid, then adding 0.5 gram of potassium hydroxide and 5 cubic centimeters of alcohol in 50 cubic centimeters of water. Upon shaking the resin acids are rapidly saponified and extracted by the dilute alkaline solution as rosin soaps, while the ethyl esters remain in solution in the gasoline. Draw off the soap solution, wash the gasoline solution again with dilute alkali and unite the alkaline solutions. Decompose the alkaline soap solution with an excess of hydrochloric acid and weigh the resin acids liberated as in the determination of total fatty acids.

According to Lewkowitsch, the results obtained by the volumetric method which assumes a combining weight of 346 for resin acids, are very likely to be high. On the other hand those obtained by the gravimetric method are too low.

Leiste and Stiepel[1] have devised a simpler method for the determination of rosin. They make use of the fact that the resin acids as sodium soaps are soluble in acetone and particularly acetone containing two per cent. water, while the fatty acid soaps are soluble in this solvent to the extent of only about 2 per cent. First of all it is necessary to show that the sample to be analyzed contains a mixture of resin and fatty acids. This may be done by the Liebermann-Storch reaction already described. Glycerine interferes with the method. Two grams of fatty acids or 3 grams of soap are weighed in a nickel crucible and dissolved in 15-20 cubic centimeters of alcohol. The solution is then neutralized with alcoholic sodium hydroxide, using phenolphthalein as an indicator. The mass is concentrated by heat over an asbestos plate until a slight film

[1] Seifensieder Ztg. (1913) No. 46.

forms over it. Then about 10 grams of sharp, granular, ignited sand are stirred in by means of a spatula, the alcohol further evaporated, the mixture being constantly stirred and then thoroughly dried in a drying oven. The solvent for the cooled mass is acetone containing 2 per cent. water. It is obtained from acetone dried by ignited sodium sulfate and adding 2 per cent. water by volume. One hundred cubic centimeters of this solvent are sufficient for extracting the above. The extraction of the rosin soap is conducted by adding 10 cubic centimeters of acetone eight times, rubbing the mass thoroughly with a spatula and decanting. The decanted portions are combined in a beaker and the suspended fatty soaps allowed to separate. The mixture is then filtered into a previously weighed flask and washed several times with the acetone remaining. The solution of rosin soap should show no separation of solid matter after having evaporated to half the volume and allowing to cool. If a separation should occur another filtration and the slightest possible washing is necessary. To complete the analysis, the acetone is completely evaporated and the mass dried to constant weight in a drying oven. The weight found gives the weight of the rosin soap. In conducting the determination, it is important to dry the mixture of soap and sand thoroughly. In dealing with potash soaps it is necessary to separate the fatty acids from these and use them as acetone dissolves too great a quantity of a potash soap.

### TOTAL ALKALI.

In the filtrate remaining after having washed the fatty acids in the determination of total fatty and resin acids all the alkali present as soap, as carbonate and as hydroxide remains in solution as sulfate. Upon titrating this solution with half normal alkali the difference between the half normal acid used in decomposing the soap and alkali used in titrating the excess of acid gives the amount of total alkali in the soap. By deducting the amount of free alkali present as carbonate or hydroxide previously found the amount of combined alkali in the soap may be calculated.

To quickly determine total alkali in soap a weighed portion of the soap may be ignited to a white ash and the ash titrated for alkalinity using methyl orange as an indicator.

### UNSAPONIFIED MATTER.

Dissolve 5 grams of soap in 50 cubic centimeters of 50 per cent. alcohol. Should any free fatty acids be present neutralize them with standard alkali. Wash into a separatory funnel with 50 per cent. alcohol and extract with 100 cubic centimeters of gasoline, boiling at 50 degrees to 60 degrees C. Wash the gasoline with water, draw off the watery layer. Run the gasoline into a weighed dish, evaporate the alcohol, dry and weigh the residue as unsaponified matter. The residue contains any hydrocarbon oils or fats not converted into soap.

### SILICA AND SILICATES.

The insoluble silicates, sand, etc., are present in the ignited residue in the determination of insoluble matter. Sodium silicate, extensively used as a filler, however, will only show itself in forming a pasty liquid. Where it is desired to determine sodium silicate, 10 grams of soap are ashed by ignition, hydrochloric acid added to the ash in excess and evaporated to dryness. More hydrochloric acid is then added and the mass is again evaporated until dry; then cooled; moistened with hydrochloric acid; dissolved in water; filtered; washed; the filtrate evaporated to dryness and again taken up with hydrochloric acid and water;

filtered and washed. The precipitates are then combined and ignited. Silicon dioxide ($SiO_2$) is thus formed, which can be calculated to sodium silicate ($Na_2Si_4O_9$). Should other metals than alkali metals be suspected present the filtrate from the silica determinations should be examined.

### GLYCERINE IN SOAP.

To determine the amount of glycerine contained in soap dissolve 25 grams in hot water, add a slight excess of sulfuric acid and keep hot until the fatty acids form as a clear layer on top. Cool the mass and remove the fatty acids. Filter the acid solution into a 25 cubic centimeter graduated flask; bring to the mark with water and determine the glycerine by the bichromate method as described under glycerine analysis.

When sugar is present the bichromate would be reduced by the sugar, hence this method is not applicable. In this case remove the fatty acids as before, neutralize an aliquot portion with milk of lime, evaporate to 10 cubic centimeters, add 2 grams of sand and milk of lime containing about 2 grams of calcium hydroxide and evaporate almost to dryness. Treat the moist residue with 5 cubic centimeters of 96 per cent. alcohol, rub the whole mass into a paste, then constantly stirring, heat on a water bath and decant into a 250 cubic centimeter graduated flask. Repeat the washing with 5 cubic centimeters of alcohol five or six times, each time pouring the washings into the flask; cool the flask to room temperature and fill to the mark with 96 per cent. alcohol, agitate the flask until well mixed and filter through a dry filter paper. Take 200 cubic centimeters of the filtrate and evaporate to a syrupy consistency over a safety water bath. Wash the liquor into a stoppered flask with 20 cubic centimeters of absolute alcohol, add 30 cubic centimeters of absolute ether 10 cubic centimeters at a time, shaking well after each addition and let stand until clear. Pour off the solution through a filter into a weighed dish and wash out the flask with a mixture of three parts absolute ether and two parts absolute alcohol. Evaporate to a syrup, dry for one hour at the temperature of boiling water, weigh, ignite and weigh again. The loss is glycerine. This multiplied by 5/4 gives the total loss for the aliquot portion taken. The glycerine may also be determined by the acetin or bichromate methods after driving off the alcohol and ether if so desired.

### SUGAR IN SOAP.

To determine sugar in soap, usually present in transparent soaps, decompose a soap solution of 5 grams of soap dissolved in 100 cubic centimeters of hot water with an excess of hydrochloric acid and separate the fatty acids as usual. Filter the acid solution into a graduated flask and make up to the mark. Take an aliquot containing approximately 1 per cent. of reducing sugar and determine the amount of sugar by the Soxhlet method.[1]

### GLYCERINE ANALYSIS.

The methods of analyzing glycerine varied so greatly due to the fact that glycerine contained impurities which acted so much like glycerine as to introduce serious errors in the determinations of crude glycerine. This led to the appointment of committees in the United States and Europe to investigate the methods of glycerine analysis. An international committee met after their investigations and decided the acetin method should control the buying and selling of glycerine, but the more convenient bichromate method in a standardized form might be used

[1] Bull 107, Bur. Chem. U. S. Dept. Agriculture.

in factory control and other technical purposes. The following are the methods of analysis and sampling as suggested by the international committee:

### SAMPLING.

The most satisfactory method available for sampling crude glycerine liable to contain suspended matter, or which is liable to deposit salt on settling, is to have the glycerine sampled by a mutually approved sampler as soon as possible after it is filled into drums, but in any case before any separation of salt has taken place. In such cases he shall sample with a sectional sampler (see appendix) then seal the drums, brand them with a number for identification, and keep a record of the brand number. The presence of any visible salt or other suspended matter is to be noted by the sampler, and a report of the same made in his certificate, together with the temperature of the glycerine. Each drum must be sampled. Glycerine which has deposited salt or other solid matter cannot be accurately sampled from the drums, but an approximate sample can be obtained by means of the sectional sampler, which will allow a complete vertical section of the glycerine to be taken including any deposit.

### ANALYSIS.

1. *Determination of Free Caustic Alkali.*—Put 20 grams of the sample into a 100 cc. flask, dilute with approximately 50 cc. of freshly boiled distilled water, add an excess of neutral barium chloride solution, 1 cc. of phenolphthalein solution, make up to the mark and mix. Allow the precipitate to settle, draw off 50 cc. of the clear liquid and titrate with normal acid ($N/1$). Calculate the percentage of $Na_2O$ existing as caustic alkali.

2. *Determination of Ash and Total Alkalinity.*—Weigh

2 to 5 grams of the sample in a platinum dish, burn off the glycerine over a luminous Argand burner or other source of heat,[1] giving a low temperature, to avoid volatilization and the formation of sulphides. When the mass is charred to the point that water will not be colored by soluble organic matter, lixiviate with hot distilled water, filter, wash and ignite the residue in the platinum dish. Return the filtrate and washings to the dish, evaporate the water, and carefully ignite without fusion. Weigh the ash.

Dissolve the ash in distilled water and titrate total alkalinity, using as indicator methyl orange cold or litmus boiling.

3. *Determination of Alkali Present as Carbonate.*—Take 10 grams of the sample, dilute with 50 cc. distilled water, add sufficient $N/1$ acid to neutralize the total alkali found at (2), boil under a reflux condenser for 15 to 20 minutes, wash down the condenser tube with distilled water, free from carbon dioxide, and then titrate back with $N/1$ NaOH, using phenolphthalein as indicator. Calculate the percentage of $Na_2O$. Deduct the $Na_2O$ found in (1). The difference is the percentage of $Na_2O$ existing as carbonate.

4. *Alkali Combined with Organic Acids.*—The sum of the percentages of $Na_2O$ found at (1) and (3) deducted from the percentage found at (2) is a measure of the $Na_2O$ or other alkali combined with organic acids.

5. *Determination of Acidity.*—Take 10 grams of the sample, dilute with 50 cc. distilled water free from carbon dioxide, and titrate with $N/1$ NaOH and phenolphthalein. Express in terms of $Na_2O$ required to neutralize 100 grams.

6. *Determination of Total Residue at* 160° *C.*—For this determination the crude glycerine should be slightly alkaline with $Na_2CO_3$ not exceeding 0.2 per cent. $Na_2O$, in

[1] Carbon is readily burned off completely, without loss of chlorides, in a gas-heated muffle furnace adjusted to a dull red heat.

order to prevent loss of organic acids. To avoid the formation of polyglycerols this alkalinity must not be exceeded.

Ten grams of the sample are put into a 100 cc. flask, diluted with water and the calculated quantity of $N/1$ HCl or $Na_2CO_3$ added to give the required degree of alkalinity. The flask is filled to 100 cc., the contents mixed, and 10 cc. measured into a weighed Petrie or similar dish 2.5 in. in diameter and 0.5 in. deep, which should have a flat bottom. In the case of crude glycerine abnormally high in organic residue a smaller amount should be taken, so that the weight of the organic residue does not materially exceed 30 to 40 milligrams.

The dish is placed on a water bath (the top of the 160° oven acts equally well) until most of the water has evaporated. From this point the evaporation is effected in the oven. Satisfactory results are obtained in an oven[1] measuring 12 ins. cube, having an iron plate 0.75 in. thick lying on the bottom to distribute the heat. Strips of asbestos millboard are placed on a shelf half way up the oven. On these strips the dish containing the glycerine is placed.

If the temperature of the oven has been adjusted to 160° C. with the door closed, a temperature of 130° to 140° can be readily maintained with the door partially open, and the glycerine, or most of it, should be evaporated off at this temperature. When only a slight vapor is seen to come off, the dish is removed and allowed to cool.

An addition of 0.5 to 1.0 cc. of water is made, and by

[1] An electric oven suitable for this work, which is readily adjusted to 160 degs. C., has been made for Mr. Low and the chairman, by the Apparatus and Specialty Company, Lansing, Mich. Its size is 9½ x 10 x 16 inches, and capacity 8 Petrie dishes. It gives a strong draft at constant temperature.

a rotary motion the residue brought wholly or nearly into solution. The dish is then allowed to remain on a water bath or top of the oven until the excess water has evaporated and the residue is in such a condition that on returning to the oven at 160° C. it will not spurt. The time taken up to this point cannot be given definitely, nor is it important. Usually two or three hours are required. From this point, however, the schedule of time must be strictly adhered to. The dish is allowed to remain in the oven, the temperature of which is carefully maintained at 160° C. for one hour, when it is removed, cooled, the residue treated with water, and the water evaporated as before. The residue is then subjected to a second baking of one hour, after which the dish is allowed to cool in a desiccator over sulphuric acid and weighed. The treatment with water, etc., is repeated until a constant loss of 1 to 1.5 mg. per hour is obtained.

In the case of acid glycerine a correction must be made for the alkali added 1 cc. *N*/1 alkali represents an addition of 0.03 gram. In the case of alkaline crudes a correction should be made for the acid added. Deduct the increase in weight due to the conversion of the NaOH and $Na_2CO_3$ to NaCl. The corrected weight multiplied by 100 gives the percentage of *total residue at* 160° *C.*

This residue is taken for the determination of the non-volatile acetylizable impurities (see acetin method).

7. *Organic residue.*—Subtract the ash from the total residue at 160° C. Report as organic residue at 160° C. (it should be noted that alkaline salts of fatty acids are converted to carbonates on ignition and that the CO thus derived is not included in the organic residue).

# ANALYTICAL METHODS

## ACETIN PROCESS FOR THE DETERMINATION OF GLYCEROL.

This process is the one agreed upon at a conference of delegates from the British, French, German and American committees, and has been confirmed by each of the above committees as giving results nearer to the truth than the bichromate method on crudes in general. It is the process to be used (if applicable) whenever only one method is employed. On pure glycerines the results are identical with those obtained by the bichromate process. For the application of this method the crude glycerine should not contain over 60 per cent. water.

### REAGENTS REQUIRED.

(*A*) *Best Acetic Anhydride.*—This should be carefully selected. A good sample must not require more than 0.1 cc. normal NaOH for saponification of the impurities when a blank is run on 7.5 cc. Only a slight color should develop during digestion of the blank.

The anhydride may be tested for strength by the following method: Into a weighed stoppered vessel, containing 10 to 20 cc. of water, run about 2 cc. of the anhydride, replace the stopper and weigh. Let stand with occassional shaking, for several hours, to permit the hydrolysis of all the anhydride; then dilute to about 200 cc., add phenolphthalein and titrate with $N/1$ NaOH. This gives the total acidity due to free acetic acid and acid formed from the anhydride. It is worthy of note that in the presence of much free anhydride a compound is formed with phenolphthalein, soluble in alkali and acetic acid, but insoluble in neutral solutions. If a turbidity is noticed toward the end of the neutralization it is an indication that the anhydride is incompletely hydrolyzed and inasmuch as the indicator is withdrawn from the solution, results may be incorrect.

Into a stoppered weighing bottle containing a known weight of recently distilled aniline (from 10 to 20 cc.) measure about 2 cc. of the sample, stopper, mix, cool and weigh. Wash the contents into about 200 cc. of cold water, and titrate the acidity as before. This yields the acidity due to the original, preformed, acetic acid plus one-half the acid due to anhydride (the other half having formed acetanilide); subtract the second result from the first (both calculated to 100 grams) and double the result, obtaining the cc. *N*/1 NaOH per 100 grams of the sample. 1 cc. *N*/NaOH equals 0.0510 anhydride.

(*B*) *Pure Fused Sodium Acetate.*—The purchased salt is again completely fused in a platinum, silica or nickel dish, avoiding charring, powdered quickly and kept in a stoppered bottle or desiccator. It is most important that the sodium acetate be anhydrous.

(*C*) *A Solution of Caustic Soda for Neutralizing, of about N/1 Strength, Free from Carbonate.*—This can be readily made by dissolving pure sodium hydroxide in its own weight of water (preferably water free from carbon dioxide) and allowing to settle until clear, or filtering through an asbestos or paper filter. The clear solution is diluted with water free from carbon dioxide to the strength required.

(*D*) *N/1 Caustic Soda Free from Carbonate.*—Prepared as above and carefully standardized. Some caustic soda solutions show a marked diminution in strength after being boiled; such solutions should be rejected.

(*E*) *N/1 Acid.*—Carefully standardized.

(*F*) *Phenolphthalein Solution.*—0.5 per cent. phenolphthalein in alcohol and neutralized.

### THE METHOD.

In a narrow-mouthed flask (preferably round-bottomed), capacity about 120 cc., which has been thoroughly cleaned and dried, weigh accurately and as rapidly as possible 1.25 to 1.5 grams of the glycerine. A Grethan or Lunge pipette will be found convenient. Add about 3 grams of the anhydrous sodium acetate, then 7.5 cc. of the acetic anhydride, and connect the flask with an upright Liebig condenser. For convenience the inner tube of this condenser should not be over 50 cm. long and 9 to 10 mm. inside diameter. The flask is connected to the condenser by either a ground glass joint (preferably) or a rubber stopper. If a rubber stopper is used it should have had a preliminary treatment with hot acetic anhydride vapor.

Heat the contents and keep just boiling for one hour, taking precautions to prevent the salts drying on the sides of the flask.

Allow the flask to cool somewhat, and through the condenser tube add 50 cc. of distilled water free from carbon dioxide at a temperature of about 80° C., taking care that the flask is not loosened from the condenser. The object of cooling is to avoid any sudden rush of vapors from the flask on adding water, and to avoid breaking the flask. Time is saved by adding the water before the contents of the flask solidify, but the contents may be allowed to solidify and the test proceeded with the next day without detriment, bearing in mind that the anhydride in excess is much more effectively hydrolyzed in hot than in cold water. The contents of the flask may be warmed to, but must not exceed, 80° C., until the solution is complete, except a few dark flocks representing organic impurities in the crude. By giving the flask a rotary motion, solution is more quickly effected.

Cool the flask and contents without loosening from the condenser. When quite cold wash down the inside of the condenser tube, detach the flask, wash off the stopper or ground glass connection into the flask, and filter the contents through an acid-washed filter into a Jena glass flask of about 1 litre capacity. Wash thoroughly with cold distilled water free from carbon dioxide. Add 2 cc. of phenolphthalein solution (*F*), then run in caustic soda solution (*C*) or (*D*) until a faint pinkish yellow color appears throughout the solution. This neutralization must be done most carefully; the alkali should be run down the sides of the flask, the contents of which are kept rapidly swirling with occasional agitation or change of motion until the solution is nearly neutralized, as indicated by the slower disappearance of the color developed locally by the alkali running into the mixture. When this point is reached the sides of the flask are washed down with carbon dioxide-free water and the alkali subsequently added drop by drop, mixing after each drop until the desired tint is obtained.

Now run in from a burette 50 cc. or a calculated excess of $N/1$ NaOH (*D*) and note carefully the exact amount. Boil gently for 15 minutes, the flask being fitted with a glass tube acting as a partial condenser. Cool as quickly as possible and titrate the excess of NaOH with $N/1$ acid (*E*) until the pinkish yellow or chosen end-point color just remains.[1] A further addition of the indicator at this point will cause an increase of the pink color; this must be neglected, and the first end-point taken.

From the $N/1$ NaOH consumed calculate the percentage of glycerol (including acetylizable impurities) after making the correction for the blank test described below.

1 cc. $N/1$ NaOH = 0.03069 gram glycerol.

The coefficient of expansion for normal solutions is

[1] A precipitate at this point is an indication of the presence of iron or alumina, and high results will be obtained unless a correction is made as described below.

0.00033 per cc. for each degree centigrade. A correction should be made on this account if necessary.

*Blank Test.*—As the acetic anhydride and sodium acetate may contain impurities which affect the result, it is necessary to make a blank test, using the same quantities of acetic anhydride, sodium acetate and water as in the analysis. It is not necessary to filter the solution of the melt in this case, but sufficient time must be allowed for the hydrolysis of the anhydride before proceeding with the neutralization. After neutralization it is not necessary to add more than 10 cc. of the $N/1$ alkali ($D$), as this represents the excess usually present after the saponification of the average soap lye crude. In determining the acid equivalent of the N/1 NaOH, however, the entire amount taken in the analysis, 50 cc., should be titrated after dilution with 300 cc. water free from carbon dioxide and without boiling.

*Determination of the Glycerol Value of the Acetylizable Impurities.*—The total residue at 160° C. is dissolved in 1 or 2 cc. of water, washed into the acetylizing flask and evaporated to dryness. Then add anhydrous sodium acetate and acetic anhydride in the usual amounts and proceed as described in the regular analysis. After correcting for the blank, calculate the result to glycerol.

### WAYS OF CALCULATING ACTUAL GLYCEROL CONTENT.

(1) Determine the apparent percentage of glycerol in the sample by the acetin process as described. The result will include acetylizable impurities if any are present.

(2) Determine the total residue at 160° C.

(3) Determine the acetin value of the residue at (2) in terms of glycerol.

(4) Deduct the result found at (3) from the percentage obtained at (1) and report this corrected figure as

glycerol. If volatile acetylizable impurities are present these are included in this figure.

Trimethylenglycol is more volatile than glycerine and can therefore be concentrated by fractional distillation. An approximation to the quantity can be obtained from the spread between the acetin and bichromate results on such distillates. The spread multiplied by 1.736 will give the glycol.

#### BICHROMATE PROCESS FOR GLYCEROL DETERMINATION. REAGENTS REQUIRED.

(*A*) *Pure potassium bichromate* powdered and dried in air free from dust or organic vapors, at 110° to 120° C. This is taken as the standard.

(*B*) *Dilute Bichromate Solution.*—7.4564 grams of the above bichromate are dissolved in distilled water and the solution made up to one liter at 15.5° C.

(*C*) *Ferrous Ammonium Sulphate.*—It is never safe to assume this salt to be constant in composition and it must be standardized against the bichromate as follows: dissolve 3.7282 grams of bichromate (*A*) in 50 cc. of water. Add 50 cc. of 50 per cent. sulphuric acid (by volume), and to the cold undiluted solution add from a weighing bottle a moderate excess of the ferrous ammonium sulphate, and titrate back with the dilute bichromate (*B*). Calculate the value of the ferrous salt in terms of bichromate.

(*D*) *Silver Carbonate.*—This is prepared as required for each test from 140 cc. of 0.5 per cent. silver sulphate solution by precipitation, with about 4.9 cc. *N*/1 sodium carbonate solution (a little less than the calculated quantity of *N*/1 sodium carbonate should be used as an excess to prevent rapid settling). Settle, decant and wash one by decantation.

(*E*) *Subacetate of Lead.*—Boil a 10 per cent. solution

of pure lead acetate with an excess of litharge for one hour, keeping the volume constant, and filter while hot. Disregard any precipitate which subsequently forms. Preserve out of contact with carbon dioxide.

(*F*) *Potassium Ferricyanide.*—A very dilute, freshly prepared solution containing about 0.1 per cent.

### THE METHOD.

Weigh 20 grams of the glycerine, dilute to 250 cc. and take 25 cc. Add the silver carbonate, allow to stand, with occasional agitation, for about 10 minutes, and add a slight excess (about 5 cc. in most cases) of the basic lead acetate (*E*), allow to stand a few minutes, dilute with distilled water to 100 cc., and then add 0.15 cc. to compensate for the volume of the precipitate, mix thoroughly, filter through an air-dry filter into a suitable narrow-mouthed vessel, rejecting the first 10 cc., and return the filtrate if not clear and bright. Test a portion of the filtrate with a little basic lead acetate, which should produce no further precipitate (in the great majority of cases 5 cc. are ample, but occasionally a crude will be found requiring more, and in this case another aliquot of 25 cc. of the dilute glycerine should be taken and purified with 6 cc. of the basic acetate). Care must be taken to avoid a marked excess of basic acetate.

Measure off 25 cc. of the clear filtrate into a flask or beaker (previously cleaned with potassium bichromate and sulphuric acid). Add 12 drops of sulphuric acid (1 : 4) to precipitate the small excess of lead as sulphate. Add 3.7282 grams of the powdered potassium bichromate (*A*). Rinse down the bichromate with 25 cc. of water and let stand with occasional shaking until all the bichromate is dissolved (no reduction will take place in the cold).

Now add 50 cc. of 50 per cent. sulphuric acid (by volume) and immerse the vessel in boiling water for two hours and keep protected from dust and organic vapors, such as alcohol, till the titration is completed. Add from a weighing bottle a slight excess of the ferrous ammonium sulphate (*C*), making spot tests on a porcelain plate with the potassium ferricyanide (*F*). Titrate back with the dilute bichromate. From the amount of bichromate reduced calculate the percentage of glycerol.

1 gram glycerol = 7.4564 grams bichromate.

1 gram bichromate = 0.13411 gram glycerol.

The percentage of glycerol obtained above includes any oxidizable impurities present after the purification. A correction for the non-volatile impurities may be made by running a bichromate test on the residue at 160° C.

### NOTES.

(1) It is important that the concentration of acid in the oxidation mixture and the time of oxidation should be strictly adhered to.

(2) Before the bichromate is added to the glycerine solution it is essential that the slight excess of lead be precipitated with sulphuric acid, as stipulated.

(3) For crudes practically free from chlorides the quantity of silver carbonate may be reduced to one-fifth and the basic lead acetate to 0.5 cc.

(4) It is sometimes advisable to add a little potassium sulphate to insure a clear filtrate.

### SAMPLING CRUDE GLYCERINE.

The usual method of sampling crude glycerine hitherto has been by means of a glass tube, which is slowly lowered into the drum with the object of taking as nearly as possible a vertical section of the glycerine contained in the drum. This method has been found unsatisfactory, owing to the fact that in cold climates glycerine runs into the tube very slowly, so that, owing to the time occupied, it is impossible to take a complete section of the crude. Another objection to the glass tube is that it fails to take anything approaching a correct proportion of any settled salt contained in the drum.

The sampler which is illustrated herewith has been devised with the object of overcoming the objections to the glass tube as far as possible. It consists of two brass tubes, one fitting closely inside the other. A number of ports are cut out in each tube in such a way that when the ports are opened a continuous slot is formed which enables a complete section to be taken throughout the entire length of the drum. By this arrangement the glycerine fills into the sampler almost instantaneously. There are a number of ports cut at the bottom of the sampler which render it possible to take a proportion of the salt at the bottom of the drum. The instrument is so constructed that all the ports, including the bottom ones, can be closed simultaneously by the simple action of turning the handle at the top; a pointer is arranged which indicates on a dial when the sampler is open or closed. In samplers of larger section (1 in.) it is possible to arrange a third motion whereby the bottom ports only are open for emptying, but in samplers of smaller dimensions (5/8 in.) this third motion must be dispensed with, otherwise the dimensions of the ports have to be so small that the sampler would not be efficient.

In using the sampler it is introduced into the drum with the ports closed, and when it has touched the bottom, the ports are opened for a second or two, then closed and withdrawn, and the sample discharged into the receiving vessel by opening the ports. When the drum contains salt which has deposited, the ports must be opened before the sampler is pushed through the salt, thus enabling a portion to be included in the sample. It is, however, almost impossible to obtain a correct proportion of salt after it has settled in the drum and it is therefore recommended that the drum be sampled before any salt has deposited. A sampler 1 in. in diameter withdraws approximately 10 oz. from a 110-gal. drum. A sampler ⅝ in. in diameter will withdraw about 5 oz.

# CHAPTER VII

## Standard Methods for the Sampling and Analysis of Commercial Fats and Oils[1]

The following report of the *Committee on Analysis of Commercial Fats and Oils* of the *Division of Industrial Chemists and Chemical Engineers* of the American Chemical Society was adopted April 14, 1919, by unanimous vote:

W. D. RICHARDSON, *Chairman*, Swift and Co., Chicago, Ill.
R. W. BAILEY, Stillwell and Gladding, New York City.
W. J. GASCOYNE, W. J. Gascoyne and Co., Baltimore, Md.
I. KATZ,* Wilson and Co., Chicago, Ill.
A. LOWENSTEIN,* Morris and Co., Chicago, Ill.
H. J. MORRISON, Proctor and Gamble Co., Ivorydale, Ohio.
J. R. POWELL, Armour Soap Works, Chicago, Ill.
R. J. QUINN,* Midland Chemical Co., Argo, Ill.
PAUL RUDNICK, Armour and Co., Chicago, Ill.
L. M. TOLMAN, Wilson and Co., Chicago, Ill.
E. TWITCHELL,* Emery Candle Co., Cincinnati, Ohio.
J. J. VOLLERTSEN, Morris and Co., Chicago, Ill.

*Resigned.

## Scope, Applicability and Limitations of the Methods.

SCOPE.

These methods are intended to aid in determining the commercial valuation of fats and fatty oils in their purchase and sale, based on the fundamental assumption commonly recognized in the trade, namely, that the product is true to name and is not adulterated. For methods for determining the identity of oils and fats, the absence of adulterants therein and for specific tests used in particular industries, the chemist is referred to standard works on the analysis of fats and oils.

---

[1] Approved by the Supervisory Committee on Standard Methods of Analysis of the American Chemical Society.

#### APPLICABILITY.

The methods are applicable in commercial transactions involving fats and fatty oils used in the soap, candle and tanning industries, to edible fats and oils and to fats and fatty oils intended for lubricating and burning purposes. The methods are applicable to the raw oils used in the varnish and paint industry with the exceptions noted under limitations, but special methods have not been included.

#### LIMITATIONS.

The methods have not been developed with special reference to waxes (beeswax, carnauba wax, wool wax, etc.) although some of them may be found applicable to these substances. The Committee considers the Wijs method superior to the Hanus method for the determination of iodine number of linseed oil as well as other oils, although the Hanus method has been considered standard for this work for some time and has been adopted by the American Society for Testing Materials and in various specifications. It has been customary to use the Hübl method for the determination of iodine value of tung oil (China wood oil) but the Committee's work indicates that the Wijs method is satisfactory for this determination.

## Sampling.

#### TANK CARS.

1. Sampling While Loading—Sample shall be taken at discharge of pipe where it enters tank car dome. The total sample taken shall be not less than 50 lbs. and shall be a composite of small samples of about 1 pound each, taken at regular intervals during the entire period of loading.

The sample thus obtained is thoroughly mixed and uniform 3-lb. portions placed in air-tight 3-lb. metal containers. At least three such samples shall be put up, one for the buyer, one for the seller, and the third to be sent to a referee chemist in case of dispute. All samples are to be promptly and correctly labeled and sealed.

2. SAMPLING FROM CAR ON TRACK[2]—(*a*) *When contents are solid.*[3] In this case the sample is taken by means of a large tryer measuring about 2 in. across and about 1½ times the depth of the car in length. Several tryerfuls are taken vertically and obliquely toward the ends of the car until 50 lbs. are accumulated, when the sample is softened, mixed and handled as under (1). In case the contents of the tank car have assumed a very hard condition, as in Winter weather, so that it is impossible to insert the tryer, and it becomes necessary to soften the contents of the car by means of the closed steam coil (in nearly all tank cars the closed steam coil leaks) or by means of open steam in order to draw a proper sample, suitable arrangements must be made between buyer tnd seller for the sampling of the car after it is sufficiently softened, due consideration being given to the possible presence of water in the material in the car as received and also to the possible addition of water during the steaming. The Committee knows of no direct method for sampling a hard-frozen tank car of tallow in a satisfactory manner.

(*b*) *When contents are liquid.* The sample taken is to be a 50-lb. composite made up of numerous small samples taken from the top, bottom and intermediate points by means of a bottle or metal container with removable stopper or top. This device attached to a suitable pole is lowered to the various desired depths, when the stopper or top is removed and the container allowed to fill. The 50-lb. sample thus obtained is handled as under (1).

---

[2] Live steam must not be turned into tank cars or coils before samples are drawn, since there is no certain way of telling when coils are free from leaks.

[3] If there is water present under the solid material this must be noted and estimated separately.

In place of the device described above, any sampler capable of taking a sample from the top, bottom, and center, or from a section through car, may be used.

(*c*) *When contents are in semi-solid condition, or when stearine has separated from liquid portions.* In this case, a combination of (*a*) and (*b*) may be used or by agreement of the parties the whole may be melted and procedure (*b*) followed.

BARRELS, TIERCES, CASKS, DRUMS, AND OTHER PACKAGES.

All packages shall be sampled, unless by special agreement the parties arrange to sample a lesser number; but in any case not less than 10 per cent of the total number shall be sampled. The total sample taken shall be at least 20 lbs. in weight for each 100 barrels, or equivalent.

1. BARRELS, TIERCES AND CASKS—(*a*) *When contents are solid.* The small samples shall be taken by a tryer through the bunghole or through a special hole bored in the head or side for the purpose, with a 1-in. or larger auger. Care should be taken to avoid and eliminate all borings and chips from the sample. The tryer is inserted in such a way as to reach the head of the barrel, tierce, or cask. The large sample is softened, mixed and handled according to TANK CARS (1).

(*b*) *When contents are liquid.* In this case use is made of a glass tube with constricted lower end. This is inserted slowly and allowed to fill with the liquid, when the upper end is closed and the tube withdrawn, the contents being allowed to drain into the sample container. After the entire sample is taken it is thoroughly mixed and handled according to TANK CARS (1).

(*c*) *When contents are semi-solid.* In this case the tryer or a glass tube with larger outlet is used, depending on the degree of fluidity.

(*d*) *Very hard materials, such as natural and artificial stearines.* By preference the barrels are stripped and samples obtained by breaking up contents of at least 10 per cent of the packages. This procedure is to be followed also in the case of cakes shipped in sacks. When shipped in the form of small pieces in sacks they can be sampled by grab sampling and quartering. In all cases the final procedure is as outlined under TANK CARS (1).

2. DRUMS—Samples are to be taken as under (1), use being made of the bunghole. The tryer or tube should be sufficiently long to reach to the ends of the drum.

3. OTHER PACKAGES—Tubs, pails and other small packages not mentioned above are to be sampled by tryer or tube (depending on fluidity) as outlined above, the tryer or tube being inserted diagonally whenever possible.

4. MIXED LOTS AND PACKAGES—When lots of tallow or other fats are received in packages of various shapes and sizes, and especially wherein the fat itself is of variable composition, such must be left to the judgment of the sampler. If variable, the contents of each package should be mixed as thoroughly as possible and the amount of the individual samples taken made proportional to the sizes of the packages.

## Analysis.

### SAMPLE.

The sample must be representative and at least three pounds in weight and taken in accordance with the STANDARD METHODS FOR THE SAMPLING OF COMMERCIAL FATS AND OILS. It must be kept in an air-tight container, in a dark, cool place.

Soften the sample if necessary by means of a gentle heat, taking care not to melt it. When sufficiently softened, mix the sample thoroughly by means of a mechanical egg beater or other equally effective mechanical mixer.

### MOISTURE AND VOLATILE MATTER.

Apparatus: *Vacuum Oven*—The Committee Standard Oven.

Description—The Standard F. A. C. Vacuum Oven has been designed with the idea of affording a simple and compact vacuum oven which will give as uniform temperatures as possible on the shelf. As the figure shows, it consists of an iron casting of rectangular sections with hinged front door made tight by means of a gasket and which can be lowered on opening the oven so as to form a shelf on which samples may be rested. The oven contains but one shelf which is heated from above as well as below by means of resistance coils. Several thermometer holes are provided in order to ascertain definitely the temperature at different points on the shelf. In a vacuum oven where the heating is done almost entirely by radiation it is difficult to maintain uniform temperatures at all points, but the F. A. C. oven accomplishes this rather better than most vacuum ovens. Larger ovens containing more than one shelf have been tried by the Committee, but have been found to be lacking in temperature uniformity and means of control. The entire oven is supported by means of a 4-in. standard pipe which screws into the base of the oven and which in turn is supported by being screwed into a blind flange of suitable diameter which rests on the floor or work table.

*Moisture Dish*—A shallow, glass dish, lipped, beaker form, approximately 6 to 7 cm. diameter and 4 cm. deep, shall be standard.

Determination—Weigh out 5 grams (=0.2 g. of the prepared sample into a moisture dish. Dry to constant weight *in vacuo* at a uniform temperature, not less than 15° C. nor more than 20° C. above the boiling point of water at the working pressure, which must not exceed 100 mm. of mercury.[4] Constant weight is attained when successive

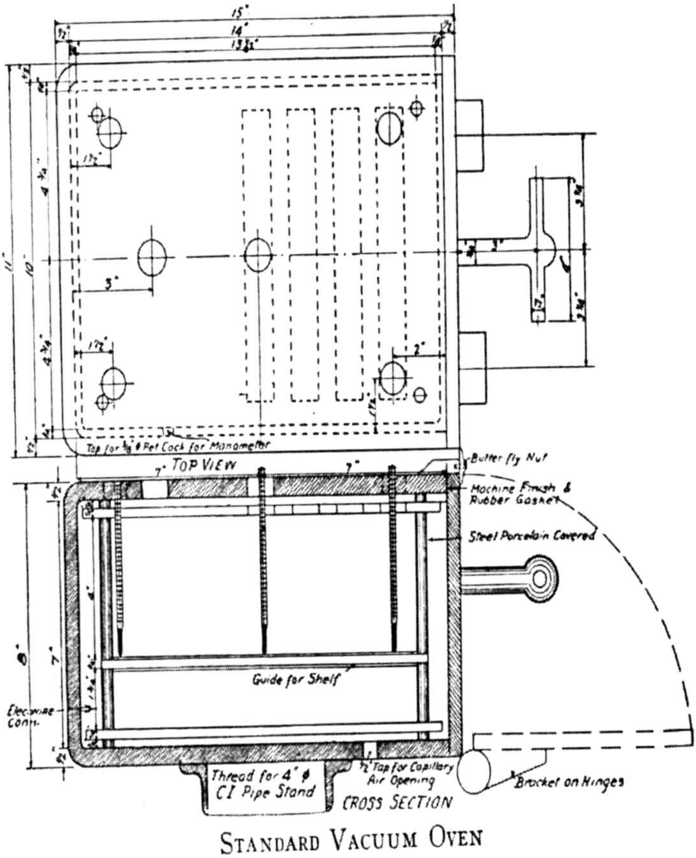


STANDARD VACUUM OVEN

dryings for 1-hr. periods show an additional loss of not more that 0.05 per cent. Report loss in weight as MOISTURE AND VOLATILE MATTER.[5]

The vacuum-oven method cannot be considered accurate in the case of fats of the coconut oil group containing free acid and the Committee recommends that it be used only for oils of this group when they contain less than 1 per cent free acid. In the case of oils of this group containing more than 1 per cent free acid, recourse should be had temporarily to the routine control method for moisture and volatile matter[6] until the Committee develops a more satisfactory method.

The air-oven method cannot be considered even approximately accurate in the case of the drying and semi-drying oils and those of the coconut oil group. Therefore, in the case of such oils as cottonseed oil, maize oil (corn oil), soy bean oil, linseed oil, coconut oil, palm kernel oil, etc., the vacuum-oven method should always be used, except in the case of fats of the coconut group containing more than 1 per cent free acid, as noted above.

### INSOLUBLE IMPURITIES.

Dissolve the residue from the moisture and volatile matter

---

[4] Boiling point of water at reduced pressures.

| Pressure Mm. Hg. | Boiling Point to 1° C. | Boiling Point + 15° C. | Boiling Point + 20° C. |
|---|---|---|---|
| 100 | 52° C. | 67° C. | 72° C. |
| 90 | 50 | 65 | 70 |
| 80 | 47 | 62 | 67 |
| 70 | 45 | 60 | 65 |
| 60 | 42 | 57 | 62 |
| 50 | 38 | 53 | 58 |
| 40 | 34 | 49 | 54 |

[5] Results comparable to those of the Standard Method may be obtained on most fats and oils by drying 5-g. portions of the sample, prepared and weighed as above, to constant weight in a well-constructed and well-ventilated air oven held uniformly at a temperature of 105° to 110° C. The thermometer bulb should be close to the sample. The definition of constant weight is the same as for the Standard Method.

determination by heating it on a steam bath with 50 cc. of kerosene. Filter the solution through a Gooch crucible properly prepared with asbestos,[7] wash the insoluble matter five times with 10-cc. portions of hot kerosene, and finally wash the residual kerosene out thoroughly with petroleum ether. Dry the crucible and contents to constant weight, as in the determination of moisture and volatile matter and report results as INSOLUBLE IMPURITIES.

SOLUBLE MINERAL MATTER.

Place the combined kerosene filtrate and kerosene washings from the insoluble impurities determination in a platinum dish. Place in this an ashless filter paper folded in the form of a cone, apex up. Light the apex of the cone, whereupon the bulk of the kerosene burns quietly. Ash the residue in a muffle, to constant weight, taking care that the decomposition of alkaline earth carbonates is complete, and report the result as SOLUBLE MINERAL MATTER.[8] When the percentage of soluble mineral matter amounts to more than 0.1 per cent, multiply the percentage by 10 and add this amount to the percentage of free fatty acids as determined.[9]

[6] The following method is suggested by the Committee for routine control work: Weigh out 5- to 25-g. portions of prepared sample into a glass or aluminum (*Caution*: Aluminum soap may be formed) beaker or casserole and heat on a heavy asbestos board over burner or hot plate, taking care that the temperature of the sample does not go above 130° C. at any time. During the heating rotate the vessel gently on the board by hand to avoid sputtering or too rapid evolution of moisture. The proper length of time of heating is judged by absence of rising bubbles of steam, by the absence of foam or by other signs known to the operator. Avoid overheating of sample as indicated by smoking or darkening. Cool in desiccator and weigh.

By co-operative work in several laboratories, the Committee has demonstrated that this method can be used and satisfactory results obtained on coconut oil even when a considerable percentage of free fatty acids is present, and the method is recommended for this purpose. Unfortunately on account of the very great personal factor involved, the Committee cannot establish this method as a preferred method. Nevertheless, after an operator has learned the technique of the method, it gives perfectly satisfactory results for ordinary oils and fats, butter, oleomargarine and coconut oil, and deserves more recognition than it has heretofore received.

FREE FATTY ACIDS.

The ALCOHOL[10] used shall be approximately 95 per cent ethyl alcohol, freshly distilled from sodium hydroxide, which with phenolphthalein gives a definite and distinct end-point.

DETERMINATION—Weigh 1 to 15 g. of the prepared sample into an Erlenmeyer flask, using the smaller quantity in the case of dark-colored, high acid fats. Add 50 to 100 cc. hot, neutral alcohol, and titrate with *N*/2, *N*/4 or *N*/10 sodium hydroxide depending on the fatty acid content, using phenolphthalein as indicator. Calculate to oleic acid, except that in the case of palm oil the results may also be expressed in terms of palmitic acid, clearly indicating the two methods of calculation in the report. In the case of coconut and palm kernel oils, calculate to and report in terms of lauric acid in addition to oleic acid, clearly indicating the two methods of calculation in the report. In the case of fats or greases containing more than 0.1 per cent of soluble mineral matter, add to the percentages of free fatty acids as determined 10 times the percentage of bases in the soluble mineral matter as determined.[9] This addition gives the equivalent of fatty acids combined with the soluble mineral matter.

---

[7] For routine control work, filter paper is sometimes more convenient than the prepared Gooch crucible, but must be very carefully washed, especially around the rim, to remove the last traces of fat.

[8] For routine work, an ash may be run on the original fat, and the soluble mineral matter obtained by deducting the ash on the insoluble impurities from this. In this case the Gooch crucible should be prepared with an ignited asbestos mat so that the impurities may be ashed directly after being weighed. In all cases ignition should be to constant weight so as to insure complete decomposition of carbonates.

[9] See note on Soluble Mineral Matter following these methods. When the ash contains phosphates the factor 10 cannot be applied, but the bases consisting of calcium oxide, etc., must be determined, and the factor 10 applied to them.

[10] For routine work methyl or denatured ethyl alcohol of approximately 95 per cent strength may be used. With these reagents the end-point is not sharp.

## TITER.

Standard Thermometer—The thermometer is graduated at zero and in tenth degrees from 10° C to 65° C., with one auxiliary reservoir at the upper end and another between the zero mark and the 10° mark. The cavity in the capillary tube between the zero mark and the 10° mark is at least 1 cm. below the 10° mark, the 10° mark is about 3 or 4 cm. above the bulb, the length of the thermometer being about 37 cm. over all. The thermometer has been annealed for 75 hrs. at 450° C. and the bulb is of Jena normal 16''' glass, or its equivalent, moderately thin, so that the thermometer will be quick-acting. The bulb is about 3 cm. long and 6 mm. in diameter. The stem of the thermometer is 6 mm. in diameter and made of the best thermometer tubing, with scale etched on the stem, the graduation is clear-cut and distinct, but quite fine. The thermometer must be certified by the U. S. Bureau of Standards.

Glycerol Caustic Solution—Dissolve 250 g. potassium hydroxide in 1900 cc. dynamite glycerin with the aid of heat.

Determination—Heat 75 cc. of the glycerol-caustic solution to 150° C. and add 50 g. of the melted fat. Stir the mixture well and continue heating until the melt is homogeneous, at no time allowing the temperature to exceed 150° C. Allow to cool somewhat and carefully add 50 cc. 30 per cent sulfuric acid. Now add hot water and heat until the fatty acids separate out perfectly clear. Draw off the acid water and wash the fatty acids with hot water until free from mineral acid, then filter and heat to 130° C. as rapidly as possible while stirring. Transfer the fatty acids, when cooled somewhat, to a 1-in. by 4-in. titer tube, placed in a 16-oz. salt-mouth bottle of clear glass, fitted with a cork that is perforated so as to hold the tube rigidly when in position. Suspend the titer thermometer so that it can be used as a stirrer and stir the fatty acids slowly (about 100 revolutions per minute) until the mercury remains stationary for 30 seconds. Allow the thermometer to hang quietly with the bulb in the center of the tube and report the highest point to which the mercury rises as the titer of the fatty acids. The titer should be made at about 20° C. for all fats having a titer above 30° C. and at 10° C. below the titer for all other fats. Any convenient means may be used for obtaining a temperature of 10° below the titer of the various fats. The committee recommends first of all a chill room for this purpose; second, an artificially chilled small chamber with glass window; third, immersion of the salt-mouth bottle in water or other liquid of the desired temperature.

### UNSAPONIFIABLE MATTER.

Extraction Cylinder—The cylinder shall be glass-stoppered, graduated at 40 cc., 80 cc. and 130 cc., and of the following dimensions: diameter about 1⅜ in., height about 12 in.

Petroleum Ether—Redistilled petroleum ether, boiling under 75° C., shall be used. A blank must be made by evaporating 250 cc. with about 0.25 g. of stearine or other hard fat (previously brought to constant weight by heating) and drying as in the actual determination. The blank must not exceed a few milligrams.

Determination—Weigh 5 g. (±0.20 g.) of the prepared sample into a 200-cc. Erlenmeyer flask, add 30 cc. of redistilled 95 per cent (approximately) ethyl alcohol and 5 cc. of 50 per cent aqueous potassium hydroxide, and boil the mixture for one hour under a reflux condenser. Transfer to the extraction cylinder and wash to the 40-cc. mark with redistilled 95 per cent ethyl alcohol. Complete the transfer, first with warm, then with cold water, till the total volume amounts to 80 cc. Cool the cylinder and contents to room temperature and add 50 cc. of petroleum ether. Shake *vigorously* for one minute and allow to settle until both layers are clear, when the volume of the upper layer should be about 40 cc. Draw off the petroleum ether layer as closely as possible by means of a slender glass siphon into a separatory funnel of 500 cc. capacity. Repeat extraction at least four more times, using 50 cc. of petroleum ether each time. More extractions than five are necessary where the unsaponifiable matter runs high, say over 5 per cent, and also in some cases where it is lower than 5 per cent, but is extracted with difficulty. Wash the combined extracts in a separatory funnel three times with 25-cc. portions of 10 per cent alcohol, shaking vigorously each time. Transfer the petroleum ether extract to a wide-mouth tared flask or beaker, and evaporate the petroleum ether on a steam bath in an air current. Dry as in the method for MOISTURE AND VOLATILE MATTER. Any blank must be deducted from the weight before calculating unsaponifiable matter. Test the final residue for solubility in 50 cc. petroleum ether at room temperature. Filter and wash free from the insoluble residue, if any, evaporate and dry in the same manner as before. The Committee wishes to emphasize the necessity of thorough and vigorous shaking in order to secure accurate results. The two phases must be brought into the most intimate contact possible, otherwise low and disagreeing results may be obtained.

### IODINE NUMBER—WIJS METHOD.

PREPARATION OF REAGENTS—*Wijs Iodine Solution*—Dissolve 13.0 g. of resublimed iodine in one liter of C. P. glacial acetic acid and pass in washed and dried chlorine gas until the original thiosulfate titration of the solution is not quite doubled. The solution is then preserved in amber glass-stoppered bottles, sealed with paraffin until ready for use.

Mark the date on which the solution is prepared on the

bottle or bottles and do not use Wijs solution which is more than 30 days old.

There should be no more than a slight excess of iodine, and no excess of chlorine. When the solution is made from iodine and chlorine, this point can be ascertained by not quite doubling the titration.[11]

The glacial acetic acid used for preparation of the Wijs solution should be of 99.0 to 99.5 per cent strength. In case of glacial acetic acids of somewhat lower strength, the Committee recommends freezing and centrifuging or draining as a means of purification.

*N/10 Sodium Thiosulfate Solution*—Dissolve 24.8 g. of C. P. sodium thiosulfate in recently boiled distilled water and dilute with the same to one liter at the temperature at which the titrations are to be made.

*Starch Paste*—Boil 1 g. of starch in 200 cc. of distilled water for 10 min. and cool to room temperature.

An improved starch solution may be prepared by autoclaving 2 g. of starch and 6 g. of boric acid dissolved in 200 cc. water at 15 lbs. pressure for 15 min. This solution has good keeping qualities.

---

[11] P. C. McIlhiney, *J. Am. Chem. Soc.*, 29 (1917), 1222, gives the following details for the preparation of the iodine monochloride solution:

The preparation of the iodine monochloride solution presents no great difficulty, but it must be done with care and accuracy in order to obtain satisfactory results. There must be in the solution no sensible excess either of iodine or more particularly of chlorine, over that required to form the monochloride. This condition is most satisfactorily attained by dissolving in the whole of the acetic acid to be used the requisite quantity of iodine, using a gentle heat to assist the solution, if it is found necessary, setting aside a small portion of this solution, while pure and dry chlorine is passed into the remainder until the halogen content of the whole solution is doubled. Ordinarily it will be found that by passing the chlorine into the main part of the solution until the characteristic color of free iodine has just been discharged there will be a slight excess of chlorine which is corrected by the addition of the requisite amount of the unchlorinated portion until all free chlorine has been destroyed. A slight excess of iodine does little or no harm, but excess of chlorine must be avoided.

*Potassium Iodide Solution*—Dissolve 150 g. of potassium iodide in water and make up to one liter.

*N/10 Potassium Bichromate*—Dissolve 4.903 g. of C. P. potassium bichromate in water and make the volume up to one liter at the temperature at which titrations are to be made.

The Committee calls attention to the fact that occasionally potassium bichromate is found containing sodium bichromate, although this is of rare occurrence. If the analyst suspects that he is dealing with an impure potassium bichromate, the purity can be ascertained by titration against re-sublimed iodine. However, this is unnecessary in the great majority of cases.

*Standardization of the Sodium Thiosulfate Solution*—Place 40 cc. of the potassium bichromate solution, to which has been added 10 cc. of the solution of potassium iodide, in a glass-stoppered flask. Add to this 5 cc. of strong hydro-chloric acid. Dilute with 100 cc. of water, and allow the *N*/10 sodium thiosulfate to flow slowly into the flask until the yellow color of the lquid has almost disappeared. Add a few drops of the starch paste, and with constant shaking continue to add the *N*/10 sodium thiosulfate solution until the blue color just disappears.

DETERMINATION—Weigh accurately from 0.10 to 0.50 g. (depending on the iodine number) of the melted and filtered sample into a clean, dry, 16-oz. glass-stoppered bottle containing 15-20 cc. of carbon tetrachloride or chloroform. Add 25 cc. of iodine solution from a pipette, allowing to drain for a definite time. The excess of iodine should be from 50 per cent to 60 per cent of the amount added, that is, from 100 per cent to 150 per cent of the amount absorbed. Moisten the stopper with a 15 per cent potassium iodide solution to prevent loss of iodine or chlorine but guard against an amount sufficient to run down inside the bottle. Let the bottle stand in a dark place for ½ hr. at a uniform temperature. At the end of that time add 20 cc. of 15 per cent potassium iodide solution and 100 cc. of distilled water. Titrate the iodine with *N*/10 sodium thiosulfate solution which is added gradually, with constant shaking, until the yellow color of the solution has almost disappeared. Add a few drops of starch paste and continue titration until the blue color has entirely disappeared. Toward the end of the reaction stopper the bottle and shake violently so that any iodine remaining in solution in the tetrachloride or chloroform may be taken up by the potassium iodide solution. Conduct two determinations on blanks which must be run in the same manner as the sample except that no fat is used in the blanks. Slight variations in temperature quite appreciably affect the titer of the iodine solution, as acetic acid has a high coefficient of expansion. It is, therefore, essential that the blanks and determinations on the sample be made at the same time. The number of cc. of standard thiosulfate solution required by the blank, less the amount used in the determination, gives the thiosulfate equivalent of the iodine absorbed by the amount of sample used in the determination. Calculate to centigrams of iodine absorbed by 1 g. of sample (= per cent iodine absorbed).

DETERMINATION, TUNG OIL—Tung oil shows an erratic behavior with most iodine reagents and this is particularly noticeable in the case of the Hanus reagent which is entirely unsuitable for determining the iodine number of this oil since extremely high and irregular results are obtained. The Hübl solution shows a progressive absorption up to 24 hrs. and probably for a longer time but the period required is entirely too long for a chemical determination. The Wijs solution gives good results if the following precautions are observed:

Weigh out 0.15 ± 0.05 g., use an excess of 55 ± 3 per

cent Wijs solution. Conduct the absorption at a temperature of 20-25° C. for 1 hr. In other respects follow the instructions detailed above.

## SAPONIFICATION NUMBER (KOETTSTORFER NUMBER).

PREPARATION OF REAGENTS. *N/2 Hydrochloric Acid*—Carefully standardized.

*Alcoholic Potassium Hydroxide Solution*—Dissolve 40 g. of pure potassium hydroxide in one liter of 95 per cent redistilled alcohol (by volume). The alcohol should be redistilled from potassium hydroxide over which it has been standing for some time, or with which it has been boiled for some time, using a reflux condenser. The solution must be clear and the potassium hydroxide free from carbonates.

DETERMINATION—Weigh accurate about 5 g. of the filtered sample into a 250 to 300 cc. Erlenmeyer flask. Pipette 50 cc. of the alcoholic potassium hydroxide solution into the flask, allowing the pipette to drain for a definite time. Connect the flask with an air condenser and boil until the fat is completely saponified (about 30 minutes). Cool and titrate with the *N*/2 hydrochloric acid, using phenolphthalein as an indicator. Calculate the Koettstorfer number (mg. of potassium hydroxide required to saponify 1 g. of fat). Conduct 2 or 3 blank determinations, using the same pipette and draining for the same length of time as above.

## MELTING POINT.

APPARATUS—*Capillary tubes* made from 5 mm. inside diameter thin-walled glass tubing drawn out to 1 mm. inside diameter. Length of capillary part of tubes to be about 5 cm. Length of tube over all 8 cm.

*Standard thermometer* graduated in tenths of a degree.

*600 cc. beaker.*

DETERMINATION—The sample should be clear when melted

and entirely free from moisture, or incorrect results will be obtained.

Melt and thoroughly mix the sample. Dip three of the capillary tubes above described in the oil so that the fat in the tube stands about 1 cm. in height. Now fuse the capillary end carefully by means of a small blast flame and allow to cool. These tubes are placed in a refrigerator over night at a temperature of from 40 to 50° F. They are then fastened by means of a rubber band or other suitable means to the bulb of a thermometer graduated in tenths of a degree. The thermometer is suspended in a beaker of water (which is agitated by air or other suitable means) so that the bottom of the bulb of the thermometer is immersed to a depth of about 3 cm. The temperature of the water is increased gradually at the rate of about 1° per minute.

The point at which the sample becomes opalescent is first noted and the heating continued until the contents of the tube becomes uniformly transparent. The latter temperature is reported as the melting point.

Before finally melting to a perfectly clear fluid, the sample becomes opalescent and usually appears clear at the top, bottom, and sides before becoming clear at the center. The heating is continued until the contents of the tube become uniformly clear and transparent. This temperature is reported as the melting point.[12] It is usually only a fraction of a degree above the opalescent point noted. The thermometer should be read to the nearest ½° C., and in addition this temperature may be reported to the nearest degree Fahrenheit if desired.

#### CLOUD TEST.

PRECAUTIONS—(1) The oil must be perfectly dry, because

---

[12] The melting point of oils may be determined in general according to the above procedure, taking into consideration the lower temperature required.

the presence of moisture will produce a turbidity before the clouding point is reached.

(2) The oil must be heated to 150° C. over a free flame, immediately before making the test.

(3) There must not be too much discrepancy between the temperature of the bath and the clouding point of the oil. An oil that will cloud at the temperature of hydrant water should be tested in a bath of that temperature. An oil that will cloud in a mixture of ice and water should be tested in such a bath. An oil that will not cloud in a bath of ice and water must be tested in a bath of salt, ice, and water.

Determination—The oil is heated in a porcelain casserole over a free flame to 150° C., stirring with the thermometer. As soon as it can be done with safety, the oil is transferred to a 4 oz. oil bottle, which must be perfectly dry. One and one-half ounces of the oil are sufficient for the test. A dry centigrade thermometer is placed in the oil, and the bottle is then cooled by immersion in a suitable bath. The oil is constantly stirred with the thermometer, taking care not to remove the thermometer from the oil at any time during the test, so as to avoid stirring air bubbles into the oil. The bottle is frequently removed from the bath for a few moments. The oil must not be allowed to chill on the sides and bottom of the bottle. This is effected by constant and vigorous stirring with the thermometer. As soon as the first permanent cloud shows in the body of the oil, the temperature at which this cloud occurs is noted.

With care, results concordant to within ½° C. can be obtained by this method. A Fahrenheit thermometer is sometimes used because it has become customary to report results in degrees Fahrenheit.

The oil must be tested within a short time after heating to 150° C. and a re-test must always be preceded by reheating to that temperature. The cloud point should be approached as quickly as possible, yet not so fast that the oil is frozen on the sides or bottom of the bottle before the cloud test is reached.

## Notes on the Above Methods.

### SAMPLING.

The standard size of sample adopted by the committee is at least 3 lbs. in weight. The committee realizes that this amount is larger than any samples usually furnished even when representing shipments of from 20,000 to 60,000 lbs. but it believes that the requirement of a larger sample is desirable and will work toward uniform and more concordant results in analysis. It will probably continue to be the custom of the trade to submit smaller buyers' samples than required by the committee, but these are to be considered only as samples for inspection and not for analysis. The standard analytical sample must consist of 3 lbs. or more.

The reasons for keeping samples in a dark, cool place are obvious. This is to prevent any increase in rancidity and any undue increase in free fatty acids. In the case of many fats the committee has found in its co-operative analytical work that free acid tends to increase very rapidly. This tendency is minimized by low temperatures.

### MOISTURE AND VOLATILE MATTER.

After careful consideration the committee has decided that moisture is best determined in a vacuum oven of the design which accompanies the above report. Numerous results on check samples have confirmed the committee's conclusions. The oven recommended by the committee is constructed on the basis of well-known principles and it is hoped that this type will be adopted generally by chemists who are called upon to analyze fats and oils. The experiments of the committee indicate that it is a most difficult matter to design a vacuum oven which will produce uniform temperatures throughout; and one of the principal ideas in the design adopted is uniformity of temperature over the entire single shelf. This idea has not quite been realized in practice but, nevertheless, the present design approaches much closer to the ideal than other vacuum ovens commonly used. In the drawing the essential dimensions are those between the heating units and the shelf and the length and breadth of the outer casting. The standard Fat Analysis Committee Oven (F. A. C. Oven) can be furnished by Messrs. E. H. Sargent & Company, 125 West Lake street, Chicago.

The committee realizes that for routine work a quicker method is desirable and has added one such method and has also stated the conditions under which comparable results can be obtained by means of the ordinary well-ventilated air oven held at 105 to 110° C. However, in accordance with a fundamental principle adopted by the committee at its first meeting, only one standard method is adopted and declared official for each determination.

The committee realizes that in the case of all methods for determining moisture by means of loss on heating there may be a loss due to volatile matter (especially fatty acids) other than water. The title of the determination MOISTURE AND VOLATILE MATTER indicates this idea, but any considerable error from this source may occur only in the case of high acid fats and oils and particularly those containing lower fatty acids such as coconut and palm kernel oil. In the case of extracted greases which have not been properly purified, some of the solvent may also be included in the moisture and volatile matter determination, but inasmuch as the solvent, usually a petroleum product, can only be considered as foreign matter, for commercial purposes, it is entirely proper to include it with the moisture.

The committee has also considered the various distillation methods for the determination of moisture in fats and oils, but since according to the fundamental principles which it was endeavoring to follow it could only standardize one method, it was decided that the most desirable one on the whole was the vacuum-oven method as given. There are cases wherein a chemist may find it desirable to check a moisture determination or investigate the moisture content of a fat or oil further by means of one of the distillation methods.

However, in co-operative work the distillation method in various types of apparatus has not yielded satisfactory results. The difficulties appear to be connected with a proper choice of solvent and particularly with the tendency of drops of water to adhere to various parts of the glass apparatus instead of passing on to the measuring device. When working on coconut oil containing a high percentage of free fatty acids, concordant results could not be obtained by the various members of the committee when working with identical samples, solvents and apparatus.

On the other hand, the committee found by individual work, co-operative work and collaborative work by several members of the committee in one laboratory, that the old, well-known direct heating method (which the committee has designated the hot plate method) yielded very satisfactory results on all sorts of fats and oils including emulsions such as butter and oleomargarine and even on coconut oil samples containing 15 to 20 per cent free fatty acids and 5 to 6 per cent of moisture. Unfortunately, this method depends altogether on the operator's skill and while the method may be taught to any person whether a chemist or not so that he can obtain excellent results with it, it is difficult to give a sufficiently complete description of it so that any chemist anywhere after reading the description could follow it successfully. The method is undoubtedly worthy of much confidence in careful hands. It is quick, accurate and reliable.

It is probably the best single method for the determination of moisture in all sorts of samples for routine laboratory work. On account of this fact the committee desires to announce its willingness to instruct any person in the proper use of the method who desires to become acquainted with it and who will visit any committee member's laboratory.

### INSOLUBLE IMPURITIES.

This determination, the title for which was adopted after careful consideration, determines the impurities which have generally been known as dirt, suspended matter, suspended solids, foreign solids, foreign matter, etc., in the past. The first solvent recommended by the committee is hot kerosene to be followed by petroleum ether kept at ordinary room temperature. Petroleum ether, cold or only slightly warm, is not a good fat and metallic soap solvent, whereas hot kerosene dissolves these substances readily, and for this reason the committee has recommended the double solvent method so as to exclude metallic soaps which are determined below as soluble mineral matter.

### SOLUBLE MINERAL MATTER.

Soluble mineral matter represents mineral matter combined with fatty acids in the form of soaps in solution in the fat or oil. Formerly, this mineral matter was often determined in combination by weighing the separated metallic soap or by weighing it in conjunction with the insoluble impurities. Since the soaps present consist mostly of lime soap, it has been customary to calculate the lime present therein by taking 0.1 the weight of the total metallic soaps. The standard method as given above is direct and involves no calculation. The routine method given in the note has been placed among the methods for the reason that it is used in some laboratories, but has not been adopted as a standard method in view of the fact that the committee has made it a rule to adopt only one standard method. It should be pointed out, however, that the method cannot be considered accurate for the reason that insoluble impurities may vary from sample to sample to a considerable extent and the error due to the presence of large particles of insoluble impurities is thus transferred to the soluble mineral matter. The committee has found one type of grease (naphtha bone grease) which shows most unusual characteristics. The type sample contains 4.3 per cent soluble mineral matter by the committee method which would be equivalent to 43.0 per cent free fatty acid. The kerosene and gasoline filtrate was particularly clear, nevertheless the ash was found to contain 36.43 per cent $P_2O_5$ equivalent to 79.60 per cent of $Ca_3(PO_4)_2$ and 9.63 per cent of $Fe_2O_3$. The method, therefore, determines the soluble mineral matter in this case satisfactorily but the factor 10 is not applicable for calculating the fatty acids combined therewith. It is necessary, therefore, in order to determine the fatty acids combined with soluble mineral matter in the original sample to determine the actual bases in the soluble mineral matter as obtained by ashing the kerosene and gasoline filtrate. To the bases so determined the factor 10 can then be applied.

### FREE FATTY ACID.

The fatty acid method adopted is sufficiently accurate for commercial purposes. In many routine laboratories the fat or oil is measured and not weighed, but the committee recommends weighing the sample in all cases. For scientific purposes the result is often expressed as "acid number," meaning the number of milligrams of KOH required to neutralize the free acids in one gram of fat, but the commercial practice has been, and is, to express the fatty acids as oleic acid or in the case of palm oil, as palmitic acid, in some instances. The committee sees no objection to the continuation of this custom so long as the analytical report clearly indicates how the free acid is expressed. For a more exact expression of the free acid in a given fat, the committee recommends that the ratio of acid number to saponification number be used. This method of expressing results is subject to error when unsaponifiable fatty matter is present, since the result expresses the ratio of free fatty acid to total saponifiable fatty matter present.

### TITER.

At the present time the prices of gycerol and caustic potash are abnormally high, but the committee has considered that the methods adopted are for normal times and normal prices. For routine work during the period of high prices the following method may be used for preparing the fatty acids and is recommended by the committee:

Fifty grams of fat are saponified with 60 cc. of a solution of 2 parts of methyl alcohol to 1 of 50 per cent NaOH. The soap is dried, pulverized and dissolved in 1000 cc. of water in a porcelain dish and then decomposed with 25 cc. of 75 per cent sulphuric acid. The fatty acids are boiled until clear oil is formed and then collected and settled in a 150-cc. beaker and filtered into a 50-cc. beaker. They are then heated to 130° C. as rapidly as possible with stirring, and transferred, after they have cooled somewhat, to the usual 1-in. by 4-in. titer tube.

The method of taking the titer, including handling the thermometer, to be followed is the same as that described in the standard method. Even at present high prices many laboratories are using the glycerol-caustic potash method for preparing the fatty acids, figuring that the saving of time more than compensates for the extra cost of the reagents. Caustic soda cannot be substituted for caustic potash in the glycerol method.

UNSAPONIFIABLE MATTER.

The committee has considered unsaponifiable matter to include those substances frequently found dissolved in fats and oils which are not saponified by the caustic alkalies and which at the same time are soluble in the ordinary fat solvents. The term includes such substances as the higher alcohols, such as cholesterol which in found in animal fats, phytosterol found in some vegetable fats, paraffin and petroleum oils, etc. UNSAPONIFIABLE MATTER should not be confused in the lay mind with INSOLUBLE IMPURITIES OR SOLUBLE MINERAL MATTER.

The method adopted by the committee has been selected only after the most careful consideration of other methods, such as the dry extraction method and the wet method making use of the separatory funnel. At first consideration the dry extraction process would seem to offer the best basis for an unsaponifiable matter method, but in practice it has been found absolutely impossible, for different analysts to obtain agreeing results when using any of the dry extraction methods proposed. Therefore, this method had to be abondoned after numerous trials, although several members of the committee strongly favored it in the beginning.

IODINE NUMBER—The iodine number adopted by the committee is that determined by the well-known Wijs method. This method was adopted after careful comparison with the Hanus and Hübl methods. The Hübl method was eliminated from consideration almost at the beginning of the committee's work for the reason that the time required for complete absorption of the iodine is unnecessarily long and, in fact, even after absorption has gone on over night, it is apparently not complete. In the case of the Hanus and Wijs methods complete absorption takes place in from 15 minutes to an hour, depending on conditions. Formerly, many chemists thought the Hanus solution rather easier to prepare than the Wijs solution, but the experience of the committee was that the Wijs solution was no more difficult to prepare than the Hanus. Furthermore, absorption of iodine from the Wijs solution appeared to take place with greater promptness and certainty than from the Hanus and was complete in a shorter time. Results by the Wijs method were also in better agreement in the case of oils showing high iodine absorption than with the Hanus solution and showed a slightly higher iodine absorption for the same length of time. However, the difference was not great. The committee investigated the question of substitution since it has been suggested that in case of the Wijs solution substitution of iodine in the organic molecule might occur, and found no evidence of this in the time required for the determination, namely, ½ hr., or even for a somewhat longer period. One member of the committee felt that it was not desirable to introduce the Wijs method into these standard methods since the Hanus method was already standardized by the Association of Official Agricultural Chemists, but the committee felt that it must follow the principle established at the commencement of its work, namely, that of adopting the method which appeared to be the best from all standpoints, taking into consideration accuracy, convenience, simplicity, time, expense, etc., without allowing precedent to have the deciding vote.

IODINE NUMBER, TUNG OIL—The committee has made an extensive study of the application of the Wijs method to the determination of iodine value in the case of tung oil with the result that it recommends the method for this oil but has thought it desirable to limit the conditions under which the determination is conducted rather narrowly, although reasonably good results are obtained by the committee method without making use of the special limitations.

The co-operative work of the committee and the special

investigations conducted by individual members bring out the following points:

*Influence of Temperature*—From 16° C. to 30° C. there is a moderate increase in the absorption, but above 30° the increase is rather rapid so that it was thought best to limit the temperature in the case of tung oil to 20° to 25° C.

*Influence of Time*—The absorption increases with the time but apparently complete absorption, so far as unsaturated bonds are concerned, occurs well within one hour's time. Consequently, one hour was set as the practical limit.

*Influence of Excess*—The excess of iodine solution also tends to increase the iodine number, hence the Committee thought it necessary to limit the excess rather rigidly to 55 ± 3 per cent, although with greater latitude results were reasonably good.

*Influence of Age of Solution*—Old solutions tend to give low results although up to 2 mo. no great differences were observed. Nevertheless, it was thought best to limit the age of the solution to 30 days—long enough for all practical purposes.

*Amount of Sample*—As a practical amount of sample to be weighed out the Committee decided on 0.15 g. with a tolerance of 0.05 g. in either direction according to preference. In other words, the amount of sample to be taken for the determination to be from 0.1 to 0.2 g. in the discretion of the analyst.

The Committee's study of the Hübl method which has been adopted by the Society for Testing Materials in the case of tung oil indicates that this method when applied to tung oil is subject to the same influences as the Wijs method and it has the additional very serious disadvantage of requiring a long period of time for absorption which cannot be considered reasonable for a modern analytical method. When using the Hübl solution, the absorption is not complete in the case of tung oil at 3, 7, 18 or even 24 hrs.

The Hanus method in the case of tung oil gives very high and erratic results, as high as 180 to 240 in ordinary cases for an oil whose true iodine number is about 165.

### MELTING POINT.

A melting point is the temperature at which a solid substance assumes the liquid condition. If the solid is a pure substance in the crystalline condition the melting point is sharp and well defined for any given pressure. With increased pressure the melting point is lowered or raised, depending on whether the substance contracts or expands in melting. The lowering or raising of the melting point with pressure is very slight and ordinarily is not taken into consideration. Melting-point determinations are commonly carried out under ordinary atmospheric pressures without correction. The general effect of soluble impurities is to lower the melting point, and this holds true whether the impurity has a higher or lower melting point than the pure substance (solvent). Thus if a small amount of stearic acid be added to liquid palmitic acid and the solution frozen, the melting point of this solid will be lower than that of palmitic acid. Likewise the melting point of stearic acid is lowered by the addition of a small amount of palmitic acid. A eutectic mixture results when two components solidify simultaneously at a definite temperature. Such a mixture has a constant melting point and because of this and also because both solid and liquid phases have the same composition, eutectic mixtures were formerly looked upon as compounds. The phenomenon of double melting points has been observed in the case of a number of glycerides. Such a glyceride when placed in the usual capillary tube and subjected to increasing temperature quickly resolidifies only to melt again and remain melted at a still higher temperature. This phenomenon has not yet been sufficiently investigated to afford a satisfactory explanation.

Non-crystalline substances such as glass, sealing wax and various other waxes and wax mixtures, and most colloidal substances do not exhibit a sharp melting point, but under the application of heat first soften very gradually and at a considerably higher temperature melt sufficiently to flow. This phenomenon of melting through a long range of temperature may be due to the amorphous nature of the substance or to the fact that it consists of a very large number of components of many different melting points.

The fats and oils of natural origin, that is, the animal and vegetable fats and oils, consist of mixtures of glycerides and, generally speaking, of a considerable number of such components. These components are crystalline and when separated in the pure state have definite melting points, although some exhibit the phenomenon of double melting point. For the most part the naturally occurring glycerides are mixed glycerides. In the natural fats and oils there are present also certain higher alcohols, of which cholesterol is characteristic of the animal fats and oils and phytosterol of many of the vegetable fats and oils. In addition to the crystalline glycerides and the higher alcohols present in neutral fats, there are in fats of lower grade, fatty acids, which are crystalline, and also various non-crystalline impurities of an unsaponifiabe nature, and the presence of these impurities tends to lower the melting point. They also tend to induce undercooling and when the liquid fat or oil is being chilled for purposes of solidification or in determination of titer.

The presence of water, especially when this is thoroughly mixed or emulsified with a fat or oil, also influences the melting point to a marked extent, causing the mixture to melt through a longer range of temperatures than would be the case if the water were absent. This is particularly true of emulsified fats and oils, such as butter and oleomargarine, both of which contain, besides water, the solids naturally present in milk or cream and including casein, milk sugar, and salts. The melting-point method recommended by the Committee is not applicable to such emulsions or other watery mixtures and the Committee has found it impossible to devise an accurate method for making softening-point or melting-point determinations on products of this nature. Not only the amount of water present but also the fineness of its particles, that is, its state of subdivision and distribution, in a fat or oil influences the softening point or melting point and causes it to vary widely in different samples.

As a consequence of the foregoing facts, natural fats and oils do not exhibit a definite melting point, composed as they are of mixtures of various crystalline glycerides, higher alcohols, fatty acids, and non-cystalline substances. Therefore, the term melting point when applied to them requires further definition. They exhibit first a lower melting point (the melting point of the lowest melting component) or what might be called the softening point and following this the fat softens through a shorter or longer range of temperature to the final melting point at which temperature the fat is entirely liquid. This is the melting point determined by the Committee's melting-point method. The range between the softening point and the final melting point varies greatly with the different fats and oils depending on their chemical components, the water associated with them, emulsification, etc. In the case of coconut oil the range between softening point and final melting point is rather short; in the case of butter, long. Various methods have been devised to determine the so-called melting point of fats and oils. Most of these methods, however, determine, not the melting point, but the softening point or the flow point of the fat and the great difficulty has been in the past to devise a method which would determine even this point with reasonable accuracy and so that results could be easily duplicated. It has been the aim of the Committee to devise a simple method for the determination of the melting point of fats and oils, but it should be understood that the term melting point in the scientific sense is not applicable to natural fats and oils.

# PLANT AND MACHINERY

Illustrations of machinery and layouts of the plant of a modern soap-making establishment.

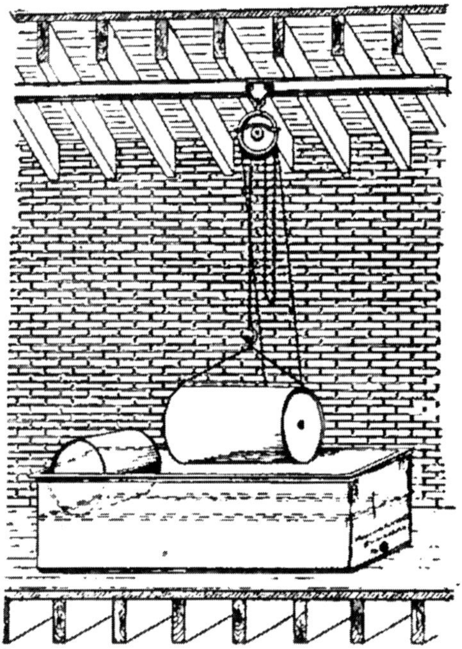

Hoist, Lye Tank, etc.

Melting-Out Trough

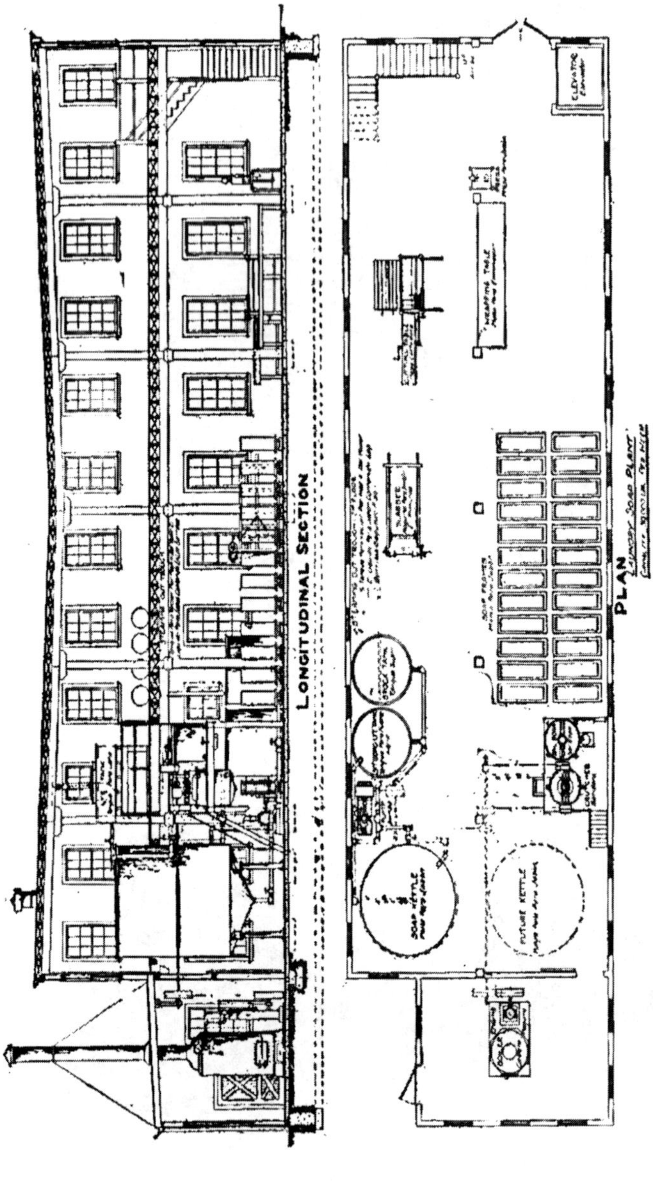


LAUNDRY SOAP PLANT

DRYING RACK

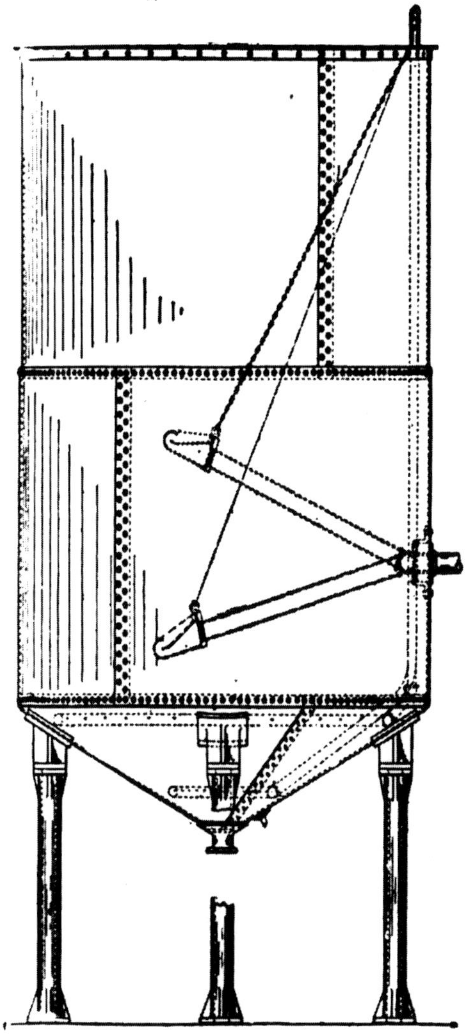

SOAP KETTLE

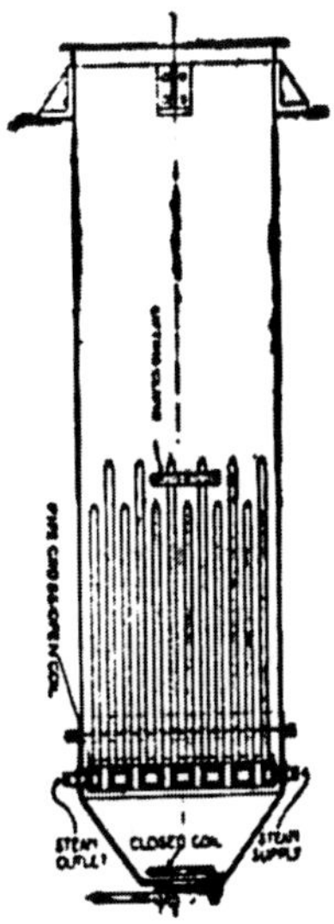


REMELTER

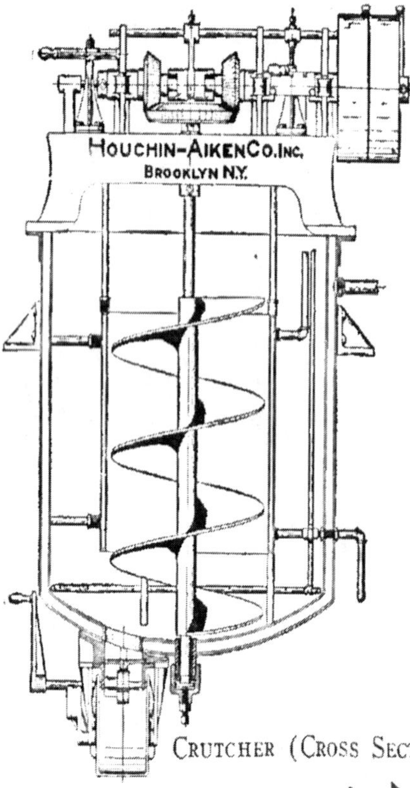


CRUTCHER (CROSS SECTION)

HORIZONTAL CRUTCHER

CRUTCHER

WRAPPING MACHINE
(LAUNDRY SOAP)

SLABBER

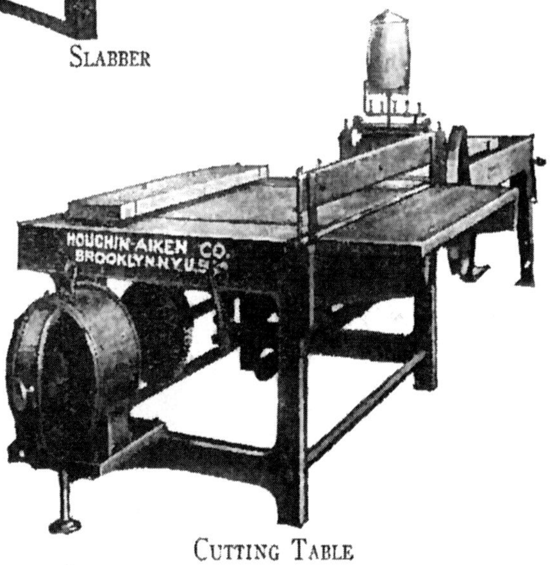


CUTTING TABLE

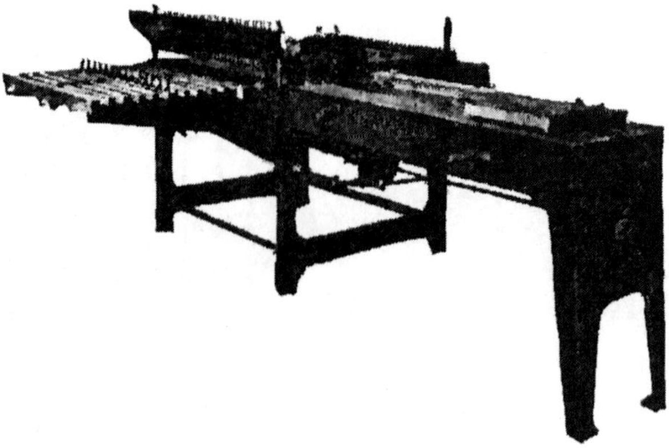

Automatic Power Cutting Table

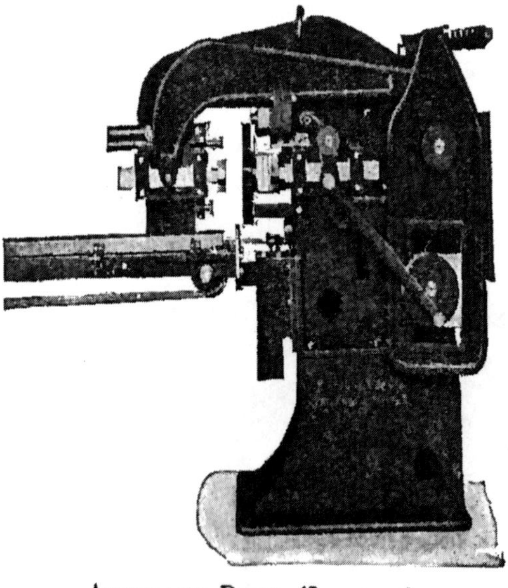

Automatic Press (Laundry)

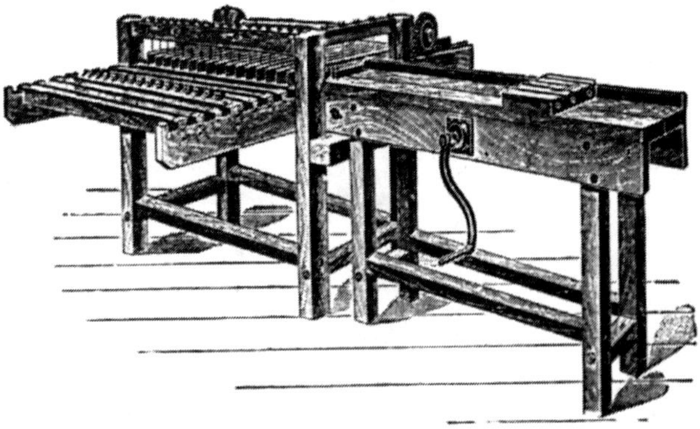

Cutting Table (Hand)

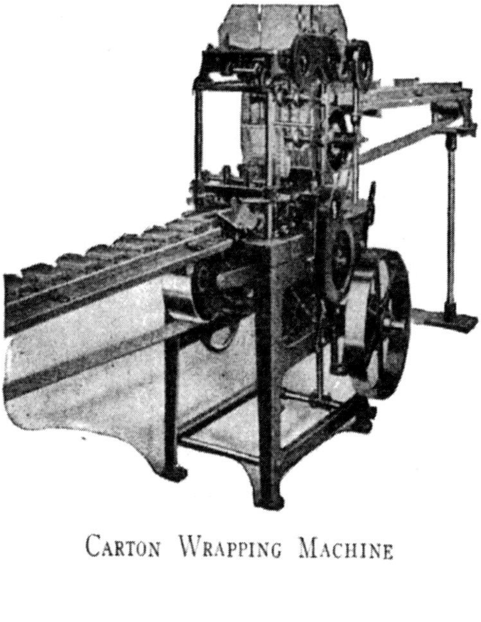

Carton Wrapping Machine

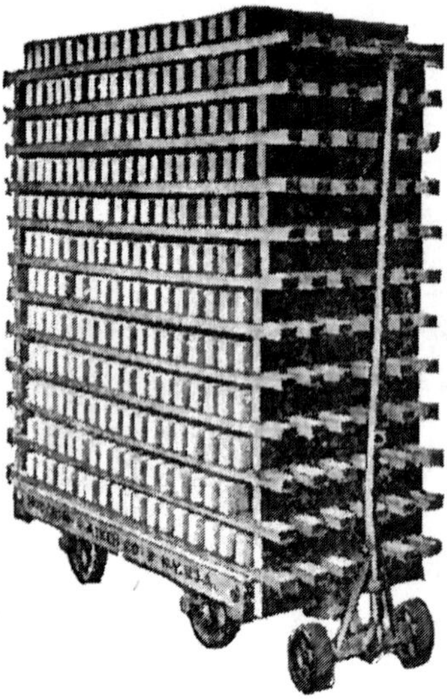

Drying Racks

Soap Powder Box

Scouring Soap Press

Frame

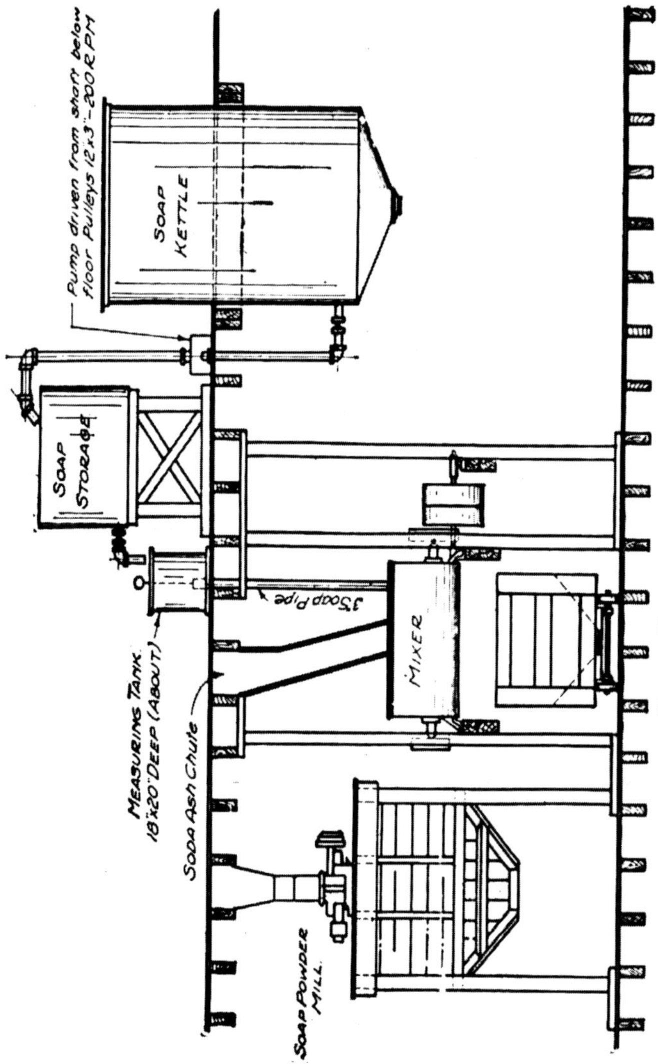


Soap Powder Equipment

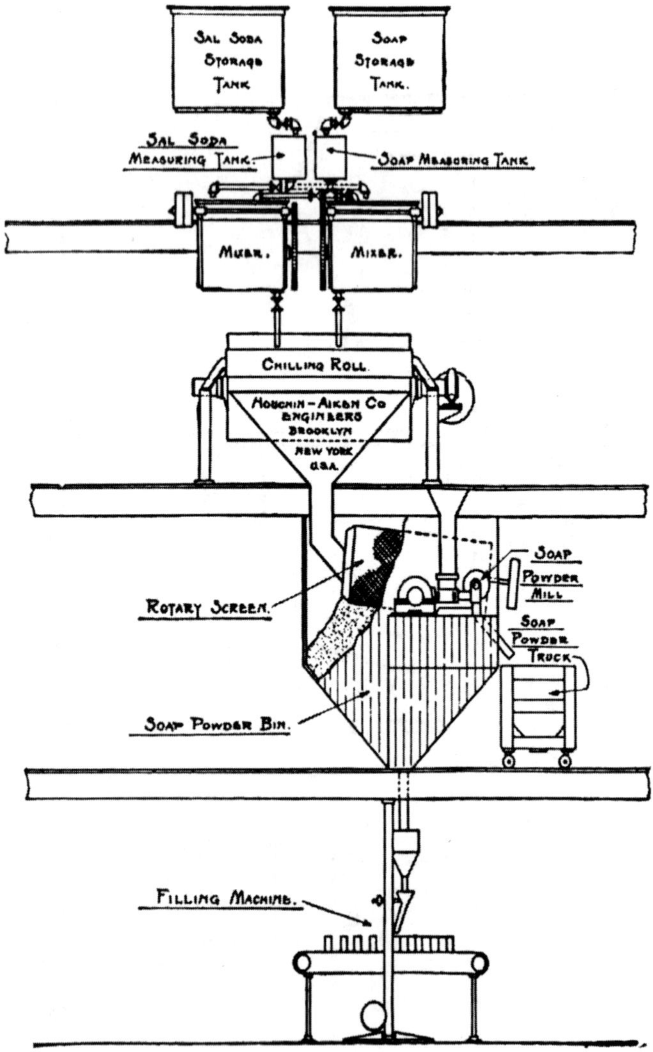


FLUFFY SOAP POWDER EQUIPMENT

Soap Powder Mixer

Soap Powder Mill

Toilet Soap Equipment

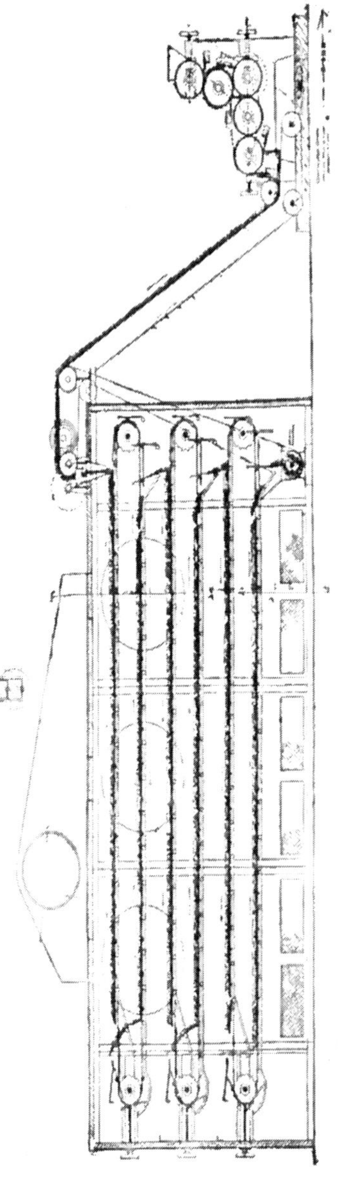

Toilet Soap Dryer

Amalgamator

Milling Box

Toilet Soap Mill

Toilet Soap Mill

CHIPPER

PLODDER

HORIZONTAL CHIPPER

AMALGAMATOR (IMPROVED)

PRESS (LETTERING ON 4 SIDES OF CAKE)

PRESS (FOOT)

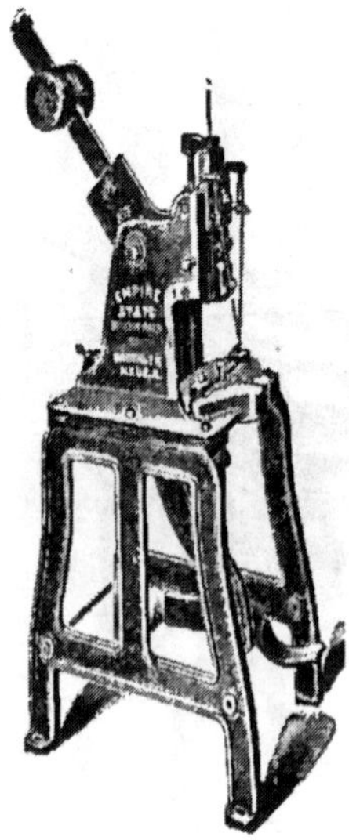

PRESS (FOOT)

PLODDER

AUTOMATIC PRESS (TOILET)

MULTIPLE CAKE CUTTER

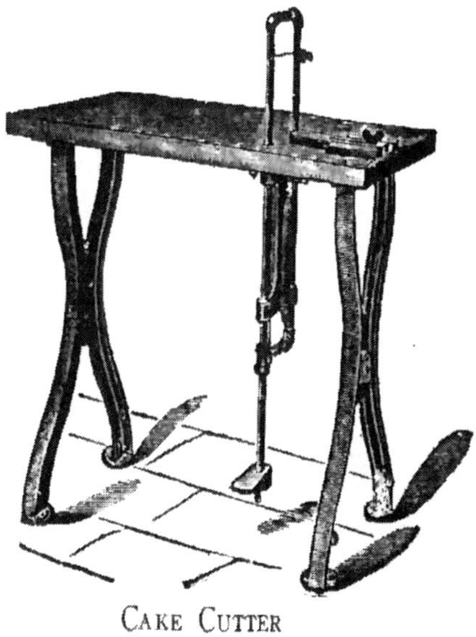

CAKE CUTTER

CHIPPER

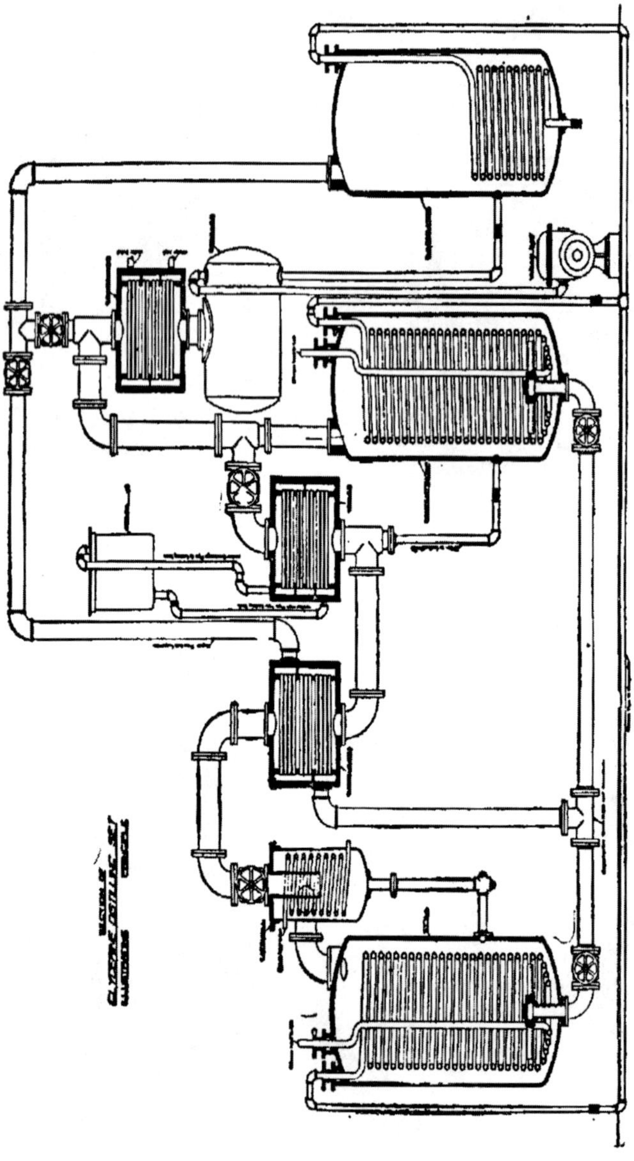

GLYCERINE DISTILLING PLANT

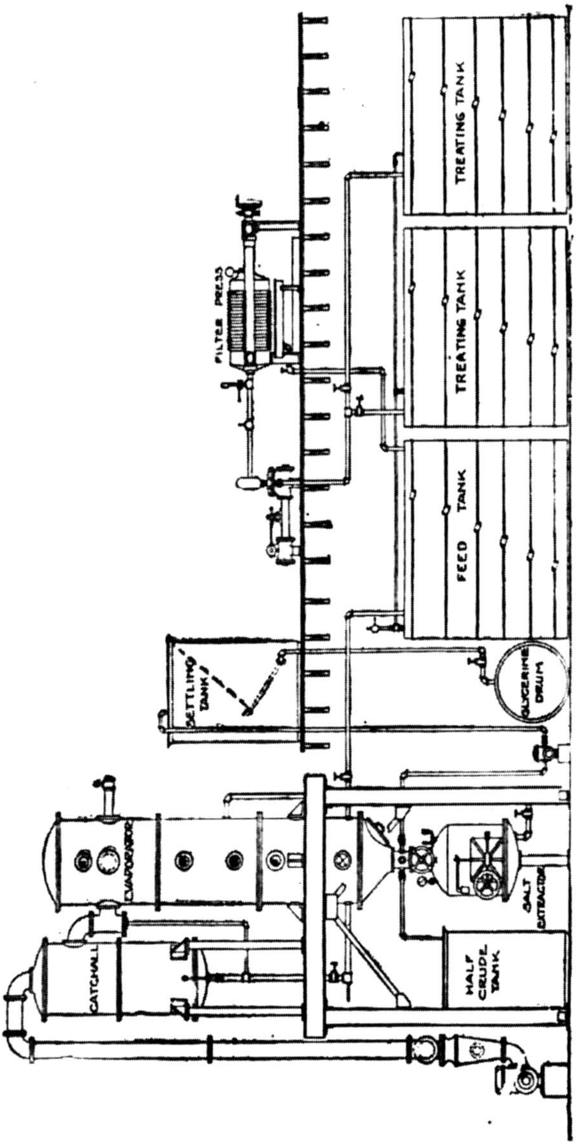


CRUDE GLYCERINE PLANT

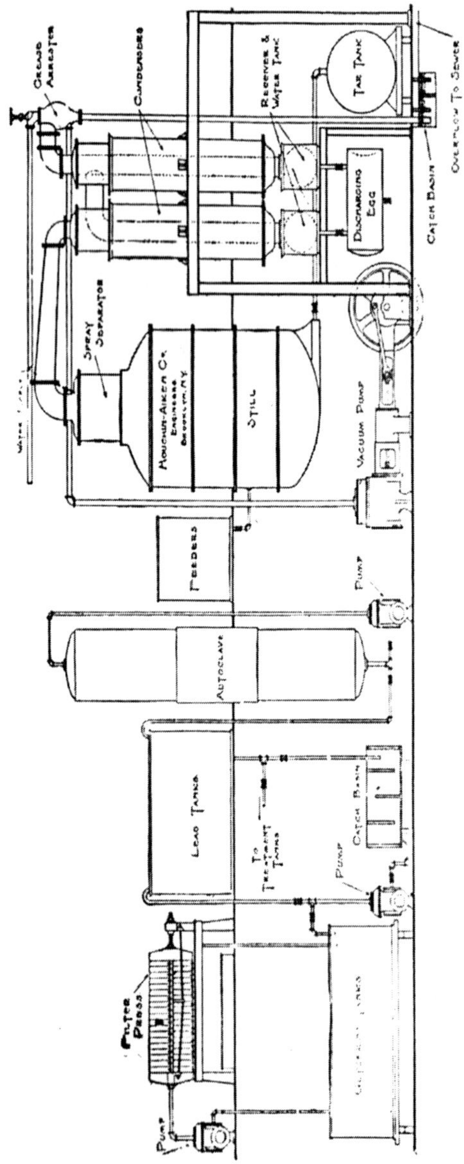


II-A Fatty Acid Distilling Plant

# Appendix

Tables marked * are taken from the German Year Book for Soap Industry.

## (U. S. BUREAU OF STANDARDS) THE METRIC SYSTEM.

The fundamental unit of the metric system is the meter (the unit of length). From this the units of mass (gram) and capacity (liter) are derived. All other units are the decimal sub-divisions or multiples of these. These three units are simply related, so that for all practical purposes the volume of one kilogram of water (one liter) is equal to one cubic decimeter.

| Prefixes. | Meaning. | | Units. |
|---|---|---|---|
| Milli- = | one thousandth 1-1000 | .001 | |
| Centi- = | one hundredth 1-100 | .01 | Meter for length. |
| Deci- = | one tenth 1-10 | .1 | |
| Unit = | one | 1. | Gram for mass. |
| Deka- = | ten 10-1 | 10. | |
| Hecto- = | one hundred 100-1 | 100. | Liter for capacity. |
| Kilo- = | one thousand 1000-1 | 1000. | |

The metric terms are formed by combining the words "Meter," "Gram" and "Liter" with the six numerical prefixes.

### LENGTH

10 milli-meters mm = 1 centi-meter ................cm
10 centi-meters .... = 1 deci-meter ..................dm
10 deci-meters .... = 1 meter (about 40 inches)....m
10 meters .......... = 1 deka-meter ..............dkm
10 deka-meters .... = 1 hecto-meter .................hm
10 hecto-meters .... = 1 kilo-meter (about 5/8 mile)..km

## APPENDIX

### Mass.

| | | |
|---|---|---|
| 10 milli-grams. m g | = 1 centi-gram | c g |
| 10 centi-grams | = 1 deci-gram | d g |
| 10 deci-grams | = 1 gram (about 15 grains) | g |
| 10 grams | = 1 deka-gram | d k g |
| 10 Deka-grams | = 1 hecto-gram | h g |
| 10 hecto-grams | = 1 kilo-gram (about 2 pounds) | k g |

### Capacity.

| | | |
|---|---|---|
| 10 milli-liters ...m l | = 1 centi-liter | c l |
| 10 centi-liters | = 1 deci-liter | d l |
| 10 deci-liters | = 1 liter (about 1 quart) | l |
| 10 liters | = 1 deka-liter | d k l |
| 10 deka-liters | = 1 hecto-liter (about a barrel) | h l |
| 10 hecto-liters | = 1 kilo-liter | k l |

The square and cubic units are the squares and cubes of the linear units.

The ordinary unit of land area is the Hectare (about 2½ acres).

## U. S. BUREAU OF STANDARDS TABLE OF METRIC EQUIVALENTS

Meter = 39.37 inches.

Legal Equivalent Adopted by Act of Congress July 28, 1866.

### LENGTH.

| | | | |
|---|---|---|---|
| Centimeter | = | 0.3937 | inch |
| Meter | = | 3.28 | feet |
| Meter | = | 1.094 | yards |
| Kilometer | = | 0.621 | statute mile |
| Kilometer | = | 0.5396 | nautical mile |
| Inch | = | 2.540 | centimeters |
| Foot | = | 0.305 | meter |
| Yard | = | 0.914 | meter |
| Statute mile | = | 1.61 | kilometers |
| Nautical mile | = | 1.853 | kilometers |

### AREA.

| | | | |
|---|---|---|---|
| Sq. centimeter | = | 0.155 | sq. inch |
| Sq. meter | = | 10.76 | sq. feet |
| Sq. meter | = | 1.196 | sq. yards |
| Hectare | = | 2.47 | acres |
| Sq. kilometer | = | 0.386 | sq. mile |
| Sq. inch | = | 6.45 | sq. centimeters |
| Sq. foot | = | 0.0929 | sq. meter |
| Sq. yard | = | 0.836 | sq. meter |
| Acre | = | 0.405 | hectare |
| Sq. mile | = | 2.59 | sq. kilometers |

# APPENDIX

## Weight.

| | | | |
|---|---|---|---|
| Gram | = | 15.43 | grains |
| Gram | = | 0.772 | U. S. apoth. scruple |
| Gram | = | 0.2572 | U. S. apoth. dram |
| Gram | = | 0.0353 | avoir. ounce |
| Gram | = | 0.03215 | troy ounce |
| Kilogram | = | 2.205 | avoir. pounds |
| Kilogram | = | 2.679 | troy pounds |
| Metric ton | = | 0.984 | gross or long ton |
| Metric ton | = | 1.102 | short or net tons |
| Grain | = | 0.064 | gram |
| U. S. apoth. scruple | = | 1.296 | grams |
| U. S. apoth. dram | = | 3.89 | grams |
| Avoir. ounce | = | 28.35 | grams |
| Troy ounce | = | 31.10 | grams |
| Avoir. pound | = | 0.4536 | kilogram |
| Troy pound | = | 0.373 | kilogram |
| Gross or long ton | = | 1.016 | metric tons |
| Short or net ton | = | 0.907 | metric ton |

## Volume.

| | | | |
|---|---|---|---|
| Cu. centimeter | = | 0.0610 | cu. inch |
| Cu. meter | = | 35.3 | cu. feet |
| Cu. meter | = | 1.308 | cu. yards |
| Cu. inch | = | 16.39 | cu. centimeters |
| Cu. foot | = | 0.283 | cu. meter |
| Cu. yard | = | 0.765 | cu. meter |

### Capacity.

| | | | |
|---|---|---|---|
| Millimeter | = | 0.0338 | U. S. liq. ounce |
| Millimeter | = | 0.2705 | U. S. apoth. dram |
| Liter | = | 1.057 | U. S. liq. quarts |
| Liter | = | 0.2642 | U. S. liq. gallon |
| Liter | = | 0.908 | U. S. dry quart |
| Dekaliter | = | 1.135 | U. S. pecks |
| Hectoliter | = | 2.838 | U. S. bushels |
| U. S. liq. ounce | = | 29.57 | millimeters |
| U. S. apoth. dram | = | 3.70 | millimeters |
| U. S. liq. quarts | = | 0.946 | liter |
| U. S. dry quarts | = | 1.101 | liters |
| U. S. liq. gallon | = | 3.785 | liters |
| U. S. peck | = | 0.881 | dekaliter |
| U. S. bushel | = | 0.3524 | hectoliter |

## AVOIRDUPOIS WEIGHT.

1 pound = 16 ounces = 256 drams
1 ounce = 16 "

## TROY (APOTHECARIES') WEIGHT (U. S.)

1 pound = 12 ounces = 96 drams = 288 scruples = 5,760 grains
1 ounce = 8 drams = 24 scruples = 480 grains
1 dram = 3 scruples = 60 grains
1 scruple = 20 grains

## WINE (APOTHECARIES) LIQUID MEASURE (U. S.)

1 gallon = 8 pints = 128 fl. ozs. = 1,024 fl. drams = 61,440 minims
1 pint = 16 fl. ozs. = 128 fl. drams = 7,689 minims
1 fl. oz. = 8 fl. drams = 480 minims
1 fl. dram = 60 minims

*To find diameter of a circle* multiply circumference by .31831.

*To find circumference of a circle,* multiply diameter by 3.1416.

*To find area of a circle,* multiply square of diameter by .7854.

*To find surface of a ball,* multiply square of diameter by 3.1416.

*To find side of an equal square,* multiply diameter by .8862.

*To find cubic inches in a ball,* multiply cube of diameter by .5236.

*Doubling the diameter of a pipe,* increases its capacity four times.

*One cubic foot of anthracite coal* weighs about 53 lbs.

*One cubic foot of bituminous coal* weighs from 47 to 50 pounds.

*A gallon of water* (U. S. standard) weighs 8 1/3 pounds and contains 231 cubic inches.

*A cubic foot of water* contains 7½ gallons, 1728 cubic inches and weighs 62½ pounds.

*To find the number of pounds of water a cylindrical* tank contains, square the diameter, multiply by .785 and then by the height in feet. This gives the number of cubic feet which multiplied by 62½ gives the capacity in pounds of water. Divide by 7½ and this gives the capacity in gallons.

*A horse-power* is equivalent to raising 33,000 pounds 1 foot per minute, or 550 pounds 1 foot per second.

*The friction of water in pipes* is as the square of velocity. The capacity of pipes is as the square of their diameters; thus, doubling the diameter of a pipe increases its capacity four times.

*To find the diameter of a pump cylinder* to move a given quantity of water per minute (100 feet of piston being the standard of speed), divide the number of gallons by 4, then extract the square root, and the product will be the diameter in inches of the pump cylinder.

*To find the horse-power necessary to elevate water* to a given height, multiply the weight of the water elevated per minute in pounds by the height in feet, and divide the product by 33,000 (an allowance should be added for water friction, and a further allowance for loss in steam cylinder, say from 20 to 30 per cent).

*To compute the capacity of pumping engines,* multiply the area of water piston, in inches, by the distance it travels, in inches, in a given time. Deduct 3 per cent for slip and rod displacement. The product divided by 231 gives the number of gallons in time named.

*To find the velocity in feet per minute* necessary to discharge a given volume of water in a given time, multiply the number of cubic feet of water by 144 and divide the product by the area of the pipe in inches.

*To find the area of a required pipe,* the volume and velocity of water being given, multiply the number of cubic feet of water by 144 and divide the product by the velocity in feet per minute. The area being found, the diameter can be learned by using any table giving the "area of circles" and finding the nearest area, opposite to which will be found the diameter to correspond.

## Physical and Chemical Constants of Fixed Oils and Fats.

(From Lewkowitsch and other authorities.)

| | Specific gravity at 15°C. | Specific gravity at 100°C. | Melting-point. C. | Solidifying-point. C. |
|---|---|---|---|---|
| Linseed oil | 0.931–0.938 | 0.880 | −16° to −26° | −16° |
| Hemp-seed oil | 0.925–0.931 | ... | ... | −27° |
| Walnut oil | 0.925–0.926 | 0.871 | ... | −27° |
| Poppy-seed oil | 0.924–0.927 | 0.873 | ... | −18° |
| Sunflower oil | 0.924–0.926 | 0.919 | ... | −17° |
| Fir-seed oil | 0.925–0.928 | ... | ... | −27° to −30° |
| Maize oil | 0.921–0.926 | ... | ... | −10° to −15° |
| Cotton-seed oil | 0.922–0.930 | 0.867 | ... | 12° |
| Sesame oil | 0.923–0.924 | 0.871 | ... | −5° |
| Rape-seed oil | 0.914–0.917 | 0.863 | ... | −2° to −10° |
| Black mustard oil | 0.916–0.920 | ... | ... | −17.5° |
| Croton oil | 0.942–0.955 | ... | ... | −16° |
| Castor oil | 0.960–0.966 | 0.910 | ... | −12° to −18° |
| Apricot-kernel oil | 0.915–0.919 | ... | ... | −14° |
| Almond oil | 0.915–0.920 | ... | ... | −10° to −20° |
| Peanut (arachis) oil | 0.916–0.920 | 0.867 | ... | −3° to −7° |
| Olive oil | 0.914–0.917 | 0.862 | ... | 2° |
| Menhaden oil | 0.927–0.933 | ... | ... | −4° |
| Cod-liver oil | 0.922–0.927 | 0.874 | ... | 0° to −10° |
| Seal oil | 0.924–0.929 | 0.873 | ... | 3° |
| Whale oil | 0.920–0.930 | 0.872 | ... | −2° |
| Dolphin oil | 0.917–0.918 | ... | ... | 5° to −3° |
| Porpoise oil | 0.926 | 0.871 | ... | −16° |
| Neat's-foot oil | 0.914–0.916 | 0.861 | ... | 0° to 1.5° |
| Cotton-seed stearine | 0.919–0.923 | 0.867 | 40° | 31° to 32.5° |
| Palm oil | 0.921–0.925 | 0.856 | 27° to 42° | ... |
| Cacao butter | 0.950–0.952 | 0.858 | 30° to 33° | 25° to 26° |
| Cocoa-nut oil | 0.925–0.926 | 0.873 | 20° to 26° | 16° to 20° |
| Myrtle wax | 0.995 | 0.875 | 40° to 44° | 39° to 43° |
| Japan wax | 0.970–0.980 | 0.875 | 51° to 54.5° | 46° |
| Lard | 0.931–0.938 | 0.861 | 41° to 46° | 29° |
| Bone fat | 0.914–0.916 | . | 21° to 22° | 15° to 17° |
| Tallow | 0.943–0.952 | 0.860 | 42° to 46° | 35° to 37° |
| Butter fat | 0.927–0.936 | 0.866 | 29.5° to 33° | 19° to 20° |
| Oleomargarine | 0.924–0.930 | 0.850 | ... | ... |
| Sperm oil | 0.875–0.884 | 0.833 | ... | −25° |
| Bottle-nose oil | 0.879–0.880 | 0.827 | ... | ... |
| Carnauba wax | 0.990–0.999 | 0.842 | 84° to 85° | 80° to 81° |
| Wool-fat | 0.973 | 0.901 | 39° to 42° | 30° to 30.2° |
| Beeswax | 0.958–0.969 | 0.822 | 62° to 64° | 60.5° to 62° |
| Spermaceti | 0.960 | 0.812 | 43.5° to 49° | 43.4° to 44.2° |
| Chinese wax | 0.970 | 0.810 | 80.5° to 81° | 80.5° to 81° |
| Tung (Chinese wood oil) | 0.936–0.942 | ... | ... | below −17° |
| Soya-bean oil | 0.924–0.927 | ... | ... | 8° to 15° |

## Physical and Chemical Constants of Fixed Oils and Fats.

(From Lewkowitsch and other authorities.)

| | Saponification value. | Maumené test. | Iodine value. | Hehner value. | Reichert value. |
|---|---|---|---|---|---|
| Linseed oil | 190–195 | 104°–111° | 175–190 | . . . | . . . |
| Hemp-seed oil | 190–193 | 95°–96° | 148 | . . . | . . . |
| Walnut oil | 195 | 96°–101° | 144–147 | . . . | . . . |
| Poppy-seed oil | 195 | 86°–88° | 134–141 | 95.38 | . . . |
| Sunflower oil | 193–194 | 72°–75° | 120–129 | 95 | . . . |
| Fir-seed oil | 191.3 | 98°–99° | 118.9–120 | . . . | . . . |
| Maize oil | 188–193 | 56°–60.5° | 117–125 | 89–95.7 | 2.5 |
| Cotton-seed oil | 191–195 | 68°–77° | 104–110 | 96–17 | . . . |
| Sesame oil | 189–193 | 64°–68° | 105–109 | 95.8 | 0.35 |
| Rape-seed oil | 170–178 | 51°–60° | 95–105 | 95 | . . . |
| Black mustard oil | 174–174.6 | 43°–44° | 96°–110 | 95.05 | . . . |
| Croton oil | 210.3–215 | . . . | 101.7–104 | 89 | 13.5 |
| Castor oil | 178–186 | 46°–47° | 83.4–85.9 | . . . | 1.4 |
| Apricot-kernel oil | 192.2–193.1 | 42.5°–46° | 100–107 | . . . | . . . |
| Almond oil | 190.5–195.4 | 51°–54° | 93–97 | 96.2 | . . . |
| Peanut (arachis) oil | 190–197 | 45°–49° | 85–98 | 95.86 | . . . |
| Olive oil | 191–196 | 41.5°–45.5° | 80.6–84.5 | 95.43 | 0.3 |
| Menhaden oil | 189.3–192 | 123°–128° | 140–170 | . . . | 1.2 |
| Cod-liver oil | 182–187 | 102°–103° | 154–180 | 95.3 | . . . |
| Seal oil | 190–196 | 92° | 127–140 | 94.2 | 0.22 |
| Whale oil | 188–193 | 91°–92° | 110–136 | 93.5 | 2.04 |
| Dolphin oil — Body oil | 197.3 | . . . | 99.5 | 93.07 | 5.6 |
| Dolphin oil — Jaw oil | 200 | . . . | 32.8 | 66.28 | 65.92 |
| Porpoise oil — Body oil | 216–218.8 | 50° | 119.4 | . . . | 23.45 |
| Porpoise oil — Jaw oil | 253.7 | . . . | 49.6 | 68.41 | 65.8 |
| Neat's-foot oil | 194.3 | 47°–48.5° | 69.3–70.4 | . . . | . . . |
| Cotton-seed stearine | 194.6–195.1 | 48° | 88.7–92.8 | 96.3 | . . . |
| Palm oil | 196.3–202 | . . . | 53–57 | 95.6 | 0.5 |
| Cacao butter | 192.2–193.5 | . . . | 32–41 | 94.59 | 1.6 |
| Cocoa-nut oil | 250–253 | . . . | 8.5–9.3 | 88.6 | 3.7 |
| Myrtle wax | 205.7–211.7 | . . . | 2.9 | . . . | . . . |
| Japan wax | 220–222.4 | . . . | 4.2–8.5 | 90.6 | . . . |
| Lard | 195.3–196.6 | 27°–32° | 57–70 | 96 | . . . |
| Bone fat | 190.9 | . . . | 46.3–49.6 | . . . | . . . |
| Tallow | 195–198 | . . . | 36–47 | 95.6 | 0.25 |
| Butter fat | 221.5–227 | . . . | 26–35 | 87.5 | 28.78 |
| Oleomargarine | 194–203.7 | . . . | 55.3–60 | 95–96 | 2.6 |
| Sperm oil | 132.5–147 | 47°–51° | 84 | . . . | 1.3 |
| Bottle-nose oil | 126–134 | 41°–47° | 77.4–82 | . . . | 1.4 |
| Carnauba wax | 80–84 | . . . | 13.5 | . . . | . . . |
| Wool-fat | 98.2–102.4 | . . . | 25–28 | . . . | . . . |
| Beeswax | 91–96 | . . . | 8.3–11 | . . . | . . . |
| Spermaceti | 128 | . . . | . . . | . . . | . . . |
| Chinese wax | 63 | . . . | . . . | . . . | . . . |
| Tung (Chinese wood oil) | 193 | . . . | 150–165 | . . . | . . . |
| Soya-bean oil | 190.6–192.9 | 59°–61° | 121.3–124 | 95.5 | . . . |

## *Temperature Correction Table for Hehner's Concentrated Bichromate Solution for Glycerine Analysis

| A<br>Temperature | f<br>Corrected Volume<br>1 c. c. | Logarithm |
|---|---|---|
| 11° C | 0.9980 ccm | 99913 |
| 12° " | 0.9985 " | 99935 |
| 13° " | 0.9990 " | 99956 |
| 14° " | 0.9995 " | 99978 |
| 15° " | 1.0000 " | 00000 |
| 16° " | 1.0005 " | 00022 |
| 17° " | 1.0010 " | 00043 |
| 18° " | 1.0015 " | 00065 |
| 19° " | 1.0020 " | 00087 |
| 20° " | 1.0025 " | 00108 |
| 21° " | 1.0030 " | 00130 |
| 22° " | 1.0035 " | 00152 |
| 23° " | 1.0040 " | 00173 |

## *Table of Important Fatty Acids

| Name | Formula | Mol. Wt. | Boiling Point | | Melting Pt. | Neutralization value Mg. KOH |
|---|---|---|---|---|---|---|
| | | | Ordinary Pressure | 100 mm Pressure | | |
| Butyric..... | $C_4H_8O_2$ | 88 | 162.3 | — | — | 637.5 |
| Caproic..... | $C_6H_{12}O_2$ | 116 | 199.7 | — | — | 483.6 |
| Caprylic..... | $C_8H_{16}O_2$ | 144 | 236—237 | — | 16.5 | 389.6 |
| Capric...... | $C_{10}H_{20}O_2$ | 172 | 268—270 | 199.5—200 | 31.3 | 326.2 |
| Lauric...... | $C_{12}H_{24}O_2$ | 200 | — | 225 | 43.6 | 280.5 |
| Myristic..... | $C_{14}H_{28}O_2$ | 228 | — | 250.5 | 53.8 | 246.1 |
| Palmitic..... | $C_{16}H_{32}O_2$ | 256 | — | 268.5 | 62 | 219.1 |
| Stearic...... | $C_{18}H_{36}O_2$ | 284 | — | 291 | 69.2 | 197.5 |
| Arachidic... | $C_{20}H_{40}O_2$ | 302 | — | — | 75 | 185.8 |
| Behenic..... | $C_{22}H_{44}O_2$ | 330 | — | — | 77–78 | 170.0 |
| Cerotic..... | $C_{27}H_{54}O_2$ | 400 | — | — | 78 | 140.25 |
| Melissic..... | $C_{30}H_{60}O_2$ | 442 | — | — | 90 | 126.5 |
| Oleic....... | $C_{18}H_{34}O_2$ | 282 | — | 185.5—286 | 14 | 198.9 |
| Erucic...... | $C_{22}H_{42}O_2$ | 338 | — | — | 33–34 | 165.9 |
| Linolic...... | $C_{18}H_{32}O_2$ | 280 | — | — | — | 200.4 |
| Linolenic.... | $C_{18}H_{30}O_2$ | 278 | — | — | — | 201.8 |
| Ricinoleic... | $C_{18}H_{34}O_3$ | 298 | — | — | — | 181.5 |

# *Comparison of Thermometer Scales

n Degree Celsius $=\frac{4}{5}$n Degree Reaumur $=32+\frac{9}{5}$n Degree Fahrenheit

n Degree Reaumur $=\frac{5}{4}$n Degree Celsius $=32+\frac{9}{4}$n Degree Fahrenheit

n Degree Fahrenheit $=\frac{5}{9}$(n—32) Degree Celsius $=\frac{4}{9}$(n—32) Deg. R

| C. | R. | F. | C. | R. | F. | C. | R. | F. | C. | R. | F. |
|---|---|---|---|---|---|---|---|---|---|---|---|
| —20 | —16 | —4 | 20 | 16 | 68 | 60 | 48 | 140 | 100 | 80 | 212 |
| —19 | —15.2 | —2.2 | 21 | 16.8 | 69.8 | 61 | 48.8 | 141.8 | 101 | 80.8 | 213.8 |
| —18 | —14.4 | —0.4 | 22 | 17.6 | 71.6 | 62 | 49.6 | 143.6 | 102 | 81.6 | 215.6 |
| —17 | —13.6 | 1.4 | 23 | 18.4 | 73.4 | 63 | 50.4 | 145.4 | 103 | 82.4 | 217.4 |
| —16 | —12.8 | 3.2 | 24 | 19.2 | 75.2 | 64 | 51.2 | 147.2 | 104 | 83.2 | 219.2 |
| —15 | —12 | 5 | 25 | 20 | 77 | 65 | 52 | 149 | 105 | 84 | 221 |
| —14 | —11.2 | 6.8 | 26 | 20.8 | 78.8 | 66 | 52.8 | 150.8 | 106 | 84.8 | 222.8 |
| —13 | —10.4 | 8.6 | 27 | 21.6 | 80.6 | 67 | 53.6 | 152.6 | 107 | 85.6 | 224.6 |
| —12 | — 9.6 | 10.4 | 28 | 22.4 | 82.4 | 68 | 54.4 | 154.4 | 108 | 86.4 | 226.4 |
| —11 | — 8.8 | 12.2 | 29 | 23.2 | 84.2 | 69 | 55.2 | 156.2 | 109 | 87.2 | 228.2 |
| —10 | — 8 | 14 | 30 | 24 | 86 | 70 | 56 | 158 | 110 | 88 | 230 |
| — 9 | — 7.2 | 15.8 | 31 | 24.8 | 87.8 | 71 | 56.8 | 159.8 | 111 | 88.8 | 231.8 |
| — 8 | — 6.4 | 17.6 | 32 | 25.6 | 89.6 | 72 | 57.6 | 161.6 | 112 | 89.6 | 233.6 |
| — 7 | — 5.6 | 19.4 | 33 | 26.4 | 91.4 | 73 | 58.4 | 163.4 | 113 | 90.4 | 235.4 |
| — 6 | — 4.8 | 21.2 | 34 | 27.2 | 93.2 | 74 | 59.2 | 165.2 | 114 | 91.2 | 237.2 |
| — 5 | — 4 | 23 | 35 | 28 | 95 | 75 | 60 | 167 | 115 | 92 | 239 |
| — 4 | — 3.2 | 24.8 | 36 | 28.8 | 96.8 | 76 | 60.8 | 168.8 | 116 | 92.8 | 240.8 |
| — 3 | — 2.4 | 26.6 | 37 | 29.6 | 98.6 | 77 | 61.6 | 170.6 | 117 | 93.6 | 242.6 |
| — 2 | — 1.6 | 28.4 | 38 | 30.4 | 100.4 | 78 | 62.4 | 172.4 | 118 | 94.4 | 244.4 |
| — 1 | — 0.8 | 30.2 | 39 | 31.2 | 102.2 | 79 | 63.2 | 174.2 | 119 | 95.2 | 246.2 |
| 0 | 0 | 32 | 40 | 32 | 104 | 80 | 64 | 176 | 120 | 96 | 248 |
| 1 | 0.8 | 33.8 | 41 | 32.8 | 105.8 | 81 | 64.8 | 177.8 | 121 | 96.8 | 249.8 |
| 2 | 1.6 | 35.6 | 42 | 33.6 | 107.6 | 82 | 65.6 | 179.6 | 122 | 97.6 | 251.6 |
| 3 | 2.4 | 37.4 | 43 | 34.4 | 109.4 | 83 | 66.4 | 181.4 | 123 | 98.4 | 253.4 |
| 4 | 3.2 | 39.2 | 44 | 35.2 | 111.2 | 84 | 67.2 | 183.2 | 124 | 99.2 | 255.2 |
| 5 | 4 | 41 | 45 | 36 | 113 | 85 | 68 | 185 | 125 | 100 | 257 |
| 6 | 4.8 | 42.8 | 46 | 36.8 | 114.8 | 86 | 68.8 | 186.8 | 126 | 100.8 | 258.8 |
| 7 | 5.6 | 44.6 | 47 | 37.6 | 116.6 | 87 | 69.6 | 188.6 | 127 | 101.6 | 260.6 |
| 8 | 6.4 | 46.4 | 48 | 38.4 | 118.4 | 88 | 70.4 | 190.4 | 128 | 102.4 | 262.4 |
| 9 | 7.2 | 48.2 | 49 | 39.2 | 120.2 | 89 | 71.2 | 192.2 | 129 | 103.2 | 264.2 |
| 10 | 8 | 50 | 50 | 40 | 122 | 90 | 72 | 194 | 130 | 104 | 266 |
| 11 | 8.8 | 51.8 | 51 | 40.8 | 123.8 | 91 | 72.8 | 195.8 | 131 | 104.8 | 267.8 |
| 12 | 9.6 | 53.6 | 52 | 41.6 | 125.6 | 92 | 73.6 | 197.6 | 132 | 105.6 | 269.6 |
| 13 | 10.4 | 55.4 | 53 | 42.4 | 127.4 | 93 | 74.4 | 199.4 | 133 | 106.4 | 271.4 |
| 14 | 11.2 | 57.2 | 54 | 43.2 | 129.2 | 94 | 75.2 | 201.2 | 134 | 107.2 | 273.2 |
| 15 | 12 | 59 | 55 | 44 | 131 | 95 | 76 | 203 | 135 | 108 | 275 |
| 16 | 12.8 | 60.8 | 56 | 44.8 | 132.8 | 96 | 76.8 | 204.8 | 136 | 108.8 | 276.8 |
| 17 | 13.6 | 62.6 | 57 | 45.6 | 134.6 | 97 | 77.6 | 206.6 | 137 | 109.6 | 278.6 |
| 18 | 14.4 | 64.4 | 58 | 46.4 | 136.4 | 98 | 78.4 | 208.4 | 138 | 110.4 | 280.4 |
| 19 | 15.2 | 66.2 | 59 | 47.2 | 138.2 | 99 | 79.2 | 210.2 | 139 | 111.2 | 282.2 |

## *Quantities of Alkali Required for Saponification of Fats of Average Molecular Weight 670

### (Cocoanut Oil, Palmkernel Oil)

| Kilos | Liters Alkali Solution Sp. Gr. 1.1 | | Liters Alkali Solution Sp. Gr. 1.2 | | Liters Alkali Solution Sp. Gr. 1.3 | | Liters Alkali Solution Sp. Gr. 1.355 | |
|---|---|---|---|---|---|---|---|---|
| | Na OH | K O H | Na OH | K O H | Na OH | K O H | Na OH | K O H |
| 1000 | 1875.83 | 1902.99 | 844.67 | 930.35 | 510.27 | 622.71 | 409.61 | 517.97 |
| 2000 | 3751.66 | 3805.97 | 1689.35 | 1860.70 | 1020.54 | 1245.41 | 819.21 | 1035.95 |
| 3000 | 5627.50 | 5708.96 | 2534.02 | 2791.04 | 1530.81 | 1868.12 | 1228.82 | 1553.92 |
| 4000 | 7503.33 | 7611.94 | 3378.69 | 3721.39 | 2041.01 | 2490.83 | 1638.43 | 2071.90 |
| 5000 | 9379.16 | 9514.93 | 4223.37 | 4651.74 | 2551.35 | 3113.54 | 2048.04 | 2589.87 |
| 6000 | 11254.99 | 11417.91 | 5068.04 | 5582.09 | 3061.61 | 3736.24 | 2457.65 | 3107.84 |
| 7000 | 13130.82 | 13320.90 | 5912.71 | 6512.44 | 3571.88 | 4358.95 | 2867.26 | 3625.82 |
| 8000 | 15006.66 | 15223.88 | 6757.38 | 7442.78 | 4082.15 | 4981.66 | 3276.86 | 4143.79 |
| 9000 | 16882.49 | 17126.87 | 7602.06 | 8373.13 | 4592.42 | 5604.36 | 3686.47 | 4661.77 |
| 10000 | 18758.32 | 19029.85 | 8446.73 | 9303.48 | 5102.69 | 6227.02 | 4096.08 | 5179.74 |

## *Quantities of Alkali Required for Saponification of Fats of Average Molecular Weight 860

### (Tallow, Cottonseed Oil, Olive Oil, Etc.)

| Kilos | Liters Alkali Solution Sp. Gr. 1.1 | | Liters Alkali Solution Sp. Gr. 1.2 | | Liters Alkali Solution Sp. Gr. 1.3 | | Liters Alkali Solution Sp. Gr. 1.355 | |
|---|---|---|---|---|---|---|---|---|
| | Na OH | K O H | Na OH | K O H | Na OH | K O H | Na OH | K O H |
| 1000 | 1461.40 | 1482.56 | 658.06 | 724.81 | 397.64 | 485.13 | 319.11 | 403.54 |
| 2000 | 2922.81 | 2965.12 | 1316.12 | 1449.61 | 795.07 | 970.27 | 638.23 | 807.08 |
| 3000 | 4384.21 | 4447.67 | 1974.18 | 2174.42 | 1192.61 | 1455.40 | 957.34 | 1210.61 |
| 4000 | 5845.62 | 5930.23 | 2632.24 | 2899.22 | 1590.14 | 1940.53 | 1276.45 | 1614.15 |
| 5000 | 7307.02 | 7412.79 | 3290.30 | 3624.03 | 1987.68 | 2425.67 | 1595.57 | 2017.69 |
| 6000 | 8768.42 | 8895.35 | 3948.35 | 4348.84 | 2385.21 | 2910.80 | 1914.68 | 2421.23 |
| 7000 | 10229.83 | 10377.91 | 4606.41 | 5073.64 | 2782.75 | 3395.93 | 2233.79 | 2824.77 |
| 8000 | 11691.23 | 11860.46 | 5264.47 | 5798.45 | 3180.28 | 3881.06 | 2552.90 | 3228.30 |
| 9000 | 13152.64 | 13343.02 | 5922.53 | 6523.25 | 3577.82 | 4366.20 | 2872.02 | 3631.84 |
| 10000 | 14614.04 | 14825.58 | 6580.59 | 7248.06 | 3975.35 | 4851.33 | 3191.13 | 4035.38 |

## DENSITY AND STRENGTH OF SULPHURIC ACID (SIDERSKY).

| Degrees Twaddell | Sp. Gr. at 15° C. | % of pure acid ($H_2SO_4$). | Equivalent (in cc.) of a kilo. of pure acid. | Equivalent (in cc.) of a liter of pure acid. |
|---|---|---|---|---|
| 1 | 1.007 | 1.9 | 52.620 | 96.930 |
| 3 | 1.014 | 2.8 | 35.710 | 66.450 |
| 4 | 1.022 | 3.8 | 25.650 | 47.230 |
| 6 | 1.029 | 4.8 | 20.410 | 37.582 |
| 8 | 1.037 | 5.8 | 16.670 | 30.690 |
| 9 | 1.045 | 6.8 | 14.085 | 25.938 |
| 10 | 1.052 | 7.8 | 12.198 | 22.460 |
| 12 | 1.062 | 8.8 | 10.755 | 19.803 |
| 13 | 1.067 | 9.8 | 9.524 | 17.540 |
| 15 | 1.075 | 10.9 | 8.547 | 15.740 |
| 17 | 1.083 | 11.9 | 7.752 | 14.278 |
| 18 | 1.091 | 13.0 | 7.042 | 12.969 |
| 20 | 1.100 | 14.1 | 6.452 | 11.882 |
| 22 | 1.108 | 15.2 | 5.953 | 10.962 |
| 23 | 1.116 | 16.2 | 5.526 | 10.177 |
| 25 | 1.125 | 17.3 | 5.405 | 9.954 |
| 27 | 1.134 | 18.5 | 4.76 | 8.770 |
| 29 | 1.142 | 19.6 | 4.465 | 8.223 |
| 30 | 1.152 | 20.8 | 4.184 | 7.723 |
| 32 | 1.162 | 22.2 | 3.876 | 7.138 |
| 34 | 1.171 | 23.3 | 3.663 | 6.745 |
| 36 | 1.180 | 24.5 | 3.541 | 6.521 |
| 38 | 1.190 | 25.8 | 3.258 | 5.999 |
| 40 | 1.200 | 27.1 | 3.077 | 5.666 |
| 42 | 1.210 | 28.4 | 2.907 | 5.353 |
| 44 | 1.220 | 29.6 | 2.770 | 5.102 |
| 46 | 1.231 | 31.0 | 2.618 | 4.865 |
| 48 | 1.241 | 32.2 | 2.500 | 4.604 |
| 50 | 1.252 | 33.4 | 2.392 | 4.406 |
| 53 | 1.263 | 34.7 | 2.283 | 4.205 |
| 55 | 1.274 | 36.0 | 2.179 | 4.012 |
| 57 | 1.285 | 37.4 | 2.079 | 3.829 |
| 60 | 1.297 | 38.8 | 1.988 | 3.661 |
| 62 | 1.308 | 40.2 | 1.905 | 3.508 |
| 64 | 1.320 | 41.6 | 1.821 | 3.354 |
| 66 | 1.332 | 43.0 | 1.745 | 3.214 |
| 69 | 1.345 | 44.4 | 1.665 | 3.085 |
| 71 | 1.357 | 45.5 | 1.621 | 2.985 |
| 74 | 1.370 | 46.9 | 1.558 | 2.869 |
| 77 | 1.383 | 48.3 | 1.497 | 2.757 |
| 80 | 1.397 | 49.8 | 1.436 | 2.646 |
| 82 | 1.410 | 51.2 | 1.386 | 2.551 |
| 85 | 1.424 | 52.6 | 1.335 | 2.459 |
| 88 | 1.438 | 54.0 | 1.287 | 2.370 |
| 91 | 1.453 | 55.4 | 1.237 | 2.270 |
| 94 | 1.468 | 56.9 | 1.195 | 2.200 |
| 97 | 1.483 | 58.3 | 1.156 | 2.130 |
| 100 | 1.498 | 59.6 | 1.116 | 2.050 |
| 103 | 1.514 | 61.0 | 1.080 | 1.980 |
| 106 | 1.530 | 62.5 | 1.045 | 1.930 |
| 108 | 1.540 | 64.0 | 1.010 | 1.860 |
| 113 | 1.563 | 65.5 | 0.975 | 1.800 |
| 116 | 1.580 | 67.0 | 0.950 | 1.740 |
| 120 | 1.597 | 68.6 | 0.917 | 1.690 |
| 123 | 1.615 | 70.0 | 0.888 | 1.630 |
| 127 | 1.634 | 71.6 | 0.855 | 1.570 |
| 130 | 1.652 | 73.2 | 0.845 | 1.520 |
| 134 | 1.671 | 74.7 | 0.800 | 1.470 |
| 138 | 1.691 | 76.4 | 0.774 | 1.430 |
| 142 | 1.711 | 78.1 | 0.749 | 1.390 |
| 146 | 1.732 | 79.9 | 0.722 | 1.320 |
| 151 | 1.753 | 81.7 | 0.705 | 1.280 |
| 155 | 1.774 | 84.1 | 0.672 | 1.235 |
| 160 | 1.798 | 86.5 | 0.639 | 1.190 |
| 164 | 1.819 | 89.7 | 0.609 | 1.130 |
| 168 | 1.842 | 100.0 | 0.544 | 1.000 |

## *Densities of Potassium Carbonate Solutions at 15 C (Gerlach)

| Sp. Gr. | Per cent of pure $K_2CO_3$ | Sp. Gr. | Per cent of pure $K_2CO_3$ | Sp. Gr. | Per cent of pure $K_2CO_3$ |
|---|---|---|---|---|---|
| 1.00914 | 1 | 1.18265 | 19 | 1.38279 | 37 |
| 1.01829 | 2 | 1.19286 | 20 | 1.39476 | 38 |
| 1.02743 | 3 | 1.20344 | 21 | 1.40673 | 39 |
| 1.03658 | 4 | 1.21402 | 22 | 1.41870 | 40 |
| 1.04572 | 5 | 1.22459 | 23 | 1.43104 | 41 |
| 1.05513 | 6 | 1.23517 | 24 | 1.44338 | 42 |
| 1.06454 | 7 | 1.24575 | 25 | 1.45573 | 43 |
| 1.07396 | 8 | 1.25681 | 26 | 1.46807 | 44 |
| 1.08337 | 9 | 1.26787 | 27 | 1.48041 | 45 |
| 1.09278 | 10 | 1.27893 | 28 | 1.49314 | 46 |
| 1.10258 | 11 | 1.28999 | 29 | 1.50588 | 47 |
| 1.11238 | 12 | 1.30105 | 30 | 1.51861 | 48 |
| 1.12219 | 13 | 1.31261 | 31 | 1.53135 | 49 |
| 1.13199 | 14 | 1.32417 | 32 | 1.54408 | 50 |
| 1.14179 | 15 | 1.33573 | 33 | 1.55728 | 51 |
| 1.15200 | 16 | 1.34729 | 34 | 1.57048 | 52 |
| 1.16222 | 17 | 1.35885 | 35 | 1.57079 | 53.024 |
| 1.17243 | 18 | 1.37082 | 36 | | |

## *Constants of Certain Fatty Acids and Triglycerides

| Triglycerides of | Mol. Wt. of Fatty Acid | Mol. Wt. of Triglycerides | Per cent Yield | |
|---|---|---|---|---|
| | | | Fatty Acid | Glycerine |
| Stearic Acid........... | 284 | 890 | 95.73 | 10.34 |
| Oleic Acid............. | 282 | 884 | 95.70 | 10.41 |
| Margaric Acid......... | 270 | 848 | 95.52 | 10.85 |
| Palmitic Acid.......... | 256 | 806 | 95.28 | 11.42 |
| Myristic Acid.......... | 228 | 722 | 94.47 | 12.74 |
| Lauric Acid............ | 200 | 638 | 94.04 | 14.42 |
| Capric Acid............ | 172 | 594 | 93.14 | 15.48 |
| Caproic Acid........... | 116 | 386 | 90.16 | 23.83 |
| Butyric Acid........... | 88 | 302 | 87.41 | 30.46 |

PERCENTAGES OF SOLID CAUSTIC SODA AND CAUSTIC POTASH IN CAUSTIC LYES ACCORDING TO BAUME SCALE.

| Degrees Baume. | % NaOH | % KOH | Degrees Baume. | % NaOH | % KOH |
|---|---|---|---|---|---|
| 1 | 0.61 | 0.90 | 26 | 19.58 | 24.20 |
| 2 | 0.93 | 1.70 | 27 | 20.59 | 25.10 |
| 3 | 2.00 | 2.60 | 28 | 21.42 | 26.10 |
| 4 | 2.71 | 3.50 | 29 | 22.64 | 27.00 |
| 5 | 3.35 | 4.50 | 30 | 23.67 | 28.00 |
| 6 | 4.00 | 5.60 | 31 | 24.81 | 28.90 |
| 7 | 4.556 | 6.286 | 32 | 25.80 | 29.80 |
| 8 | 5.29 | 7.40 | 33 | 26.83 | 30.70 |
| 9 | 5.87 | 8.20 | 34 | 27.80 | 31.80 |
| 10 | 6.55 | 9.20 | 35 | 28.83 | 32.70 |
| 11 | 7.31 | 10.10 | 36 | 29.93 | 33.70 |
| 12 | 8.00 | 10.90 | 37 | 31.22 | 34.90 |
| 13 | 8.68 | 12.00 | 38 | 32.47 | 35.90 |
| 14 | 9.42 | 12.90 | 39 | 33.69 | 36.90 |
| 15 | 10.06 | 13.80 | 40 | 34.96 | 37.80 |
| 16 | 10.97 | 14.80 | 41 | 36.25 | 38.90 |
| 17 | 11.84 | 15.70 | 42 | 37.53 | 39.90 |
| 18 | 12.64 | 16.50 | 43 | 38.80 | 40.90 |
| 19 | 13.55 | 17.60 | 44 | 39.99 | 42.10 |
| 20 | 14.37 | 18.60 | 45 | 41.41 | 43.40 |
| 21 | 15.13 | 19.50 | 46 | 42.83 | 44.60 |
| 22 | 15.91 | 20.50 | 47 | 44.38 | 45.80 |
| 23 | 16.77 | 21.40 | 48 | 46.15 | 47.10 |
| 24 | 17.67 | 22.50 | 49 | 47.58 | 48.25 |
| 25 | 18.58 | 23.30 | 50 | 49.02 | 49.40 |

GLYCERINE CONTENT OF MORE COMMON OILS AND FATS USED IN SOAP MAKING.

| Kind. | Theoretical Yield of Pure Glycerine of Neutral Oil or Fat. | Average Free Fatty Acid in Commercial Oil. | % Pure Glycerine in Commercial Oil. | Yield Soap Lye 80% Crude Glycerine. |
|---|---|---|---|---|
| Beef Tallow | 10.7 | 5 | 10.2 | 12.75 |
| Bone Grease | 10.5 | 20—50 | 5.2— 8.4 | 6.5 —10.5 |
| Castor Oil | 9.8 | 0.5—10 | 8.8— 9.8 | 11.0 —12.45 |
| Cocoanut Oil | 13.9 | 3—5 | 13.2—13.5 | 16.5 —16.9 |
| Cocoanut Oil Off | .... | 15—40 | 8.3—11.8 | 10.37—14.75 |
| Corn Oil | 10.4 | 1—10 | 9.3—10.3 | 11.62—12.9 |
| Cottonseed Oil | 10.6 | Trace | 10.6 | 13.25 |
| Hog Grease | 10.6 | 0.5—1 | 10.5—10.6 | 13.12—13.25 |
| Horse Grease | 10.6 | 1—3 | 10.5—10.6 | 13.12—13.25 |
| Olive Oil | 10.3 | 2—25 | 7.7—10.2 | 9.62—12.75 |
| Olive Foots | .... | 30—60 | 4—7 | 5— 8.75 |
| Palm Oil | 11.0 | 10—50 | 5.5—10 | 6.87—12.5 |
| Palmkernel Oil | 13.3 | 4—8 | 12.2—12.8 | 15.25—16 |
| Peanut Oil | 10.4 | 5—20 | 8.3— 9.9 | 10.37—12.37 |
| Soya Bean Oil | 10.4 | 2 | 10.2 | 12.75 |
| Train Oil | 10.0 | 2—20 | 8— 9.8 | 10.0 —12.25 |
| Vegetable Tallow | 10.9 | 1—3 | 10.5—10.8 | 13.12—13.5 |

## *Table of Specific Gravities of Pure Commercial Glycerine with Corresponding Percentage of Water. Temperature 15 C.

| Sp. Gr. | | |
|---|---|---|
| 1.262 | 0 | Water |
| 1.261 | 1% | " |
| 1.258 | 2 " | " |
| 1.255 | 3 " | " |
| 1.2515 | 4 " | " |
| 1.250 | 5 " | " |
| 1.2467 | 6 " | " |
| 1.2450 | 7 " | " |
| 1.243 | 8 " | " |
| 1.241 | 9 " | " |
| 1.237 | 10 " | " |
| 1.235 | 11 " | " |
| 1.2324 | 12 " | " |
| 1.229 | 13 " | " |
| 1.2265 | 14 " | " |
| 1.2245 | 15 " | " |
| 1.2225 | 16 " | " |
| 1.2185 | 17 " | " |
| 1.2174 | 18 " | " |
| 1.2142 | 19 " | " |
| 1.211 | 20 " | " |
| 1.207 | 21 " | " |
| 1.203 | 22 " | " |
| 1.2004 | 23 " | " |
| 1.198 | 24 " | " |
| 1.195 | 25 " | " |
| 1.1923 | 26 " | " |
| 1.189 | 27 " | " |
| 1.188 | 28 " | " |
| 1.1846 | 29 " | " |
| 1.182 | 30 " | " |
| 1.179 | 31 " | " |
| 1.176 | 32 " | " |
| 1.1734 | 33 " | " |
| 1.171 | 34 " | " |
| 1.168 | 35 " | " |
| 1.165 | 36 " | " |
| 1.163 | 37 " | " |
| 1.160 | 38% | Water |
| 1.157 | 39 " | " |
| 1.155 | 40 " | " |
| 1.152 | 41 " | " |
| 1.149 | 42 " | " |
| 1.1464 | 43 " | " |
| 1.1437 | 44 " | " |
| 1.141 | 45 " | " |
| 1.1377 | 46 " | " |
| 1.1353 | 47 " | " |
| 1.1326 | 48 " | " |
| 1.1304 | 49 " | " |
| 1.127 | 50 " | " |
| 1.125 | 51 " | " |
| 1.1224 | 52 " | " |
| 1.1204 | 53 " | " |
| 1.117 | 54 " | " |
| 1.114 | 55 " | " |
| 1.112 | 56 " | " |
| 1.109 | 57 " | " |
| 1.106 | 58 " | " |
| 1.103 | 59 " | " |
| 1.1006 | 60 " | " |
| 1.088 | 65 " | " |
| 1.075 | 70 " | " |
| 1.0623 | 75 " | " |
| 1.049 | 80 " | " |
| 1.0365 | 85 " | " |
| 1.0243 | 90 " | " |
| 1.0218 | 91 " | " |
| 1.0192 | 92 " | " |
| 1.0168 | 93 " | " |
| 1.0147 | 94 " | " |
| 1.0125 | 95 " | " |
| 1.01 | 96 " | " |
| 1.0074 | 97 " | " |
| 1.0053 | 98 " | " |
| 1.0026 | 99 " | " |

## *Table of Percentage, Specific Gravity and Beaume Degree of Pure Glycerine Solutions

| Per cent Water | Sp. Gr. Champion and Pellet | Degree Beaume (Berthelot) | Per cent Water | Sp. Gr. Champion and Pellet | Degree Beaume (Berthelot) |
|---|---|---|---|---|---|
| 0 | 1.2640 | 31.2 | 11.0 | 1.2350 | 28.6 |
| 0.5 | 1.2625 | 31.0 | 11.5 | 1.2335 | 28.4 |
| 1.0 | 1.2612 | 30.9 | 12.0 | 1.2322 | 28.3 |
| 1.5 | 1.2600 | 30.8 | 12.5 | 1.2307 | 28.2 |
| 2.0 | 1.2585 | 30.7 | 13.0 | 1.2295 | 28.0 |
| 2.5 | 1.2575 | 30.6 | 13.5 | 1.2280 | 27.8 |
| 3.0 | 1.2560 | 30.4 | 14.0 | 1.2270 | 27.7 |
| 3.5 | 1.2545 | 30.3 | 14.5 | 1.2255 | 27.6 |
| 4.0 | 1.2532 | 30.2 | 15.0 | 1.2242 | 27.4 |
| 4.5 | 1.2520 | 30.1 | 15.5 | 1.2230 | 27.3 |
| 5.0 | 1.2505 | 30.0 | 16.0 | 1.2217 | 27.2 |
| 5.5 | 1.2490 | 29.9 | 16.5 | 1.2202 | 27.0 |
| 6.0 | 1.2480 | 29.8 | 17.0 | 1.2190 | 26.9 |
| 6.5 | 1.2465 | 29.7 | 17.5 | 1.2177 | 26.8 |
| 7.0 | 1.2455 | 29.6 | 18.0 | 1.2165 | 26.7 |
| 7.5 | 1.2440 | 29.5 | 18.5 | 1.2150 | 26.5 |
| 8.0 | 1.2427 | 29.3 | 19.0 | 1.2137 | 26.4 |
| 8.5 | 1.2412 | 29.2 | 19.5 | 1.2125 | 26.3 |
| 9.0 | 1.2400 | 29.0 | 20.0 | 1.2112 | 26.2 |
| 9.5 | 1.2390 | 28.9 | 20.5 | 1.2100 | 26.0 |
| 10.0 | 1.2375 | 28.8 | 21.0 | 1.2085 | 25.0 |
| 10.5 | 1.2362 | 28.7 | | | |

## *Table of Specific Gravities of Pure Glycerine Solutions with Corresponding Beaume Degree and Percent Water

| Per cent Water | Sp. Gr. | Degree Beaume | Per cent Water | Sp. Gr. | Degree Beaume |
|---|---|---|---|---|---|
| 0.0 | 1.2640 | 31.2 | 1.0 | 1.2612 | 30.9 |
| 0.5 | 1.2625 | 31.0 | 1.5 | 1.2600 | 30.8 |
| 2.0 | 1.2585 | 30.7 | 12.0 | 1.2322 | 28.3 |
| 2.5 | 1.2575 | 30.6 | 12.5 | 1.2307 | 28.2 |
| 3.0 | 1.2560 | 30.4 | 13.0 | 1.2295 | 28.0 |
| 3.5 | 1.2545 | 30.3 | 13.5 | 1.2280 | 27.8 |
| 4.0 | 1.2532 | 30.2 | 14.0 | 1.2270 | 27.7 |
| 4.5 | 1.2520 | 30.1 | 14.5 | 1.2255 | 27.6 |
| 5.0 | 1.2505 | 30.0 | 15.0 | 1.2242 | 27.4 |
| 5.5 | 1.2490 | 29.9 | 15.5 | 1.2230 | 27.3 |
| 6.0 | 1.2480 | 29.8 | 16.0 | 1.2217 | 27.2 |
| 6.5 | 1.2465 | 29.7 | 16.5 | 1.2202 | 27.0 |
| 7.0 | 1.2455 | 29.6 | 17.0 | 1.2190 | 26.9 |
| 7.5 | 1.2440 | 29.5 | 17.5 | 1.2177 | 26.8 |
| 8.0 | 1.2427 | 29.3 | 18.0 | 1.2165 | 26.7 |
| 8.5 | 1.2412 | 29.2 | 18.5 | 1.2150 | 26.5 |
| 9.0 | 1.2400 | 29.0 | 19.0 | 1.2137 | 26.4 |
| 9.5 | 1.2390 | 28.9 | 19.5 | 1.2125 | 26.3 |
| 10.0 | 1.2375 | 28.8 | 20.0 | 1.2112 | 26.2 |
| 10.5 | 1.2362 | 28.7 | 20.5 | 1.2100 | 26.0 |
| 11.0 | 1.2350 | 28.6 | 21.0 | 1.2085 | 25.9 |
| 11.5 | 1.2335 | 28.4 | | | |

# INDEX

# INDEX

# INDEX